The
Transcendental
Turn

The Transcendental Turn

THE FOUNDATION OF KANT'S IDEALISM

MOLTKE S. GRAM

University Presses of Florida
UNIVERSITY OF FLORIDA PRESS/Gainesville
UNIVERSITY OF SOUTH FLORIDA PRESS/Tampa

Library of Congress Cataloging in Publication Data

Gram, Moltke S.
  The transcendental turn.

  Includes index.
  1. Kant, Immanuel, 1772–1804—Addresses, essays,
lectures. I. Title.
B2798.G683 1984   193   84–22047
ISBN 0–8130–0787–9 (alk. paper)

UNIVERSITY PRESSES OF FLORIDA is the central agency for scholarly publishing
of the State of Florida's university system, producing books selected for publication by
the faculty editorial committees of Florida's nine public universities: Florida A&M Uni-
versity (Tallahassee), Florida Atlantic University (Boca Raton), Florida International Uni-
versity (Miami), Florida State University (Tallahassee), University of Central Florida (Or-
lando), University of Florida (Gainesville), University of North Florida (Jacksonville),
University of South Florida (Tampa), University of West Florida (Pensacola).

ORDERS for books published by all member presses of University Presses of Florida
should be addressed to University Presses of Florida, 15 NW 15th Street, Gainesville, FL
32603

CONTENTS

v

W. H. WERKMEISTER

in tiefer kollegialer Verbundenheit zugeeignet

ACKNOWLEDGMENTS

SOME OF my essays on Kant have prepared the way for this book, but it is not a collection of those essays. Much of what appears here can be traced to an ancestral formulation that has appeared elsewhere. The relation between what appears here and what it was in its original version, however, is tenuous. Once I began putting my discussions of these themes into the context of a unified theory, I discovered that the form in which I had originally presented them had to undergo significant change, not only in the manner of presentation but also in the conclusions that I had at first drawn from the evidence I had presented and evaluated elsewhere. For example, a much earlier version of chapter 1 originally appeared as "The Myth of Double Affection," in *Reflections on Kant's Philosophy*, edited by W. H. Werkmeister (Gainesville: University Presses of Florida, 1975), pp. 29–63, but it appears here changed in its formulation and greatly expanded in the conclusions that I originally drew from my consideration of the theory of double affection.

Chapters 2 and 3 constitute a greatly transformed version of what appeared as a series of articles in *Ratio* 18 (1976). The change here is especially significant because the context in which I ultimately placed the discussion forced me to put the conclusion I originally drew in a quite different perspective. Chapter 5, chronologically the first of these studies, appeared in *Monist* 51 (1967); but there the conclusion of the natal version was excessively restricted, and here it is greatly extended in the light of the more general relations of its theme to Kant's distinction between appearances and things in themselves.

Chapter 6 first appeared in *Dialectica* 34 (1980). It is justifiably the longest of these studies because it knits together the theories of affection, causation, and the distinction between things in themselves and appearances in Kant's epistemology. It thus provides not only independent confirmation of the views I develop in the earlier chapters but also a demonstration of how those views can be used as a heuristic tool for uncovering the structure of Kant's argument for transcendental idealism.

I am grateful for the permission of the various editors of these sources to reprint portions of what has previously appeared.

INTRODUCTION

Caveat Lector

THESE STUDIES attempt to provide a unified account of themes in Kant's epistemology that have previously been discussed in mutual isolation. Kant gives us a theory of causation. He also gives us a theory of what he calls affection. The nature and cogency of both have been obscured by the assimilation of affection to causation and the attendant neglect of the problem of relating what are, as I shall show, two quite different, distinctive theories about two different problems. Kant also distinguishes between things in themselves and appearances. But the nature of that relation and the viability of his theory about that relation have both been lost. The issues surrounding the distinction have been discussed without attention to the fact that Kant distinguishes sharply, although not always explicitly, between causation and affection. Both the distinction between affection and causation on the one hand as well as the nature of the relation between a thing in itself and an appearance on the other have been further obscured by a deep historical overlay of philsophical interpretation and controversy—much of which has taken place in neglect or ignorance of those distinctions—from Kant's day to the present. And, finally, Kant's statement

I

and resolution of the First and Third Antinomies have suffered because the independent corroboration they give of these distinctions in Kant's general theory of knowledge has been ignored in the traditional assessment of Kant's views in his discussion of those antinomies.

The isolation has had serious consequences. It has been responsible for historical as well as philosophical blunders in our understanding of Kant's views taken individually. It has provoked grave objections to Kant's central epistemological theories. And it has encouraged attempts to answer those objections that have spawned them. Both objections and rebuttals have fed upon one another, for both of them alike have been guided by common assumptions about the distinction between causation and affection as well as the relation between a thing in itself and an appearance that lies at a deeper level of Kant's thought.

The objections cluster around Kant's alleged surreptitious application of the categories to things in themselves. This has become an issue only because the critics have repeatedly assumed that what Kant calls affection is only a kind of causation. The relational answer to those objections, encapsulated in the notion of double affection, succeeds in dissociating causation from affection only at the prohibitive cost of making causation into a kind of affection. This erroneous coupling distorts the clarification of Kant's theory, for, as we shall see, it distinguishes affection from causation only in the end to allow the distinction to deliquesce. Both the objection and its traditional remedy neglect a deeper level in Kant's thought. The exploration of that level is the purpose of this book.

The argument of the book divides into four parts.

1. For the Kant of the Second Analogy, causation is a necessary succession of events according to a rule. But this omits something that Kant repeatedly alludes to in his exposition of the relation between intuitions and what is responsible for their appearance under any form of intuition at all. It should be remembered that Kant also says that intuitions are the result of the action on us of objects that affect our sensibility, and this conflicts sharply with what he claims causation to be. If what takes place when something affects our sensibility is a case of causation, then we have what would seem to be a blatant violation of what Kant tells us about the nature of causation in his exposition and defense of the Second Analogy.

The conflict arises in this way. Whatever else a Kantian causal connection may be, it is at least a relation between two events one of which is temporally prior to the other. But the relation of affection does not fit this model of causation. It cannot be explained as a case of temporal succession between events governed by a rule. This no more explicates the relation of affection than affection explains the relation of temporal succession. Affection obtains between each individual occurrence given in a temporally ordered series and whatever is responsible for its appearing to us as it does. To ask about what affects us is to inquire not about what events follow temporally on other events but rather about the epistemic relation in which we stand to each of those events taken separately.

The ineradicable fact is that we are confronted here with two different kinds of relation. There is, first, the relation of one occurrence to another. And there is, second, the quite different relation of any one of these occurrences to what is presented to us by that occurrence. The former cannot be the same relation as the latter, for the latter relation is logically prior to the former. The relation of affection must, then, be assumed if we are to define the notion of what it is to be any occurrence that is a link in a causal chain. And if affection is not a case of causation, then the philosophically important question for Kant's theory is how any object can be said to act non-causally on our sensibility.

2. The theory of affection is the basis of the present inquiry. Once the relations of causation and affection have been separated from each other, we can ask whether a Kantian thing in itself and an appearance are related by causation or affection. This problem has been handed down to us in a state that is even more serious than the neglect or ignorance of the affection-causation distinction. We have inherited two principal ways of accounting for the distinction between things in themselves and appearances. We have been given what I shall call the Two Worlds Theory, according to which a thing in itself is something that lacks the characteristics of our forms of intuition, whereas an appearance is a numerically different object that has these characteristics.

The Two Worlds Theory, as we shall see, makes problematic the distinction it is supposed to explicate philosophically. In the first place, it does not explain the relation between an object that lacks the characteristics of any form of intuition whatever to the characteristics of any such form. If this relation is causal, it must be temporal. And this transforms a thing in itself into an appearance among appearances. Both are in time. If there is no relation at all between a thing in itself and an appearance, then the theory does not reveal whether the mutual independence of things in themselves and appearances applies merely to our forms of intuition or whether that independence holds for any possible forms of intuition at all. The Two Worlds Theory cannot, in any case, explain the relation between a thing in itself and an appearance because it succeeds only in abolishing the very relation it is supposed to explain.

The Two Descriptions Theory, the major traditional alternative, fares no better than its rival. It tells us that there are two descriptions that one and the same object can satisfy. One such description specifies our forms of intuition; the other, characteristics that the object may have under other forms of intuition. But here, again, flaws flourish. The very notion of a description satisfiable in a possible world that is not the same as our world gives us a faulty account of the relation between things in themselves and appearances. Such a description fails to explain the relation that is supposed to hold between a thing in itself and an appearance in our world. An object that appears under our forms of intuition may be able to appear under other forms of intuition. But this merely perpetuates the problem that the distinction between the two descriptions of the same object is supposed to solve. An object can satisfy different descriptions with a change in the forms of our intuition. But the relation between things in themselves and appearances remains with every change. The forms may change. The problem of explaining the relation does not. If the problem is to be solved at all, it must be solved for our world as well as for other, possible worlds.

These theoretical alternatives are diametrically opposed. To say that a thing in itself is an object with no relation at all to any forms of intuition is totally different from saying that such an object can stand in some relation to a potentially infinite number of forms of intuition. But both are false. Neither can provide an adequate account of the relation of affection. The Two Worlds Theory founders because it fails to account for affection altogether. Things in themselves and appearances are numerically different objects with none of the characteristics in common that are the necessary condition for instantiating the affection relation. And the Two Descriptions Theory fares no better. It states the problem of the relation between things in themselves and appearances only to postpone its solution to infinity by deferring an explication of what must be explained in our world to the context of other possible worlds.

Both of these theories fail for superficially different reasons. One explicates the relation between a thing in itself and appearance by implicitly denying that there is any relation to be explicated. The other explicates that relation by transferring the problem to other contexts. But the theories have common ground. Neither takes the successful explication of the affection relation as an implied condition of any creditable explication of the relation between things in themselves and appearances. If you accept the Two Worlds Theory, you implicitly deny that there is any such distinction in the world governed by our forms of intuition. Affection is an epistemic relation. To say that one term of that relation cannot be related epistemically to the other term is to deny that the relation applies to those terms. This makes it impossible for us to use the relation of affection in order to relate things in themselves and appearances. If we accept the Two Descriptions Theory as it has been traditionally set forth, we postpone the original problem by transporting it, *mutatis mutandis*, to a world in which the distinction between things in themselves and appearances arises all over again. In either case, then, you deny a necessary condition that exists if the distinction between things in themselves and appearances is to be made.

3. The philosophical tradition has bequeathed this problem to us. We have inherited two strands of exegesis and interpretation through which much of what has been accepted as Kant's distinction between things in themselves and appearances has been filtered. Both alternatives have been imputed to Kant. Both have been attacked on philosophical grounds, and both have been questioned with no less severity on philological grounds: philosophically, because each of them assumes the existence of an epistemic relation that cannot apply to the epistemic situation they describe; philologically, because the characterization to which each alternative appeals distorts Kant's text. And both are wrong for the same reason.

We have been traditionally and repeatedly told, in the first place, that things in themselves relate to appearances as objects relate to the sensations they produce in us. We are then told that the causal relation involves a temporal connection between objects that generate the sensations we have, that a thing in itself cannot stand in a temporal relation to anything we perceive without ceasing to be what it is and that there are, therefore, no things in themselves. This part of the hermeneutical tradition first assimilates the relation between things in themselves and appearances to causation and then quite correctly points out that a relation thus assimilated ceases to be what it purports to be.

The conclusion is admittedly sound, but it must be greatly modified. One large segment of the tradition tells us that there is no distinction between things in themselves and appearances because any such distinction must be causal. The mistake can be traced to a more basic blunder in the assimilation of affection to causation. And so this strand of the tradition, as we shall see, provides us not with an argument for the rejection of the distinction it is supposed to explicate but rather and quite ironically with a demonstration that the distinction must be something quite different from what it has been said to be.

The tradition has given us a second strand, according to which a thing in itself must relate to appearances as a substratum or bearer of properties relates to the properties that inhere in it. But a substratum cannot be given independently of the properties that inhere in them. Thus no substratum can be an object of possible experience. Yet it can cause us to perceive what we do by producing the properties that we perceive under our forms of intuition by acting on our sensibility.

This story is as traditional as it is familiar. It is not, however, an illustrious chapter in the history of philosophical interpretation. None of it correctly states Kant's theory of the distinction it supposedly explicates. And none of it draws the proper conclusions demanded by the interpretation that it hands down to us. The distinction between a thing in itself and an appearance is first assimilated to a thing and its properties. That, we shall see, is the first and most serious error in this strand of interpretation. The distinction between a thing and its properties can be drawn with respect to phenomenal substances. The relation between a thing in itself and an appearance must turn on the relation of what we call a phenomenal substance to a thing in itself. That is a condition if not the solution of the successful explication of the relation between a thing in itself and appearances. The thing-property relation is irrelevant to it.

This mistake is accompanied by others. A thing that has properties is now identified in the course of the argument with a substratum or bearer of properties. That substratum is, in turn, assimilated to a thing in itself. But a substratum cannot be an object of possible experience. All we ever perceive is a cluster of the properties that are said to inhere in it. A thing in itself cannot be an object of possible experience. Thus the notion of a thing in itself, we are told, is theoretically superfluous.

But is it? Emphatically not. The account of a thing in itself that dominates this strand of interpretation is superfluous. The justification of that theory was intended to reside in the fact that it can be an object of possible experience. Even if the relation between a substratum and its properties were read back into Kant's distinction between a thing in itself and an appearance, we would not be forced to jettison the latter distinction. A substratum cannot be an object of possible experience. While we cannot perceive it in isolation from the properties inhering in it, it does not follow that we are unable to perceive it at all. This has a direct but traditionally neglected application to the relation between a thing in itself and the objects we perceive. We can perceive an object under various descriptions. We may not be able to perceive it under all or most of the descriptions that it satisfies. But it does not follow that we are unable to perceive the same object when we perceive it under different descriptions. This is crucial to our understanding of Kant's distinction between a thing in itself and an appearance. It is also fatal to the second historical strand of interpretation.

These traditional theoretical alternatives are diametrically opposed. It is one thing to say that a thing in itself is an object with no relation to any forms of intuition. It is quite another to say that a thing in itself can stand in relation to any of a potentially infinite range of forms of intuition. As I stated above, both alternatives are false because neither adequately explicates the affection relation. The Two Worlds Theory fails to account for epistemic affection altogether. And the Two Descriptions Theory states the problem only to postpone the solution to infinity.

The surface dispute between the two types of theory cannot be settled until we have an adequate theory of affection. If affection is causation, nothing can save the Two Worlds Theory from the problems that undermine it. The affection relation can hold only between things and our forms of intuition. The Two Worlds Theory forbids this. The Two Descriptions Theory escapes this difficulty only to break down on an unacceptable alternative. That theory either postpones the solution of the problem to infinity by appealing to possible worlds or transforms affection into a relation between appearances. The former re-creates the problem it is meant to solve. The latter abolishes the distinction between things in themselves and appearances altogether.

4. The arguments of the First and Third Antinomies independently support the conclusion that affection is not causation. They also expose the deficiency of what both the Two Worlds and the Two Descriptions Theories tell us about the relation between things in themselves and appearances. The argument of the First Antinomy is supposed to prove the transcendental ideality of our forms of intuition. But that argument admits of two different interpretations of the relation be-

tween things in themselves and appearances. The ontological interpretation of the argument requires us to believe that a thing in itself is a kind of substance or accident that is neither spatial nor temporal. The criteriological or epistemic interpretation of the argument, however, entails only that we do not know whether things apart from our forms of intuition have the characteristics that we perceive them to have under those forms.

Both interpretations are at work in the First and the Third Antinomies. I introduce the distinction between an ontological and an epistemic interpretation of those arguments because it exhibits a proof structure that Kant himself obscures when he describes what he does in his discussion of the antinomies. They do not arise, as Kant tells us, because time and space are supposed to be transcendentally real. And Kant's resolution of those antinomies does not give us an independent proof of the transcendental ideality of space and time.

This, as we shall see, is not disastrous to the argument of either antinomy. The argument of the First Antinomy does prove that we can never know that the world exists as a thing in itself. For we cannot know it to be either finite or actually infinite. The world as such cannot be shown to exist at all. The conclusion of the First Antinomy runs counter to both of the received theories of the distinction between things in themselves and appearances. To say that the world as such cannot be known to exist because it cannot be either finite or infinite is to deny that there is any relation between things in themselves and appearances at all. The solution of the problem, on the ontological interpretation of Kant's argument, abolishes the very relation it is supposed to explicate.

The traditional version of the Two Descriptions Theory gains no support from the way in which Kant describes his argument in the First Antinomy. We are asked on that theory to believe that a thing in itself relates to an appearance as something in a possible world that appears under forms of intuition that we lack in our world. The assumption here is that there is something that appears. The dispute is how to explain the relation between what appears to us and its appearances. It is not Kant's own intepretation of the antinomy that a dispute about whether the world as a thing in itself is either a substance or an accident. And even less is it a controversy about whether the world as a whole can appear to us differently under forms of intuition given to us in different possible worlds.

There is another reason for rejecting both the traditional version of the epistemic interpretation and the ontological interpretation of Kant's argument in the First and Third Antinomies. Both of them duplicate the problem that they purport to solve. The problem arises primarily about the relation between things in themselves and appearances. If we accept the Two Worlds Theory of that relation, we not only abolish the possibility of that relation in our own world but raise it all over again with respect to those things that inhabit a world that is neither spatial nor temporal but that nonetheless can relate to some forms of intuition or other. And the Two Descriptions Theory duplicates the problem in the same way.

Kant's resolution of the Third Antinomy marks the most important stage of the argument. Here both the problems of relating causation to affection and things in themselves to appearances merge. The argument of that antinomy confirms the integrity of the affection-causation distinction. But if we are to accept either of the two main theories of the relation between things in themselves and appearances that we have inherited from the tradition, Kant's enterprise in the Third Antinomy is nothing more than a philosophical disaster. The duplication problem enters again. And this can be shown in detail once we try to see the argument of that antinomy through the spectacles supplied by either the Two Worlds Theory or the Two Descriptions Theory of the distinction between things in themselves and appearances.

None of these problems arises, however, if we revise the epistemic version of Kant's theory and reject what the tradition has given to us in both the ontological and the epistemic interpretations of the relation between things in themselves and appearances. The revision I propose gives us a coherent general account of the distinction between things in themselves and appearances. It also provides, as its predecessors do not, a textually intelligible and philosophically defensible account of Kant's argument in the First and Third Antinomies.

The revisionist strategy is to define the distinction between things in themselves and appearances independently of what forms of intuition we have. What distinguishes a thing in itself from an appearance does not turn on whether it either has or lacks the characteristics of the forms of intuition we have. The reason for the strategy is the record of philosophical-cum-exegetical difficulties of the strategy assumed by its antecedents. Both the Two Worlds Theory and the Two Descriptions Theory tacitly and falsely assume that the ground of the distinction between a thing in itself and an appearance must be found in the peculiarities of our forms of intuition. We shall see how this assumption is responsible for the objectionable consequences of both theories. And we shall discover how its removal prevents such consequences from arising. Affection is to provide the source of specifying the distinction. The relation of affection is independent of any specific form of intuition. We say, *apud* Kant, that things are subject to our forms of intuition. We also say that these forms are spatial and temporal. But this implies at most that we cannot be immediately aware of an object without also being aware of its spatial and temporal characteristics. It does not imply that our being aware of the latter is a necessary condition of the existence of the former.

Epistemic revision has equally important consequences. It explains why a causal explanation of our epistemic relation to a perceptual object is both textually and philosophically inadequate to Kant's theory of knowledge. Affection may be accompanied by causal relations, but it cannot be defined solely in terms of those relations. The explication of the causal relation assumes the affection relation. It does not define that relation. The epistemic revision of the relation between things in themselves and appearances will enable us to separate affection from causation, to account for what this does in Kant's arguments in the antinomies, and to show the philosophical basis of his transcendental idealism.

1. Double Affection

*T*HE THEORY of double affection (call it *DA* for short) is a classical attempt to rescue Kant's account of perceptual awareness from what is alleged to be a glaring inconsistency. But *DA* arises with the notion of affection and can be stated in the form of a dilemma neither horn of which is compatible with Kant's theory of perception. The problem generates the dilemma in the following way. To be affected by anything, so the Kantian account goes, is to experience what Kant calls "the effect of an object upon the faculty of representation."[1] The notion of affection does not, however, become fully clear unless we can specify the kind of object that can stand in such a relation to our sensibility. There are two possibilities open to the theory, neither of which would seem to make the notion of affection any more intelligible than the other. That is, I shall argue, the dilemma to which *DA* has been proposed as an answer. But I do this only to show that the difficulty with *DA* arises, not from the Kantian notion or theory of affection itself, but rather from a faulty theory of what affection is supposed to be and how it fits into Kant's account of the relation between things in themselves and appearances. I shall also argue that the dilemma is ultimately spurious.

Let me begin the construction of the dilemma by ignoring a complication in the notion of affection that is irrelevant to the issue facing *DA*. Kant describes affection as the experience of the *effect* of an object on our sensory apparatus. The dilemma facing Kant's theory has nothing to do with the quite separate issue of whether what is related to sensibility is the effect of an object rather than the object itself. The issue concerns the nature of the object that is immediately present to preceptual awareness rather than the causal relation in which it might stand to some further object.

With this restriction in mind consider what the dilemma is. Suppose we say that what affects our sensibility is a thing in itself.[2] This account of what affects us, however, prevents us from distinguishing between a case in which somebody perceives an object and the quite different case in which an object exerts a merely causal influence on the body of the perceiver. This can be seen by consulting an elementary fact of perception. The fact is that to perceive anything is to perceive it under a certain description. If this were not the case, then we could not distinguish between the perceiving of one object rather than another. But if we must always perceive something under a description, to say that we are affected by a thing in itself when we perceive anything would imply that we perceive that objects satisfy certain descriptions. And this would contradict the claim that we cannot be perceptually acquainted with a thing in itself.

It will do no good here to say that a thing in itself can act upon our sensory organs even though we cannot perceive it to satisfy any description at all. If this were the case, we would not be able to distinguish between a situation in which an object causally affects our bodies in certain ways and we do not perceive the effect of that action from the quite different situation in which the object exerts such an influence and we do perceive it. This, then, is the first horn of the dilemma. If the affection relation is to hold between a thing in itself and an act of perceptual awareness, we would have to be able to perceive things in themselves under descriptions appropriate to them or obliterate the distinction between causation and perceptual awareness. In either case, the candidature of things in themselves for one of the relata of the affection relation would serve only to destroy the theory on which it is erected.

There is, however, another candidate for one of the relata of the affection relation. Suppose we say that what affects our sensibility is a phenomenal object, allowing anything that has spatial or temporal characteristics to count as such an object.[3] This alternative, it would seem, succeeds in rescuing the theory of affection from the disastrous implication that we can perceive objects that cannot be in our sensory fields.

The gain, however, is illusory. Such a claim would conflict with Kant's assertion that space and time are forms of our sensibility. Consider how the conflict arises. Sensibility, we are told, is "[t]he capacity (receptivity) for receiving representations through the mode in which we are affected by objects."[4] But what Kant calls the mode of affection here is the form of sensuous intuition that is, in turn, the way in which the subject is affected.[5] And this merely implies that affection is to be partially defined in terms of a relation in which an object stands to certain spatio-temporal forms; hence, there can be no such relation between a *phenomenal* object and such forms. For the relation is specified in terms of a connection between an object and these forms, not in terms of an object exhibiting these forms and sensibility. What makes a phenomenal object an even unlikelier candidate for one of the relata of the affection relation is that such an assumption leads us back to the equally unacceptable candidature of the thing itself. If the object that affects the forms of our sensibility cannot itself have spatio-temporal characteristics, then what affects us must, on Kant's theory, be a thing in itself. Thus replacing things in themselves with phenomenal objects merely returns us to all of the difficulties of the first horn of the dilemma.

The theory of *DA* purports to supply a remedy for the foregoing dilemma. It purports to show that both things in themselves and phenomenal objects can affect the perceiving subject, albeit in different ways. The claim for double affection is made to rest on two kinds of evidence. There is, first, the claim that assuming *DA* defuses the dilemma that I have just sketched. And, second, there is the claim that several of the most characteristic doctrines of the *Kritik* imply the existence of double affection.[6] But neither of these claims is true. For one thing, the *Kritik* does not commit Kant to such a doctrine. For another, imputing it to Kant's theory of perception does not remove the dilemma facing the theory. This does not, however, leave us with an insuperable dilemma. For what generates the dilemma is a confusion between two different conceptions of what a thing in itself is and how it relates to our sensibility. The confusion is not Kant's. It is, rather, the result of an imperfect understanding of the concept of intuition in his theory of perception.

1. The Principal Parts of *DA*

Let me begin by formulating the claims that proponents of *DA* have traditionally tried to defend. I distinguish three such claims: (1) appearances in themselves stand in a relation of empirical affection to the empirical ego;[7] (2) things in themselves transcendently affect the ego in itself;[8] (3) the result of (2) is the world of perceptual objects that are presented to the empirical ego.[9] Consider how these claims contrive to remove the dilemma. We are faced with the problem that neither phenomenal objects nor things in themselves can affect our sensibility. The former cannot do this because it leads us back to things in themselves. The latter cannot do this because it would seem to require that we can perceive things in themselves independent of any forms of intuition at all once we say that they affect our sensibility. *DA* must, accordingly, show how something can affect our sensibility without acquiring spatio-temporal characteristics. It must also show how what we do perceive to have such characteristics can affect our sensibility without once again driving us back to the untenable position that what we are perceiving in such a case is something that lacks such characteristics. In order to accomplish this, the demonstration relies on the crucial distinction between empirical and transcendent affection. The former does not require that the objects in our sensory field lack spatio-temporal characteristics. And the latter countenances the existence of objects that affect egos in themselves. It thereby seeks to avoid the difficulty issuing from the claim that things in themselves affect our sensibility.

The claim is initially plausible. If affection can hold between things in themselves and egos that are not in time and space, the dilemma I have just sketched would seem to me to be removed. For we would seem not to face the problem of an object that must but cannot be spatio-temporal if we are to meet the requirements of perceiving an object. Things in themselves affect the ego in itself; phenomenal things, the phenomenal ego. One and the same object would no longer be pressed into the impossible service of being perceived to have spatio-temporal characteristics and being perceived not to have them. But the distinction between two kinds of affection is a myth. It is not implied by the other parts of Kant's theory of perception. Nor can it escape the dilemma facing that theory. Consider the evidence for such a distinction.

2. The Status of Appearances in Themselves

DA relies essentially on the distinction between what Adickes calls an appearance in itself and a thing in itself. The term "appearance in it-self" is, however, an invention of the *DA* theory. It is not to be found in so many words in the *Kritik*. But there is another term that is both present in so many words in the *Kritik* and that designates a state of affairs that the *DA* theorist exploits as prima facie evidence for his theory. In the *Kritik* Kant speaks of an appearance as a thing in itself in the empirical understanding (*ein Ding an sich selbst im empirischen Verstande*).[10] This is the textual foundation for claiming, as the *DA* theorist does, that there are appearances in themselves. For there are things, if the theory is right, that both have the properties of space and time—existing, as Kant says, *im empirischen Verstande*—and which are nonetheless things in themselves.

The notion of an appearance in itself, founded though it is in the text, still functions as a theoretical term for *DA*. It is a way of characterizing a situation acknowledged by Kant's description of the perceptual situation that generates a critical difficulty for that theory. That there are appearances in themselves is crucial to *DA* if it is to make a serious claim to our attention. For the plausibility of that theory derives from the fact that there are entities that both have spatio-temporal characteristics and are relata of the affection relation. The critical issue can be put in this way. *DA* seems to be required once you say that something with spatio-temporal characteristics stands in the affection relation to a perceiver and, further, that what stands in such a relation to a perceiver is really a thing in itself. These claims generate a contradiction, for something cannot stand in the affection relation to a perceiver and be both a thing in itself and a phenomenal entity. That is the difficulty that the notion of an appearance in itself signals.

DA depends, then, on the notion of an appearance in itself even though that notion surfaces in the *Kritik* in different semantical garb. The absence of the phrase "appearance in itself" does not prevent the issue to which *DA* is meant as an answer from arising. But there is, nonetheless, an argument to show that the very notion of an appear-

ance in itself is internally incoherent and, further, that no such theory—not even one as complicated as *DA*—is needed to solve a problem in Kant's theory of perception. The argument runs like this: The
very notion of an appearance in itself is said to be self-contradictory.
To say that anything is an appearance is, according to this argument,
to say that somebody stands in an epistemic relation to whatever is
called an appearance. Whatever we choose to call an appearance cannot, therefore, be anything in itself just because it cannot be what it is
outside of the relation in which it stands to a perceiver. But to say of
anything that it has some status implies that it can satisfy the description it does outside of the relation in which it may stand to any perceiver. An appearance cannot satisfy this condition; therefore, there
can be no appearances in themselves. And if there can be no such entities, there is no textual necessity to import a theory like *DA* to account for the existence of such entities to our sensibility.

The notion of an appearance in itself cannot be undermined so
easily. The attempt to avert the difficulties of *DA* by disqualifying the
very notion of an appearance in itself breaks down on a fatal ambiguity inherent in that notion. Something can stand in an epistemic relation to a perceiver and be called an appearance. But whatever might
stand in that relation to a perceiver is not an appearance but something that can be neutrally described as an object. In this case what we
perceive can stand outside the epistemic relation it may have to a perceiver without ceasing to be what it is. This is not the case, however, in
the situation that I have just described as a case of an appearance that
appears to somebody.

The distinction I have just made shows the true threat of the problem of which *DA* is one solution. It shows that something can appear
to us without being an appearance. The notion of an appearance in
itself entails a contradiction only on the assumption that an appearance is an object that stands in some relation to a perceiver. But if that
object is not an appearance but, rather, something else that is not essentially described as an appearance, then what stands in such a relation is not an appearance but something else that can exist and satisfy
a description outside that relation. What appears, in other words, is
not an appearance. It is an object that appears. And this is what frees
the notion of an appearance in itself from the difficulties that would
otherwise undermine it at the very outset.

The notion of an appearance in itself does not render the *DA* theory
superfluous. That notion is used to support *DA* by the following line

of argument.[11] If there were only one kind of affection, there would be only one kind of object affecting the ego. But, so the argument goes, Kant provides two kinds of objects that affect the self. There are, in the second place, appearances in themselves that act on our sensibility. Appearances in themselves exist independently of the sensory apparatus of whoever perceives them. They are, therefore, independent of whatever characteristics attach to our sensory receptors. But at the same time appearances in themselves also have spatio-temporal properties. The former characteristic enables them to affect our sensibility; the latter, to be directly present in our sensory field without contradicting the claim that things in themselves cannot be objects of such awareness. Appearances in themselves are like things in themselves in that they are independent of the existence of our sensory receptors. They are unlike things in themselves in that they have spatio-temporal characteristics.

There are two kinds of evidence on which *DA* draws to support this use of appearances in themselves in Kant's theory of perception. In the first place, we are reminded that Kant cites the example of a rose that can appear to different observers in different ways depending upon the peculiarities of their sensory apparatus.[12] The rose is an appearance because it has spatio-temporal characteristics; but since it can appear to various observers in different ways under different circumstances, it can affect the sensibility of different observers in various ways without ceasing to be a spatio-temporal object.

The same point can be put in a different way. Objects that can appear to have characteristics that they lack show that they are independent of the features of our sensibility. That fact, as far as the present example goes, is enough to show that there can be appearances that share at least one feature in common with things in themselves; namely, both exist independently of the characteristics of our sensibility. But at the same time appearances in themselves still retain spatio-temporal properties.

Does this kind of example provide evidence for *DA*? I think not. At A28=B45 Kant begins to discuss the variability of our perceptions of color and concludes that they

> cannot rightly be regarded as properties of things, but only as changes in the subject, changes which may, indeed, be different for different men. In such examples as these, that which is originally itself only appearance, for instance, a rose, is being treated

by the empirical understanding as a thing in itself, which, never-theless, can appear differently to every observer. The transcen-dental concept of appearances in space, on the other hand, is a reminder that nothing in space is a thing in itself, that space is not a form inhering in things in themselves as their intrinsic property.

What this shows is that physical objects like roses can exist inde-pendently of the *accidental* features of the sensory apparatus of each observer. An object can appear to have properties it lacks, for ex-ample, if the organism of the observer is diseased or temporarily al-tered by some other means. It does not show that spatio-temporal ob-jects affect the self in one way and things in themselves in another. The same fact of perceptual relativity could be explained on the assumption that what appears to our sensibility is a thing in itself; hence, the dis-tinction that Kant draws between what is a thing in itself for the em-pirical understanding and what counts as a thing in itself *simpliciter* can draw no support from the fact of perceptual variability.

The same point can be put in a different way. The rose example shows that phenomenal objects can appear to have properties that they lack. A rose that is red can, under certain circumstances of per-ception, appear to be, say, yellow. But this neither requires nor sup-ports the distinction between two kinds of affection. All it requires is that we recognize the distinction between affecting and appearing. To affect our perceptual apparatus is for an object to stand in a relation to our sensibility that, in our case, is characterized by space and time. Yet the object given to us under these forms can appear to be other than it is and might still be a thing in itself. To say that something is a thing in itself for the empirical understanding does not, therefore, imply two relations of affection. All it does imply is that spatio-temporal objects independent of our sensory apparatus can appear to have properties they lack. And this is silent about what it is, exactly, that can appear other than it is.

This is not all. Even if you say that appearances in themselves affect us in one way and things in themselves in another, the dilemma with which we began still faces Kant's theory once you have imported such a distinction into his argument. Suppose we say that a thing in itself transcendently affects the ego in itself and an appearance in itself. If an appearance in itself is just a thing in itself affecting the ego, we have the difficulty of explaining how things in themselves are knowable.

And if an appearance in itself is a spatio-temporal object affecting the forms of our sensibility, then we have the equally great difficulty of explaining how we can avoid the assumption of a thing in itself that stands in the affection relation to the perceiver.

But *DA* dies hard. Suppose we try to repair the foregoing difficulty by invoking the distinction between two kinds of ego. What faces *DA* is the difficulty of explaining how an appearance in itself can affect our sensibility without resolving itself into a relation of a thing in itself to the perceiver. It might be argued, however, that an appearance in itself affects the empirical ego while a thing in itself affects the ego in itself. The claim, crucial to *DA*, that there are two kinds of affection would then be made to rest on the difference between two kinds of ego. A thing in itself would not, accordingly, affect our sensibility. For it would stand in relation only to the ego in itself. What does affect our sensibility is an appearance in itself; and this, so the argument might run, no longer requires a *DA* theorist to admit that all cases of affection are ultimately relations of things in themselves to the forms of our sensibility. And so, the conclusion would seem to be that *DA* can remove the dilemma facing Kant's theory of perception.

Invoking the distinction between two kinds of ego serves, however, only to delay the demise of *DA*. The problem that arises for the *objects* of perceptual awareness is merely transferred to the *subjects* of that awareness. Consider how this comes about. What distinguishes the ego in itself from the empirical ego is that it can apprehend individuals without the forms of space and time that characterize our sensibility and thus becomes a phenomenal object. But both still have something in common: Both must have some forms or other of sensibility. Kant does not explicitly claim this, but an argument can be constructed to show that his distinction between positive and negative noumena commits him to it. A negative noumenon is anything just insofar as it is not the object of our sensuous intuition; a positive noumenon, just insofar as it is an object of a nonsensuous intuition.[13]

Let us suppose, as *DA* requires us to do, that transcendent affection is some kind of epistemic relation holding between a thing in itself and the ego in itself. What should be noticed here is that, even in the case of transcendent affection, there is a kind of intuition. And this requires that there be a sensibility for the ego in itself with characteristics of its own. If this were not the case, then *DA* could not explain, as it must, how transcendent affection gives the ego a relation to a *particular* rather than, say, only to a concept. The doctrine of transcendent affection requires the notion of a positive noumenon. Without such a notion the theory must also recognize, not the mere absence of sensibility, but merely a different kind of sensibility characterized by its own forms.[14]

The distinction between transcendent and empirical affection must be drawn, then, in terms of two ways in which particulars are received. The distinction cannot be drawn in terms of the presence or absence of any intuitive faculty at all. But once it is seen that even an ego in itself has a sensibility if it is to be perceptually aware of particulars, the problem that the distinction between two kinds of ego was introduced to solve breaks out all over again with respect to an ego that does not have our forms of intuition. Even if we assume that the ego itself lacks the forms of sensibility that distinguish it from the empirical ego, we must assume that it has some forms of sensibility or other. The rejection of this assumption would prevent the ego in itself from being affected at all. But the acceptance of this assumption would merely raise all of the problems facing the notion of an appearance in itself at another level. What makes the notion so problematic is that, as I have argued, we are forced to account for it in terms of the relation in which something not having the forms of our sensibility stands to those forms.

Consider how this recapitulation comes about. The dilemma to which *DA* is supposed to be the solution arises over the relation of sensibility to the doctrine of affection. On the one hand, the object affecting us would seem to be a thing in itself, and this is impossible because we would then have to perceive something that, on Kant's theory, we cannot. On the other hand, what stands in that relation to us would seem necessarily to be what Kant calls a phenomenal object, and this is impossible because affection is defined as the relation of an object to the forms of our sensibility; hence, that relation precludes the object's having spatial or temporal characteristics. What generates the foregoing dilemma is Kant's assessment of the forms of sensibility. The difficulty in finding an acceptable relatum to stand in the affection relation to an ego issues from the fact that any candidate would seem both to have and not to have the characteristics of sensibility. It must be a thing in itself because it affects the ego and cannot be characterized by forms of intuition. But it must also be a phenomenal object because it must be characterized by some forms of intuition or other if it is to affect the ego at all. And this problem does not disappear by appealing to the notion of transcendent affection even though the forms of such a sensibility would be different from those of the empirical ego.[15] They are, after all, still forms that qualify the way in which the ego in itself must be affected by a thing in itself. Thus a change in the character of sensibility does not give *DA* a way of removing the dilemma. Both kinds of ego must have forms of sensibility if they are to be affected by *particulars*.

All that an appeal to two kinds of ego can accomplish for the *DA* theorist, then, is to show that both kinds of affection must inevitably apply to each kind of ego, but this is to perpetuate the problem that the distinction must eliminate. I conclude, therefore, that Kant's distinction between what are things in themselves for the empirical understanding and what are transcendent things in themselves fails to imply a corresponding distinction between two kinds of affection.

Distinguishing between an appearance in itself and the variable circumstances of perceiving it lends no support to the *DA* theorist because the character of the appearing relation and its relata are precisely what is at stake here. Nor, finally, does the dilemma confronting the notion of an appearance in itself in Kant's theory of perception disappear if we allow ourselves to impute two kinds of affection to Kant's theory. Such a step merely raises the same problem all over again with respect to the relation between a thing in itself and an ego in itself.

There is, however, a second kind of example that Kant gives as a case of an appearance in itself. He cites a rainbow as a case of an appearance in itself, contrasting the way in which it appears to us with the rain constituting the object that appears. Thus he says that the "rainbow on a sunny shower may be called merely appearance, and the rain the thing itself."[16]

This must be sharply distinguished from the rose example because it gives us very different grounds for believing in appearances in themselves. In the former case, perceptual *properties* of a particular vary with changing perceptual conditions. In the latter, the distinction holds between the micro- and macro-structures of one and the same *particular*. But, as the *DA* theorist quickly points out, even the micro-structure of rainbows has spatio-temporal properties. There is, so it is concluded, a relation of empirical affection between the micro-structures of phenomenal objects and the forms of our sensibility. The micro-structure of objects like rainbows exists independently of our

forms of intuition. It is, in other words, an object that can exist independently of our sensory apparatus while at the same time having
spatio-temporal characteristics.

The distinction between micro- and macroconstituents of an object
is, however, useless to the *DA* theorist: It confuses causation with affection.[17] The rain is the partial cause of the rainbow we might see in
our visual field. What stands in a relation to the forms of our sensibility is the rainbow and not the rain because the rain does not generate the rainbow by acting on our sensory mechanism. It produces
something else that does. It is about the rainbow, not the rain, that we
must ask what its relation to the sensory mechanism is. And it is no
answer to this objection to say that the cause of the effect that does act
on our sensory mechanism is itself an item having spatio-temporal location. All this shows is that the various items of our spatio-temporal
world can be related one to another as cause to effect. It does not show
that the notion of an appearance in itself demands a theory of double
affection but merely that one phenomenal item can cause another phenomenal item to occur.

But this is not the only reason for rejecting the claim, crucial to a
DA theory, that the distinction between such entities as rain and rainbows requires the further distinction between two kinds of affection.
There are two alternatives in characterizing the rainbow case that are
conjointly exhaustive and neither of which establishes the existence of
double affection. We may suppose either that the rainbow we see in
our visual field is the same as the rain or that it is numerically different
from the rain. Neither option implies *DA*. Take them in turn.

Suppose we say that the rainbow and the rain are literally one and
the same item. This would only obliterate the distinction between an
appearance in itself and how it appears to us since the rain as opposed
to the rainbow would be the object that would occupy our perceptual fields. But in that case what was supposed to be an appearance
in itself would really be an appearance *simpliciter* that would not support the claim that appearances are items that can appear to us other
than they are. And it would also cancel out the necessity to import the
distinction between empirical and transcendent affection into Kant's
theory of perception in order to explain the relation between that per-
cipient and what he immediately perceives.

All that remains to *DA* is to assume that the two items are numerically diverse. Yet, even this shows, at most, that one spatio-temporal
item can cause another. The very fact that both items have spatio-

temporal qualities shows that an account of the relation between the two requires something more than the forms of our sensibility since both items satisfy spatio-temporal descriptions. To show, in other words, that one item in nature *causes* another is not to show that the two items *affect* us in different ways. Causation is not affection, empirical or otherwise. And this, in turn, shows that no double affection takes place in either case.[18]

I conclude, then, that Kant's distinctions between appearances and appearances in themselves, appearances and appearances of appearances, and appearances and things in themselves for the empirical understanding neither imply *DA* nor require the distinction between two kinds of affection in order to be made intelligible. The part of Kant's theory of perception to which a *DA* theorist appeals really consists of nothing more than the recognition of the phenomenon of perceptual variability. Whatever the problems that such a fact raises, they cannot be removed by imputing *DA* to Kant. Rather, such an imputation, as I have also been arguing, merely reproduces the problem it was meant to solve. Nor, finally, does the distinction between micro- and macro-structures of perceptual objects require the adoption of *DA*; in this case what is baptized as a distinction between two kinds of affection is really only a distinction between causation and affection.

3. Ideality and Subjectivity

The notion of an appearance in itself present in Kant's theory of perception is not, however, the only evidence to which *DA* theorists have appealed. Kant calls some of the items of our experience ideal and contrasts these with what he calls merely subjective items.[19] *DA* theorists like Erich Adickes claim that this distinction collapses without the recognition of two kinds of affection. And from this they infer that the ideal-subjective distinction implies *DA*.[20] The argument for this conclusion runs as follows. Kant says that items like space and time are transcendentally ideal.[21] But he also says that secondary properties like colors, tastes, and smells are merely subjective. And this is what generates the problem. Both ideality and subjectivity betoken the fact that whatever has either is dependent in some way on the characteristics of our sensory apparatus. There remains, however, the crucial distinction between the sense in which each kind of item is dependent. If something is transcendentally ideal, it depends for its existence upon a generic character of our sensibility as such. But whatever is merely subjective is dependent upon the peculiarites of some perceiver. And, so the argument concludes, if this distinction is to be preserved, we must attribute *DA* to Kant.

Does such a distinction require *DA*? I think not. Consider how Kant introduces the distinction between subjectivity and ideality. This can be inferred from what he says at A28=B44. In the first place, anything is ideal whenever it is the basis for verification of a synthetic a priori judgment. This is not the case with an item of experience that is merely subjective. In the second place, something is ideal whenever it is a necessary condition for any object's being presented to us in intuition. Distinguish, for example, between the status that Kant gives to space and, say, a color. Both are dependent for their existence, according to Kant, on our sensory apparatus. But space fulfills both of the foregoing conditions, while color can be absent from the content of our experience without making it impossible for us to experience any object whatever.

But, as it stands, the distinction between subjectivity and ideality alone offers no support to the *DA* theorist. That something in our experience is neither the necessary condition for our experiencing any object at all nor the basis for the verification of a synthetic a priori judgment does not require a distinction between two ways of our being affected by objects. It requires, at most, the recognition of two different roles that the items affecting our sensibility play in our experience. And this is still compatible with our being affected in only one way.

The distinction between subjectivity and ideality is, however, also linked with the distinction between primary and secondary properties.[22] What Kant calls secondary properties are subjective in that they allegedly have an origin different from ideal items.[23] The secondary properties of an object are the partial result of the characteristics of our sensibility. But they are also partially the result of the action of the primary properties of an object on our sensibility.[24] And yet both primary and secondary properties belong only to bodies that are spatio-temporally located. To separate primary from secondary properties as Kant does, so the *DA* theorist's argument runs, is to assume that there are qualities of spatio-temporal objects that act upon the perceiver to produce his experience of secondary qualities. Thus while both kinds of quality are ideal in that they are instantiated by objects that also have spatio-temporal characteristics, secondary qualities are subjec-

tive in that they are the effects of the causal action of primary properties on the sensibility of the perceiver. Primary qualities empirically affect the perceiver because they are in space and time. But the objects
having such qualities transcendently affect the ego because they lack
spatio-temporal characteristics.[25]

The fact is, however, that Kant's distinction between subjectivity
and ideality does not require *DA*. Consider the distinction between
primary and secondary qualities. Let us suppose that there are bodies
having, say, such properties as size, shape, and solidity that, in turn,
cause us to experience objects as having color, taste, smell, and sound.
This distinction does not require *DA*. At most it requires that we recognize the existence of certain powers or dispositional properties that
cause us to experience other properties. And this requires us, again, to
distinguish between causation and affection. Primary properties may
cause us to experience secondary properties, but this does not imply
that they affect our forms of sensibility. They may cause sensations of
certain kinds to occur in us. But this is not so much evidence of the
existence of a relation called empirical affection as it is of the fact of
causation in our perception.

That primary and secondary qualities are distinguishable does not,
however, prove even that our perception of secondary qualities is
caused by the primary properties of the bodies we perceive. That
something is a primary quality of a body does not prevent it from
being the content of an act of perceptual awareness. We can perceive
the primary qualities of a body simultaneously with the secondary
qualities that body has. That both kinds of property can be simultaneously present in our sensory field shows that they affect us in the same
way. Thus even though it may be the case that a body's possession of
both kinds of property is to be explained in terms of properties it has
that cannot be present in a spatio-temporal framework, the distinction
between primary and secondary properties does not of itself demand a
distinction between two kinds of affection.

4.   Individuals and Spatiality

The distinction between secondary and primary qualities does not, as
we have seen, demand a distinction between empirical and transcendent affection. This still does not exhaust the evidence on which the
DA theorist relies. Two kinds of affection are required, we are told, if

we are to account for the diversity of spatial shapes that the objects of our apprehension have.[26] To say, as Kant does, that space is a form of our sensibility is merely to say that it characterizes our apprehension of things in outer sense. But it does not explain why the figures of things we perceive in space have a variety of shapes. Kant explains this in two divergent ways. On the one hand, he claims that appearances in themselves determine the difference between the spatial characteristics of perceptual objects.[27] On the other hand, however, he says that what accounts for the very same fact is the character of things in themselves.[28] But he cannot say both. If what is called an appearance in itself is supposed to account for such features of our experience as spatial diversity, then there is no need to import things in themselves to account for an account that has already been given. And if things in themselves are supposed to account for the fact of spatial diversity, then there is no need to import appearances in themselves to accomplish the same task.

The *DA* theorist offers the following solution. What determines the diversity of characteristics exhibited by spatial objects is, according to *DA*, the way things in themselves are constituted.[29] But this does not contradict the claim that appearances in themselves determine such characteristics. Things in themselves *remotely* determine the spatial characteristics of the things we intuit. What we intuit in that intuition, however, is *proximately* determined by an appearance in itself. Kant does not, according to *DA*, say that both things in themselves and appearances in themselves account for spatial differences in things. That one spatial configuration is different from another is supposedly explained by the fact that some properties of a thing in itself are different from the properties that other things in themselves have. The difference in spatial properties exhibited by appearances in themselves is explained by the existence of a corresponding difference in the order of things in themselves. The contradiction disappears, according to *DA*, once we recognize that things in themselves transcendently affect the ego in itself and appearances in themselves empirically affect the empirical ego. Since they stand in relation to different things, the contradiction between claiming that appearances in themselves and things in themselves account for the diversity of spatial figures disappears.

The appeal to Kant's variant explanations of the diversity of shape breaks down on two crucial difficulties. It is not implied by Kant's explanations. And, what is even more damaging to *DA*, imputing that theory to Kant does not succeed in removing the alleged contradiction. Take these in turn. We can hold without contradiction that both things in themselves and appearances in themselves account for the diversity of spatial figures. Nothing in the concept of an appearance in itself forbids analyzing it as the content of an intuition generated whenever a thing in itself affects our sensibility.[30] There are, as I have already pointed out, philosophical difficulties with this account. But a contradiction in Kant's account of the diversity of spatial figures is not among them. What remains is to explicate the relation between an appearance in itself and a thing in itself. But the difficulty that attends such an explication must not be confused with the quite separate difficulty issuing from the claim that Kant's account of spatial diversity entails a contradiction. The former arises from Kant's account of affection in general; the latter provides fresh evidence for the problem. But since no such contradiction exists, there is no fresh evidence to support the claim that Kant's theory implies *DA*; hence, the Kantian explanation of spatial diversity does not imply *DA*.

But let us suppose, for the sake of the argument, that there is a genuine conflict with Kant's account of spatial diversity. Does *DA* remove that conflict? I think not. Let us first try to locate the place where the conflict arises. I have already shown how to interpret the relation between a thing in itself and an appearance in itself that does not entail such a conflict. Yet one might argue that, so long as we impute to Kant only one kind of affection, both a thing in itself and an appearance in itself could not stand in that relation to somebody perceiving spatial shapes. An appearance in itself is in space and time. They are the conditions of our ability to be affected at all. But this is not the case with a thing in itself. To work with only one notion of affection would, accordingly, conflict with the claim that a thing in itself and an appearance in itself can both affect us.

What does *DA* offer to relieve this conflict? We are given two relations of affection, one of which relates the thing in itself to the empirical ego. This may remove the contradiction at one level. But what results only reproduces the problem it was supposed to solve. The existence of a sensibility even for the ego in itself as a necessary condition of nonsensuously intuiting anything only permits us to raise the difference between two kinds of account of the diversity of what we see all over again for that ego. For such an appeal merely resurrects the distinction between the way in which something is constituted apart from any sensibility whatever and the way in which that object appears to a perceiver. This, we already know, follows from the fact that a noumenal ego must have a sensibility in order to be affected by a thing in itself. Since all of the distinctions that are made with respect to our sensibility and the objects that are given to it can be made with a noumenal sensibility, an appeal to a difference of affection cannot remove the alleged contradiction in Kant's account of spatial diversity. *DA* cannot, therefore, be confirmed in virtue of its power to remove that alleged conflict in Kant's account.

5. The Affinity of Appearances

But the diversity of objects with either spatial or temporal characteristics attaching to the objects we perceive is not the only difficulty that the *DA* theorist claims to remove from Kant's theory of perception. There is, it is claimed, a conflict internal to Kant's doctrine of affinity.[31] Kant says that all of our knowledge of natural laws must be derived from our experience of events in nature.[32] This follows from what Kant says about the nature of the affinity of appearances: There must be an objective ground on the basis of which we synthesize the perceptual manifold in the way we do.[33] What distinguishes a mere succession of perceptions from an ordered sequence of perceptions is that there is a ground in the object for the latter while there is none in the former. Kant claims, on this view, that our ability to distinguish between a synthesis governed by law and one that cannot be subjected to any rule is founded on something that is present in the object.

This is not all that Kant says. He also claims that all laws or rules governing the synthesis of perceptual manifolds are introduced into our perception of nature by the self.[34] That we order a manifold in one way rather than in another is explained, on this view, by a capacity of the self and not by whatever properties there are in the object. The *DA* theorist offers to reconcile this conflict in the following way.[35] What *DA* calls the objective affinity underlying sequences of all our perceptions is to be explained by the action of the ego in itself on appearances in themselves.[36] This supposedly explains the independent ground for the rules of synthesis we apply to objects. But all synthesis is, nonetheless, subjective in that what we call an appearance in itself is really a construction that we make out of a series of perceptions.[37] In this way, then, *DA* seeks to resolve the conflict in Kant's theory of affinity.

But here, again, *DA* fails. And, again, it fails on two counts. For one thing, *DA* is powerless to remove the apparent conflict between the claims Kant makes about the sources of the rules of synthesis. For another, what the *DA* theorist calls a conflict between two grounds of rules of synthesis is illusory. Let us assume, in the first place, that the ego in itself somehow acts in such a way as to bring about the affinity of appearances that justifies the application of one rule of synthesis rather than another. This would only raise the original problem all over again.

What generates the problem? According to the *DA* theorist, it is the difficulty of reconciling the existence of an affinity of appearances with the fact that all rules for combining the manifold are supplied by the ego. But to say that the ego in itself generates the order in the sequences that appearances in themselves present to us merely allows us to raise our original question all over again at the level of the activity of the ego in itself; the question, namely, of how to distinguish between the basis for an objective ordering of appearances and an ordering that is imposed on the sequence of appearances by the ego. *To invoke an action of the ego in itself on appearances in themselves to explain this distinction merely requires an explanation at another level of the distinction between those rules that the ego in itself imposes on appearances in themselves and those it does not.*

Yet the fact remains that there is no contradiction requiring the remedy offered by *DA*. No contradiction arises if we say, as Kant admittedly does, both that the self generates the rules according to which it synthesizes a perceptual manifold and that the self must always rely upon the way the world is in order to know what these rules are. This apparent contradiction dissolves once we distinguish between two different but mutually compatible claims. To say that all synthesis is an activity of the ego and not given to us by the objects we synthesize is to put forward a thinly disguised tautology. What is claimed is something about the essential feature of how we must come to know anything that is given to us in perception. To say that all synthesis is the work of the intellect is merely to claim that the way that we have of perceiving things is to unite a series of presentations. And this serves only to tell us that the self must rely on some activity or other of synthesis in order to perceive anything. It does not follow, however, that the rules in virtue of which that capacity is exercised on any particular occasion are also generated by the self. And to say that the rules of synthesis of the various objects we are given are derived from an affinity of appearances merely formulates the claim that the distinction between correctly and incorrectly synthesizing any given manifold cannot be derived from a general analysis of the nature of synthesis as such.

What emerges from the foregoing distinction is this. Our perceptual apparatus consists of whatever we bring with us to the apprehension of the objects that are given to us. This consists of the generic characteristics of the capacity to synthesize any manifold at all. These are rules for combining any manifold at all. But there are also rules for correctly combining any *given* manifold. There are general rules that any act of synthesis must satisfy in order to count as an act of synthesis. There are also specific rules that an act of synthesis must satisfy if it is to govern a correct apprehension of a given *kind* of object. The former are put into nature in that they prescribe how we must go about the apprehension of any perceptual object. The latter are derived from nature in that they prescribe the distinction between a correct and incorrect synthesis of any given kind of object. We can perform the former correctly even if we always perform the latter incorrectly. This is what marks the distinction. It is also what dissolves the contradiction to which *DA* is mistakenly meant as a remedy.[38]

6. The Dilemma Revisited

DA leaves the dilemma facing Kant's theory of perception where it was found. That dilemma, it will be remembered, comes to this. To be affected is to stand in some epistemic relation to an object. That object is either a thing in itself or a phenomenal object. If it is the former, we would be in direct epistemic contact with something that, on Kant's theory, we cannot have in our sensory fields. We would obliterate the distinction between a phenomenal object and a thing as it is apart from what we perceive it to be. If the object affecting us is phenomenal, then affection in its Kantian acceptation cannot be applied without either a vicious circle or an equally vicious infinite regress. On Kant's theory, consciousness of phenomenal objects is partially explicated in terms of a thing in itself affecting our forms of intuition. But this assumes that affection stands between a thing in itself and whatever forms of intuition we have. It cannot stand between phenomena and acts of perceptual awareness because it is used to explain how perceptual awareness of phenomenal objects is possible in the first place.

To conscript it into service as a relation between phenomenal objects and acts of awareness is to make Kant's entire theory break out into a vicious circle. We need the relation of affection if we are to give a Kantian explanation of how we get ourselves into a state of perceptual awareness. We cannot then introduce that relation all over again without circularity in the original explanation.

But there is also the problem of a vicious infinite regress in Kant's theory if we hold that what affects us is a phenomenal object. If what is required is that a phenomenal object stand in the relation of affection to a state of perceptual awareness, then that object inherits all of the difficulties of the original thing in itself. For now what was a phenomenal object at one level becomes a functional or structural thing in itself once we ask how a phenomenal object can affect us. And this goes on so long as what is given to us merely recapitulates the format of the original situation generating the difficulty. For the forms of our sensibility are, on Kant's theory, space and time. What makes an object phenomenal, on the same account, is the fact of spatio-temporal location. But in that case the notion of affection cannot be explicated in terms of the relation in which a *phenomenal* object stands to the forms of our sensibility. Such an object is already spatio-temporal and cannot, therefore, stand in the required relation to forms of sensibility like space and time.

The problem confronting the theory of double affection is really a problem that confronts the very notion of affection: there must be a justification for claiming that affection is an epistemic relation between an object and the forms of our sensibility while claiming at the same time that we cannot perceive things in themselves. But there would seem to be no hope in reconciling the two claims with each other. The problem is to find viable relata for the relation of affection. We have only two. And neither is viable. If you opt for things in themselves as the affecting agents, then you provide an object that cannot be perceived. And if you opt for phenomenal objects, you are left with the task of providing an object that cannot stand in the required relation to the forms of sensibility. In either case, the appropriate relatum is missing. And this is not a problem that can be solved by contriving, in the tradition of Adickes, Vaihinger, and their Anglo-Saxon scions, a theory of double affection. The problems that beset Kant's theory of perception arise with single affection and, as I have tried to show, can be duplicated only by a corresponding duplication of affections.

The first step in removing the prima facie contradiction that vitiates the concept of affection is to reject a plausible but ultimately un-satisfactory solution. Suppose somebody claimed that space and time can be both the forms of our sensibility and the characteristics of the objects that we sensuously apprehend.[39] There is, it might be argued, nothing in the theory that space and time are the formal characteris-tics of our sensibility to imply that they cannot also inhere in the things we perceive. Let us provisionally grant that it is not only free of contradiction but also true. There is no contradiction. But even with this concession, the same problem that undoes DA in other precincts merely emerges all over again. The problem arises again with respect to the relation that the object we perceive has to its spatio-temporal characteristics. Even if we allow the possibility that the objects we per-ceive have spatio-temporal characteristics, we do not rid ourselves of the issue with which we began.

The issue concerns the relation between what we perceive and what Kant calls the forms of sensibility. The problem is reduplicated when those forms are also implanted in the things we perceive. Whatever problem that arises in the context of the objects we perceive and the forms under which we perceive them will arise all over again when the context is shifted to the objects we perceive and the spatio-temporal characteristics they have.

The upshot is that either the notion of a thing in itself must go from Kant's theory of perception or the notion of affection must be dis-carded. And this is a situation that DA is powerless to remedy because the general strategy for applying DA must inevitably force the emer-gence of the original dilemma with respect to transcendent affection. Since we must make a distinction between what affects the sensibility of an ego in itself and what that object is in itself, we can raise all of the problems associated with affection within the context of a sen-sibility different from ours. And, what is equally disturbing for DA, to say that phenomenal objects affect the empirical ego raises the same problem with the fact that the affecting object is phenomenal that is raised about Kant's theory even without imputing DA to it. To say that space and time are forms under which we can be sensibly aware of any perceptual object does not prevent that object from satisfying spatio-temporal descriptions.

The problem about the proper description of the object that satis-fies these descriptions does not disappear. To say that something is a form under which we must perceive an object if we are to experience it at all does not imply that the object that we experience lacks the properties that are designated as forms of perception. And such a claim is also completely silent about the relation between the objects we perceive and the characteristics they exemplify.

It remains to be seen how we can intuit things in themselves without contradicting the very notion of a thing in itself or, what is equally unsatisfactory for Kant's theory, transforming a thing in itself into a phenomenal object. The dilemma facing Kant's theory can be removed when we see that his notion of intuition admits a perception of things in themselves but that such an admission is harmless. Kant specifies the content of an intuition in a way that implies nothing about the spatio-temporal character of the object we are given. He gives us two criteria. We know something by intuition, in the first place, when we stand in an immediate epistemic relation to it.[40] And we intuit something, secondly, just in case that entity is singular or, equivalently, an individual rather than a common property.[41] What is important about these criteria for the present dilemma is that neither *implies* that a content of intuition is spatial or temporal. It may be the case that the individuals that are immediately presented to us also satisfy spatio-temporal descriptions, but nothing about the notion of immediacy or singularity as such requires them to do so.

The immediacy and singularity criteria do, however, imply that the objects we intuit are at best only contingently related to the spatial or temporal characteristics they might have. And it also follows that the singular entities that we may be given in intuition satisfy descriptions just insofar as they are singular. This implies, further, that singular entities are logically independent of whatever spatial or temporal descriptions they may also satisfy. This tells us the sense in which we do intuit things in themselves when they affect our sensibility: we are immediately aware of individuals that satisfy descriptions that do not necessarily contain spatial or temporal predicates. Thus the individuals we intuit may be presented with spatio-temporal characteristics; but when we intuit the individuals that are presented with spatial or temporal characteristics, what we intuit is not something that can be identified with those other entities. This is not to deny that spatial and temporal entities might also be individuals. Kant's argument in the Aesthetic in fact requires that spaces and times be kinds of individuals. For, as everybody knows, the account he gives of space there is that it is an infinite volume with other volumes contained within that volume to infinity. He believes, in other words, in the existence of a kind of particular he calls a volume.[42]

This belief extends to another kind of particular called a moment. This is the result of his application of the volume analogy to time.[43] Spaces and times must, on the present theory, be kinds of individuals. None of this, however, undermines the conclusions I have drawn from an examination of the singularity and immediacy criteria for intuitions. All it shows is that there are some kinds of particulars that have spatio-temporal characteristics essentially. This does not show that *all* individuals have spatio-temporal characteristics essentially. That moments and volumes have temporal or spatial characteristics essentially is, therefore, the logical result of their being spatial and temporal and not the consequence of their being singular items that are immediately given to us in intuition.

There is, if the foregoing argument is sound, a sense in which we do intuit things in themselves. But it is not a sense that would require the collapse of the distinction between a thing in itself and a phenomenal object. The latter is a particular together with the spatial or temporal characteristics that it must have if it is to be a perceptual object for us. But although the particular must be connected with space and time, the particular that affects us is not itself spatial or temporal. It is, at most, connected with a volume of space or a moment in time. This preserves the distinction between a phenomenal object and a thing in itself.[44] If the connection, say, between moments, spatial volumes, and the particulars occupying a spatial volume at a moment is contingent, then what we perceive when we are aware of a perceptual particular other than a moment or a spatial volume is an entity that can exist apart from the forms of our apprehension. This makes it a thing in itself. What makes it a phenomenal particular as well is its contingent relation to volumes and moments.

But there is a sense in which we cannot perceive things in themselves. Since the object we do perceive is only contingently connected to space and time, there is at least one possible world in which the particular could exist without satisfying any spatial or temporal description at all. Whatever properties it would have in such a world could not be perceived by us. This is compatible, however, with saying that the world in which we intuit the entity having spatio-temporal characteristics and the world in which other kinds of beings intuit the entity lacking such characteristics both contain the same *particular*.

Let me apply the distinctions for which I have been arguing to the solution of the dilemma raised by Kant's theory of perception. In the first place, things in themselves can affect us without becoming phenomenal objects. What affects us is the particular that satisfies the immediacy and singularity criteria for the content of a Kantian intuition. But a thing in itself does not affect us in the sense that the possible state of affairs of which the particular we intuit can be a part stands in no epistemic relation to us. This explains how it is possible to say that a thing in itself can be intuited without contradicting the very notion of a thing in itself because that notion has two senses. We can call something a thing in itself just in case it is a particular that is only contingently related to the moments and spatial volumes that comprise our forms of perceptual awareness. Or we can call the very same particular a thing in itself when it is separated from moments and spatial volumes. The discrimination of these two senses of "thing in itself" allows an escape from the dilemma that could not have been provided by *DA*.

We are now in a position to show how Kant's theory of affection avoids both the objection of circularity and infinite regress. The theory is not circular because we can account for phenomenal awareness without having to introduce the notion of affection surreptitiously. We are given a thing in itself whenever we are aware of a phenomenal object. But we are not given a thing in itself independent of any form of intuition. An infinite regress is avoided because a thing in itself is part of the content of phenomenal awareness. We do not have to explain how a phenomenal object can affect us as a thing in itself is said to do just because it is not two objects that we are perceiving and, therefore, not two objects that stand in the relation of affection to us.

7. Residual Objections

The explication of the notion of affection that I have offered is bound to invite two plausible and initially powerful objections. Let me take them in turn.

The objection from transcendental ideality.—Some might still argue that my resolution of the dilemma ignores its most crucial objection. Space and time are, as Kant says, forms of our sensibility. They are nothing but the forms that, as Kant also says, lie a priori in the mind.[45] But if all of this is true, then somebody might contend that it is simply false to say that the particulars that we intuit satisfy spatiotemporal descriptions while still being things in themselves. Once you have said, in other words, that space and time are transcendentally ideal, then you have also said that they cannot attach to the particulars that we intuit.

The answer to this objection issues from a closer examination of Kant's argument to show that space and time are transcendentally ideal.[46] What Kant says is this: Space is not a property, relational or otherwise. He says, further, that this is equivalent to the claim that space is not "a determination which attaches to the objects themselves when abstraction has been made from all the subjective conditions of intuition."[47] Both of these claims are made to follow from this: If space were a characteristic of things in themselves rather than a subjective form of our apprehension, we would not be able to intuit it prior to the things that are in space.

What, exactly, does this argument prove? Kant's strategy here is to show that objects cannot have spatio-temporal characteristics because having them would be incompatible with our ability to intuit space prior to our acquaintances with objects in space. But the argument succeeds only on the assumption that space is to be construed as a relational or nonrelational property. If space were a property, we could not intuit it prior to the things that have it just because we cannot intuit a property that is uninstantiated. Consider, say, the relational property "to the left of." If it were intuitable apart from the entities that instantiate it, it would have to be a singular that satisfies Kant's two criteria for an intuition. But the fact is that it is multiply instantiable. It cannot, therefore, be intuited as a singular entity satisfying Kant's criteria for an intuition. It assumes, accordingly, the simultaneous intuition of the entities instantiating spatial properties. But if space is a particular like a volume, then it would not be internally contradictory to maintain both that the particulars we intuit satisfy spatial descriptions and that space is transcendentally ideal in the sense that it is an a priori intuition constituting the condition of any object's being an object for us. Since space would, in this case, be a particular among particulars, our intuition of it would not be logically dependent upon intuiting the things to which it attaches. And this would be enough to show that objects could satisfy spatial descriptions even though space is transcendentally ideal.[48]

There is, I acknowledge, a troublesome addition to this line of reasoning. I refer to Kant's conclusion that whatever is an a priori intuition is not "a determination to the objects themselves, and which remains even when abstraction has been made of all the subjective conditions of intuition."[49] This would seem to commit us to the conclusion that the objects we intuit do not, after all, satisfy spatial descriptions. But all this claim states is that space is dependent for its existence upon the existence of acts of consciousness. And all this, in turn, shows us that space would cease to exist if acts of consciousness ceased to exist. It does not show that the objects in question fail to satisfy any spatial descriptions. It merely lays down a necessary condition under which such descriptions are true of objects; hence, the appeal to subjectivity does not buttress the objection from transcendental ideality.[50]

The objection from phenomenal properties.—Someone might still argue, however, that the account I have given of the way in which we intuit things in themselves without doing irreparable damage to Kant's theory of perception succeeds only at the cost of impoverishing that theory completely. It can be maintained, so the objection might run, that the problem of numerical diversity has been solved but that the related issue of qualitative diversity has not been solved. When we perceive individuals, what we see are entities that, though they have spatio-temporal properties, do not have them essentially. But this is still silent about other features of a perceptual situation. There may be properties that perceptual individuals have that cannot be presented to us because of the peculiarities of our forms of intuition.

But this is only one part of the objection. It might also be argued that the problem of qualitative diversity serves only to raise the original dilemma facing Kant's theory all over again with respect to properties. Consider how this allegedly comes about. Distinguish between the spatio-temporal characteristics of things and such phenomenal characteristics as shape and size. If all we are allowed to introduce here is the property of spatiality, there is no way to account for the qualitative difference between, say, a square and a round shape in the spatial objects we intuit. But this demands that we add to the general notion of spatiality the phenomenal difference between different kinds of spatial characteristics. Yet such characteristics must, on Kant's theory, either be what I shall call properties in themselves or they must be manifestations of properties that cannot be intuited but that somehow act on our sensibility. Both alternatives cause difficulty for the theory. Take them in turn.

Suppose that the spatial properties are characteristics of what Kant calls things in themselves. This would disqualify them from counting as spatial or temporal because it would be the same as saying that the properties in question are phenomenal. But suppose, for the sake of the argument, that they are phenomenal. This would seem to force us back to the alternative according to which the properties that we intuit are the result of the action of properties we do not intuit on our sensibility, and this would raise the problem confronting Kant's theory all over again. That problem arose because of an impossible set of conditions placed on the perception of objects. What we perceive must be a phenomenal object. Yet what is called a phenomenal object is the result of the action of a noumenal object on our sensibility. The former condition permits us to perceive things, but the latter condition prevents us from doing so just because it requires us to have the capacity to perceive things that we cannot perceive should we accept Kant's theory. The problem, it should be noticed, can be formulated in a perfectly general way without introducing the peculiarities of any specific kind of perceptual entity: it applies to perceptual individuals as well as perceptual properties. So far I have tried to solve the problem with respect to perceptual *individuals*. But it would seem that the same problem would arise all over again for perceptual *properties*.

But does it? I think not. Nothing in Kant's argument for the transcendental ideality of space implies a distinction between how the particulars we intuit are presently constituted in themselves and how they appear to us. As far as Kant's argument goes, we are required only to distinguish between how things are presently given to us and how they might be constituted in some other possible world. To explain how one spatial figure differs from another does not, in other words, demand that we make the distinction between properties of things in themselves and properties of objects as they appear to us. All it does demand, on Kant's theory of perception, is that we distinguish between the properties things have in the world that is presented to us and those properties that can be instantiated in the possible worlds with which we are not presented. And this is enough to escape the objection from phenomenal properties. For all it says is that we do not require the distinction between a property in itself and something called a phenomenal property in order to account for the fact of qualitative diversity. We do not need such a distinction, but this does not imply a lack of need for a distinction between things in themselves and things as they are presented to us. The Objection from Phenomenal Properties does not, therefore, force us to make the impossible distinction between properties in themselves and phenomenal properties.

Before relegating *DA* to philosophy's population of theoretical myths, let me take stock of why it fails and why what it purports to

accomplish can be done without its dubious aid. It fails both exegetically and philosophically. The former failure can be traced to the
fact that the doctrines to which *DA* theorists appeal are compatible
with other, quite different, theories of affection. The latter failure can
be found in the fact that the theory that *DA* attributes to Kant duplicates the problems it is supposed to solve. In neither case does the dilemma facing that theory demand or profit from the introduction of
two kinds of affection. The proper solution must, I conclude, rely on a
different interpretation of the notion of a perceptual individual and its
relation to a thing in itself. And this, in turn, demands an interpretation of the relation of individuation to our sensibility very different
from the one on which *DA* is based. Once such an interpretation has
been given, the problem raised by the dilemma originally facing Kant's
theory disappears.

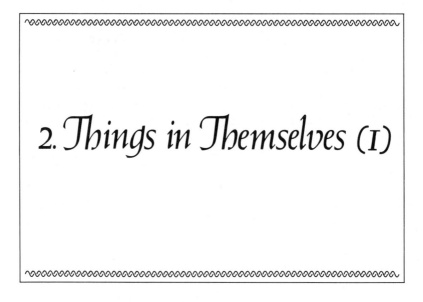

2. Things in Themselves (I)

D OUBLE AFFECTION begins with a dilemma and ends in failure. Kant claims, as we have seen, that every case of what he calls affection is also a case of causation. His theory provides us with two candidates for the relata in such a relation. We might say that things in themselves generate the relation of affection by acting on our sensibility or, alternatively, that phenomenal objects stand in this relation. Neither candidacy is successful. But the *DA* theorist postulates two relations of affection holding between the things in themselves and our noumenal egos on the one hand and holding between phenomenal objects and our empirical egos on the other.

The theory falters, as we have also seen, because Kant's examples do not support it, and its introduction into his theory conflicts with other parts of his epistemology. The notion of an appearance in itself, crucial to *DA*, founders on the evidence that is adduced to support it. The rose and the rainbow examples, when properly explicated, drive this point home. The variability of our perception of the properties of a phenomenal object like a rose shows that there is something constant despite the change of its perceptual properties. But this shows only that there is a distinction between something that is constant in perception and something else that need not be. We are not shown, as the *DA* theorist requires, that what is constant is something called an appearance in itself rather than a thing in itself. The example is entirely neutral about the relation between things in themselves and appearances. The rainbow example supplies further confirmation of this conclusion. The distinction between the macro and micro constituents of a phenomenal object is equally neutral about the issue. It is true that we can perceive the macroconstituents of an object on one occasion and the microconstituents of the same object on another. But our ability to do this shows only that we can be given two different phenomenal objects about which the problem concerning the relation between things in themselves and appearances can be raised one each occasion. Perhaps this is why Kant persistently called, however misleadingly, such objects as constant roses and variable rainbows things in themselves *in the empirical understanding*. All of this shows that, while every case of affection may be accompanied by a case of causation, the two relations are logically independent of each other. Distinguishing these two relations does not force the philosophically hazardous conclusion that there are two kinds of affection. It shows, instead, that there are two unique kinds of relation that Kant's theory accommodates side by side.

But the gain from distinguishing between affection and causation, valuable though it is, sets the stage for an even more intractible issue confronting Kant's theory. Kant distinguishes, notoriously, between things in themselves and appearances. He also distinguishes, less notoriously, between phenomenal substances and their appearances.[1] And, finally, he claims that the two distinctions are independent of each other: Phenomenal substances, unlike things in themselves, are in space and time.[2] This generates the following problem. If what Kant calls phenomenal substances appear to us, then why is the relation between a phenomenal substance and its appearances different from the putative relation between things in themselves and phenomenal substances? The answer to this question is, I believe, that there is no difference at all. There is, of course, a prima facie difference in that phenomenal substances are in space and time, while things in themselves are not. It is, in fact, the answer that Kant himself gives.[3]

The plausibility of such an answer dwindles, I shall argue, in the following considerations. For one thing, traditional accounts of the distinction between a thing in itself and an appearance cannot be given a coherent exposition unless that distinction is transformed into the distinction between a phenomenal substance and the ways in which it appears. For another, the reason why any attempt to account for the distinction between a thing in itself and an appearance in other ways must suffer the same fate is that it breaks down on the following dilemma that arises out of the way in which Kant introduces the distinction. A thing in itself must satisfy two mutually incompatible conditions. It must, first, generate an appearance by standing in some relation to the forms under which we apprehend appearances. (Call this the Affection Condition.) It cannot, secondly, be an object of sensory awareness. (Call this the Cognitivity Condition.) Both of these conditions are as essential as they are impossible conjointly to fulfill. Insofar as anything satisfies the Affection Condition, it must be an object of sensory awareness. And insofar as anything satisfies the Cognitivity Condition, it cannot stand in any relevant relation to the forms under which we apprehend appearances. The dilemma puts the notion of the thing itself, then, in an impossible position. It must either merge indistinguishably with the notion of a phenomenal thing, or it must prevent things in themselves from standing in any epistemically relevant relation to what Kant calls an appearance. This impossible position is not, however, a mere accident of the way in which Kant describes things that appear to us. It is the result of a crucial and instructive ambiguity in the very notion of transcendental ideality and affection as they have been traditionally conceived.

1. Things in Themselves: What They Must Be

Whatever else a thing in itself may be, it must satisfy what I have called the Affection and the Cognitivity Conditions. Both of these conditions emerge from the conclusion in the Aesthetic that space and time are transcendentally ideal. Kant summarizes this result of the argument as follows:

> For in an appearance the objects, nay even the properties that we ascribe to them, are always regarded as something actually given. Since, however, in the relation of the given object to the subject, such properties depend upon the mode of intuition of the subject, this object as appearance [Erscheinung] is to be distinguished from itself as object *in itself*.[4]

Things in themselves and appearances are distinguished in terms of the relation in which they stand to acts of perceiving. But to stand in such a relation to an act of perceiving is not enough to secure the distinction. This is a fact about an object that would merely distinguish possible from actual contents of such acts. It would not distinguish those contents that can stand in such a relation from those that in principle cannot do so. Something else must be added to Kant's distinction. We must be able to separate those contents that can possibly stand in some relation to an act of perceiving from those that cannot.

The foregoing requirement is met by what Kant calls a "mode of intuition." The ability to distinguish between a thing in itself and an appearance commits Kant to the following account of such a mode. It must have characteristics that are dependent for their existence upon the existence of acts of perceiving. But this alone is not enough. All this tells us is that a mode of intuition could be any sensation or other mental event that belongs essentially to the mental history of a perceiver. What must be added is that perceiving such characteristics is a necessary condition of being acquainted with any perceptual object at all. These conditions together explain how Kant can distinguish between things in themselves and appearances. To say that something is an appearance is not merely to say that it is an object of perceptual consciousness. This, we have seen, is not enough. An appearance is, rather, an object of consciousness some of whose properties depend for their existence upon the existence of acts of perceiving. And a thing in itself is an object to which such characteristics do not belong.[5]

Both the Affection and the Cognitivity Conditions follow directly from this interpretation of a mode of intuition. What I have called the Affection Condition follows from the requirement that certain characteristics of our mode of intuition depend for their existence upon acts of perceiving and, further, that these characteristics are necessary conditions of our perceiving whatever our modes of intuition. The object in question cannot, if Kant's theory is true, be what he calls a phenomenal substance, for that is an object that already has the characteristics that Kant calls modes of intuition. The object that stands in the relation of affection to the modes of intuition must lack the characteristics of these modes while yet standing in that relation to those modes. The distinction between a thing in itself and an appearance, then, requires that what counts as a thing in itself affect the modes of our intuition and thereby generate what Kant calls a phenomenal substance.

Let me anticipate an objection to this account of the Affection Condition. The following, alternative, account might be offered. To say that an object is a thing in itself is, so the account might go, to say that the object that we see spatially and temporally might exist apart from the spatial and temporal characteristics it has whenever we perceive it. And this would permit us to say that a thing in itself is not an object that differs from what Kant calls a phenomenal substance. It is the same object whose spatial and temporal properties are only contingently related to it; hence, the affection relation would hold between an object that is given to us and our acts of perceiving.

But the alternative interpretation breaks down. It fails to meet the Affection Condition essential to the distinction between things in themselves and appearances. It would entail that space and time are not, as Kant's theory requires them to be, modes of intuition. Suppose we say that spatio-temporal objects do, after all, affect acts of perceiving. This would make it impossible for space or time to be modes of intuition. For they would be constituents of what we intuit; hence, they would have to be distinguished from the way in which we intuit them. The present interpretation would, furthermore, entail that there is really no distinction between things in themselves and appearance at all. Suppose that the affection relation were to hold between spatio-temporal objects and acts of perceiving. This implies that space and time are not modes of intuition. And this, in turn, deprives Kant of his way of distinguishing between what makes an object accessible to perception and what does not.

But what about the Cognitivity Condition? Does it follow from anything that is essential to Kant's distinction between things in themselves and appearances? I think it does. The requirements are that a mode of intuition be a feature that is dependent for its existence on acts of perceiving and that such a mode be a necessary condition of our perceiving any object at all. If space and time are modes of intuition, the object given to those modes is not perceived as it is in itself, since it is not perceived apart from spatio-temporal characteristics. Yet if those characteristics belong to the way in which we perceive an object rather than to the object we perceive, then we cannot perceive the object as it is apart from space and time; hence, we cannot perceive the object as it is in itself.

Both of the conditions I have set forth are required by the conditions that Kant lays down for the distinction between things in themselves and appearances. Without the Affection Condition there can be no distinction between things as we perceive them to be and things as they are. And without the Cognitivity Condition what we perceive will inevitably be things as they are. It remains to be seen, however, whether anything can conjointly satisfy both of these conditions.

2. Things in Themselves: What They Are Not

The traditional accounts of what a thing in itself is cannot supply anything that meets both of the foregoing conditions. The first theory, argued in one form or another by Hermann Cohen and Hans Vaihinger, is that a thing in itself is a limiting concept (*Grenzbegriff*).[6] What is called a thing in itself is the total number of members belonging to the collection of which any one member is an appearance. The object that we perceive is an appearance in that it belongs to a set of appearances that cannot itself be given to perception. But since the collection consists of a potentially infinite number of appearances, it cannot itself become a content of an act of perceiving. The element-collection account of the distinction cannot, however, give a correct account of what the distinction must be if it is to fulfill both of the conditions I have set forth. For one thing, the collection does not exist. There is no such thing as a collection of all of the appearances that belong to an object just because that collection is potentially infinite; hence, no such thing can affect our mode of intuition. For another, the present theory begs the question it is supposed to answer. In order to determine which appearances are elements of any given set, we must find some way of separating those appearances that belong to one object rather than another. But if we are to distinguish between set membership among appearances, we must assume the existence of an object that is not itself a set in order to determine which appearances belong to it rather than to another set. And this raises the problem of the relation between that object and its appearances all over again. The notion of membership in a potentially infinite collection cannot, then, be used to explicate the distinction between a thing in itself and an appearance. A thing in itself is actual. A potential infinity is not. A set does not appear. A thing in itself does. The account, accordingly, satisfies the Cognitivity Condition: A set cannot be known. It fails the Affection Condition: A set cannot generate appearance.

What I shall call the Two Worlds Theory (*TWT*) purports to account for the difference between things in themselves and appearances in terms of two different kinds of objects. Appearances are objects having spatio-temporal characteristics; things in themselves are objects lacking such characteristics. Kant himself supplies the strongest piece of evidence of *TWT* when he claims that "the concept of appearances . . . already of itself establishes the objective reality of *noumena* and justifies the division of objects into *phenomena* and *noumena*."[7] If we can equate a thing in itself with a noumenon, then an object that lacks spatio-temporal characteristics is a thing in itself.

But can we? I think not. The *TWT* is unsatisfactory because it fails the Affection Condition. It feeds, in fact, on a confusion between two different kinds of objects that we cannot perceive. There are, first, objects that lack spatio-temporal characteristics and stand in no relation at all to our modes of intuition. There are, secondly, objects that also lack these characteristics but that affect our modes of intuition. The former are noumena; the latter, things in themselves properly so called. The *TWT* breaks down, therefore, on the fact that things in themselves must and noumena cannot appear to us by affecting our modes of intuition. To say, as the *TWT* requires, that a thing in itself is an entity that exists apart from spatio-temporal conditions passes the Cognitivity only to fail the Affection Condition.[8] Neither a noumenon nor a thing in itself can be known. But a thing in itself does, while a noumenon does not, affect our modes of intuition.

This is not, however, the only defect of the theory. To say, as *TWT* requires, that a thing in itself is an entity that exists without spatio-temporal characteristics succeeds only in avoiding the problem at hand. Suppose, for example, that what appears to us in space and time were a numerically different object from a thing in itself. The problem about distinguishing between an appearance and a thing in itself can be raised all over again with respect to what appears to us. The relation between a thing in itself and an appearance concerns the connection between what appears to us and the appearance of that thing; hence, the question about things in themselves already arises in the context of the distinction between a thing and its appearances. It is, therefore, independent of the issue about whether there are things that exist but that stand in no relation to the modes of our intuition.

There remains what I shall call the Two Descriptions Theory (*TDT*). D. P. Dryer gives a standard version of that theory, saying that it rests on "a distinction between two ways in which the same thing is regarded—between considering it in a certain relation, namely, as presented to the senses, and considering it apart from that relation."[9] The first thing to notice about *TDT* is that there is no disputing its firm textual basis. Kant says, for example, that "[t]he object is to be regarded in two different ways, as that which presents itself or as thing in itself."[10] This is typical of numerous other passages that can be adduced to support *TDT*. The second thing to notice is that *TDT* seems on the face of it to satisfy both the Affection and the Cognitivity Conditions. If one and the same thing can both be presented to our senses and be conceived as lacking spatio-temporal characteristics, at least one thing is clear: The thing that affects our modes of intuition is at least the same thing that can exist independently of them. What *makes* it a thing in itself may indeed be the possibility that it lacks spatio-temporal characteristics. But what has those characteristics for our mode of intuition is still the same object that might lack them. And the same holds for the Cognitivity Condition. If the theory is right, the object that appears to us to be spatio-temporal might appear without them to other modes of intuition. This is precisely what makes the object appearing to us unknowable as a thing in itself.

But the advantages of *TDT* are illusory. The crucial assumption of the theory is that one and the same object can satisfy two different descriptions. There is, if the theory is right, a description that a perceptual object satisfies when we can perceive it and another description that it can satisfy when it cannot be perceived by us at all. The theory assumes, in other words, two kinds of intuitional content. There is, first, the content that can be perceived by perceivers with our modes of intuition. There is, secondly, a content that cannot be perceived by us. The object that is perceived in either case, however, can satisfy both descriptions. This is the advantage of *TDT*; but it is also the undoing of the theory as an adequate account of what a thing in itself is. Let me explain.

Suppose that one and the same object can be described in two different ways. Consider what this requires us to say in the case of an object that can be both a thing in itself and an appearance. We must say that the object satisfies these descriptions simultaneously. This is only a consequence of the Affection Condition. If what affects our mode of intuition is a thing in itself, then the object that we perceive must satisfy descriptions appropriate to things in themselves and appearances at the same time. And this is obviously impossible. Insofar as it satisfies one description, it cannot satisfy the other; hence, the *TDT* lays down a requirement that cannot be met.

There are, however, plausible ways in which this difficulty might be avoided. We might, first of all, claim that the two descriptions need not be simultaneously satisfiable. To describe the object we perceive as a thing in itself might be merely to claim that there is a description it might but does not satisfy. The relation between the object and its spatio-temporal characteristics would then be logically contingent. And to describe something as a thing in itself would be to say that the object that has spatio-temporal characteristics could be the same object and yet lack these characteristics. But the suggestion, however true it may be, still fails to reconstruct the notion of a thing in itself. It may be true, for example, that what we perceive is only contingently related to the spatio-temporal properties it has. But if this object is what affects our modes of intuition, then space and time would not be modes of intuition. They would be part of the content of what we intuit. And this would imply the collapse of the Affection Condition, which is defined in terms of a relation of an object to spatio-temporal characteristics that characterize a mode of intuition.

Consider another way of avoiding the problems besetting *TDT*. It might be argued that spatio-temporal characteristics do not belong to an object apart from the relation in which it stands to something else. This goes well beyond the claim that space and time are contingently related to spatio-temporal things. The trouble with the preceding interpretation is that it cannot reconcile actual and possible descriptions with the Affection Condition. The present interpretation purports to repair this defect. We are asked to distinguish between two kinds of characteristics. These are those characteristics that an object has only in virtue of standing in some relation to an act of perceiving. And there are characteristics that the same object can have independently of standing in any such relation. This would seem to avoid the difficulties facing any attempt to distinguish between things in themselves and appearances by means of actual and possible states of affairs. We are given two kinds of actual states of affairs. The distinction between a thing in itself and an appearance is drawn in terms of those properties whose presence in an object depends upon the existence of acts of perceiving and those that do not. And, it might be argued, the same object can consistently have both kinds of properties. For dependent properties are assigned to an object under the condition that it stand in some relation to acts of perceiving; independent properties are assigned to that object without such a condition.

This does not, however, rescue the *TDT* from the difficulty it faces. We are, to be sure, given a case in which independent properties are actually possessed by the objects we perceive. But the attempt to save

TDT breaks down on both the Affection and the Cognitivity Conditions. It fails the Affection Condition. One and the same object may have both dependent and independent properties. This does, however, imply that the presence of one kind of property prevents us from perceiving the object to have the other kind of property. It does not even show that the presence of dependent properties is a necessary condition of our perceiving the object to have any properties at all. And, as if this were not enough, the present suggestion founders on the Cognitivity Condition as well. Nothing in the dependent-independent distinction prevents us from perceiving both kinds of properties; hence, nothing about the distinction enables us to demarcate the properties of an object that make it a thing in itself from those that make it an appearance.

None of the received accounts can explain the difference between a thing in itself and an appearance. To say that a thing in itself is a set of appearances fails because it cannot fulfill the Affection Condition. Something that does not exist cannot affect our mode of intuition. To substitute an existent entity that is neither spatial nor temporal, however, does not improve the intelligibility of a thing in itself. For the very characterization of such an entity prevents us from being affected by it. We cannot be affected by something that is definitionally disqualified from standing in any epistemic relation to our mode of intuition. And the replacement of an existing entity with a description that an existent entity might but does not satisfy is equally powerless to explain what a thing in itself is. Such an alternative merely gives us the original problem in a more elaborate form. Insofar as the description in question only possibly applies to the object we perceive, it serves no better than any other possible entity in the attempt to account for a thing in itself. And insofar as the description involved is satisfied by the object we perceive, we are not advanced beyond the difficulties facing the assumption of entities that are neither spatial nor temporal. Both fail, each in its own way, to satisfy the Affection Condition.

3. The Dilemma of Affection

The failure of the traditional accounts is not an accident. All of them illustrate the dilemma confronting any attempt to distinguish between a thing in itself and an appearance. The Affection Condition generates the problem. According to that condition, a thing in itself is responsible for the existence of what appears to us by standing in a certain epistemic relation to our forms of intuition. The problem then becomes how that relation can be both epistemic and have a thing in itself as one of its terms. Consider how this comes about. Kant tells us as much about affection as he ever does at the very beginning of the *Kritik*. He says, first, that "intuition takes place only insofar as the object is given to us."[11] He goes on to say, secondly, that "[t]his again is only possible, to man at least, insofar as the mind is affected in a certain way."[12] To be given an object, then, is to be affected in some way or other. But the tradition cannot successfully explicate such a notion. The claim is that the relation of being appeared to obtains just in case an object that we do not perceive acts on our mode of intuition and generates another perceptual content. The requirement is that an object that we cannot perceive produces a content that we can perceive. If this requirement were dropped, then there would be no distinction between what Kant calls a thing in itself and what he calls an appearance. Yet there is no such relation. Suppose we describe an object as satisfying a *phi*-description that, in turn, gives us something that we perceive under a *psi*-description. If affection is to be a special kind of relation in terms of which a thing in itself is distinguished from an appearance, *phi*- and *psi*-descriptions must be different. But if they are different, one of them cannot affect our mode of intuition. If either content is to affect our mode of intuition, it must be given to us. There would otherwise be no difference between perceiving an object under a *psi*-description rather than under a *phi*-description. Yet if the descriptions are different, then there must be such a distinction. Thus what Kant calls a relation of affection cannot be separated from what takes place when somebody is appeared to in certain ways. And this only serves to show that affection is not a unique kind of causal relation.

The dilemma, then, is this. If we are to distinguish between things in themselves and appearances, there must be a unique kind of relation that obtains between the two as Kant describes such a relation. Insofar as an object can be said to affect our mode of intuition, it must be distinguished from what we perceive. Insofar as the two are distinguished in this way, one of them cannot affect our mode of intuition. And so long as there is no relation called affection, the basis of the distinction between things in themselves and appearances collapses.

There are two ways in which the foregoing dilemma might be forestalled. Let me consider them in turn. You might object that a causal relation can hold between two states of affairs satisfying different descriptions. There is nothing objectionable about relating, say, a *phi*- and a *psi*-description causally; hence, it might be argued that what affects our mode of intuition can, after all, have a different property from what it is perceived to have.

The answer to such an attempt to avoid the dilemma is that it is true but irrelevant. There is nothing objectionable about causally relating two different properties. But explicating the affection relation in these terms *is* objectionable. If what Kant calls affection were really a causal relation between two different properties, there would be no explanation of what it is to perceive one property rather than the other. There may be causal circumstances that are indispensable conditions of our being affected by some property. Nothing about the causal relation between two properties satisfying these descriptions prevents one of those properties from being the cause of the property we perceive on one occasion and the object of perception on another. The distinction between *phi* and *psi* properties does not demarcate two kinds of *property* but rather two functions of one and the same property. This fact shows us once again that affection cannot be reduced to a kind of causation. Affection cannot be just the causal relation between *phi* and *psi* properties because either property can admittedly stand in a relation of affection to an act of perception. This possibility shows that the relation of causation presupposes the antecedent existence of the relation of affection in order to give any description of what causes us to have the kinds of perceptual content that we do. But these circumstances cannot be the same as those that affect us.

Suppose, finally, that there is another relation between two kinds of description applied to the objects we perceive. Let us assume that the object we perceive has a description that actually applies to it but a different description that we systematically misperceive to apply to it. If, say, space and time are characteristics that belong to our mode of intuition and not to objects that we perceive by means of this mode, then the difficulties of the foregoing account might be avoided. For one thing, we would perceive the object to have both kinds of characteristics. For another, when we perceive the spatio-temporal characteristics of an object, we would be seeing properties that really belong to what Kant calls our mode of intuition and not to the objects we perceive.

This avoids assimilating affection to causation only at the cost of abolishing the Affection Condition altogether. The theory requires that we distinguish between two kinds of description according to whether they are satisfied by what we perceive or the way in which we perceive it. But this implies that the properties of our mode of perceiving cannot be the result of our being affected by the properties of the object we perceive. For both properties are contents of our perception; hence, one of them cannot be used to account for the fact that we perceive the other.

Neither of the foregoing attempts to explicate the Affection Condition can avoid the dilemma that the condition raises. A causal relation between two properties is useless because it obliterates the distinction between being affected by one of the properties rather than the other. Finding distinct subjects of predication for properties is no more helpful. To say that some characteristics like space and time are really present in our mode of intuition rather than the objects we intuit fails to show how the objects we intuit affect us. For it cannot account for how what characterizes a mode of intuition is the result of the affect on us of the objects we intuit. It gives us, in other words, a way of avoiding the problem facing Kant's theory only at the cost of abolishing the Affection Condition.

4. The Background of the Dilemma

We have now canvassed two interpretations of the Affection Condition. One of them rests on the distinction between two kinds of description only at the cost of giving us a relation that is altogether different from the affection relation. The other gives us a difference in two states of enlightenment about whether one and the same description is satisfied only at the cost of doing the same thing.

The Affection Condition so essential to Kant's claim that there are things in themselves as well as phenomenal substances ultimately rests on an ambiguity in Kant's notion of transcendental ideality. There are what I shall call ontological and epistemic senses of transcendental ideality present in Kant's argument in the Aesthetic. Both of these senses figure in arguments he gives for transcendental ideality. Yet both of them are mutually exclusive and, when used in the same context, make the dilemma facing the Affection Condition with all that it implies about things in themselves a foregone conclusion.

Consider how Kant argues to his conclusion in the Aesthetic. I restrict myself to his argument concerning space. The results of that argument are readily transferable to time. Let me briefly summarize that argument. Kant moves to his conclusion by showing that our concept of space cannot be abstracted from objects in space and by showing that, as he puts it, space "underlies all outer intuitions." [13] We cannot, Kant says, acquire the concept of space by examining objects in space. For in order to acquire the notion in this way, we must be aware of numerically diverse objects in space. [14] We must, therefore, assume an awareness of space in order to derive the notion of space from objects.

Kant argues to the same conclusion in a second way. We can never represent to ourselves (uns eine Vorstellung machen) the absence of space. We can, however, think (uns denken) of space as empty of objects. [15] Kant concludes from both of the foregoing considerations that space "is nothing but the form of all appearances of outer sense. It is the subjective condition of sensibility, under which alone outer intuition is possible for us." [16] But consider just how much Kant's arguments permit him to infer. What they show is at most the epistemic dependence of our perception of objects on our perception of space. But so far from showing, as Kant concludes from his argument, that space is transcendentally ideal, the arguments are neutral about whether space exists independently of our mode of intuition. The arguments show, at most, that our mode of sensibility is dependent on space and not that space is dependent on our mode of sensibility. This is the epistemic sense of "transcendental ideality."

Kant also uses that notion in what I have called an ontological sense. He claims that calling something transcendentally ideal is just saying that it is "nothing at all, immediately we withdrew the above condition, namely, its limitation to possible experience, and so look upon it as something that underlies things in themselves." [17] Something is transcendentally ideal, then, just in case it is not a characteristic of what we perceive but rather of our mode of perception.

The ontological sense of "transcendental ideality" is both allowed by the characterization Kant gives of the conclusion he draws from the foregoing arguments and demanded by an independent argument for transcendental ideality. The argument occurs at A32–33 in his discussion of time. He puts it this way:

Were it self-subsistent, it would be something which would be actual and yet not an actual object. Were it a determination or order inhering in things themselves, it would not precede the objects as their condition.

He concludes that "time is not something which exists in itself, or which inheres in things as an objective determination, and it does not, therefore, remain when abstraction is made of all subjective conditions of intuition."[18] I do not consider the cogency of this argument and ask instead how it shows the existence of what I have called the ontological sense of "transcendental ideality." What Kant rejects here is the claim that time is a subsistent entity or that it is a property, relational or otherwise, of such entities. He concludes that it can only characterize the way in which we apprehend such entities. And this requires the ontological as distinct from the epistemic interpretation of "transcendental ideality." To say that space and time are necessary conditions of perceiving an object does not preclude them from being subsistents or properties of subsistents; hence, it does not imply that they are characteristics of our sensibility rather than the objects that we perceive. But to say that space and time can be neither subsistents nor properties of such things has quite a different implication. For it implies that, if they are to exist at all, they must somehow characterize the way in which we apprehend what we perceive rather than what we perceive.[19] Thus there arises the need to distinguish an ontological from an epistemic sense of "transcendental ideality."

This ambiguity engenders a dangerous illusion about the nature of the Affection Condition. If space and time are ontologically ideal, they cannot be part of the content of what we perceive. This follows from Kant's own account of what a mode of sensibility is. Such a mode, he says, is "the capacity (receptivity) for receiving representations through the mode in which we are affected by objects."[20] If we are to perceive an object, then, it must stand in some relation to our modes of sensibility. But if these modes were to form part of what we perceive, Kant could not explain how we can perceive the object we do by saying that the object affects these modes. Let me explain.

Suppose we say, as Kant does, that we are in an immediate epistemic relation to an object whenever we intuit it.[21] Kant explains what this immediate relation is by appealing to the affection of our modes of sensibility. But which of those modes—in this case, space and time—is also a part of the content of our intuition? What was formerly a mode of intuition would become part of what is intuited. And this implies that the fact of perceptual immediacy could not be explained by the presence of another perceptual content to our modes of sensibility. The present assumption makes space and time into objects among other objects of perceptual awareness. Once again we would be launched on an infinite regress destructive to the theory we are supposed to explicate. We have begun by saying that space and time are transcendentally ideal in the ontological sense: They are characteristics of things we perceive but are ontologically dependent upon the existence of perceptual acts. If this is so, then we cannot invoke the relation of affection to explain how we stand in an epistemic relation to an object. For we have already explicated affection in terms of modes of intuition and then implied that what is presented to us cannot be known to have those characteristics independent of possible experience. And we could not appeal to either space or time to explain how an object can stand in an epistemically immediate relation to our sensibility without obvious circularity.

But if affection were explicated in terms, not of being spatial or temporal, but rather of the relation that something that is neither spatial nor temporal has to space and time, matters would not improve. This way out of the circle would only presuppose another relation if we were to explain the fact of immediate presence to consciousness. The problem facing the Affection Condition arose because the modes of our intuition were allowed to function as objects as well as modes of intuition. Assume, however, that space and time can be modes but not objects of intuition. The restriction only postpones the problem. The content of an intuition that satisfies this restriction cannot, however, be the object that may act in some way on our modes of intuition. So long as these modes cannot themselves be objects of perception, then what we do perceive must still be somehow related to an act of awareness by a relation other than affection as it has been traditionally expounded, because that relation cannot itself be temporally or spatially connected with its relata. None of this shows, however, that there is no relation of affection or that the Affection Condition is a superfluous appendage to Kant's theory of the relation between things in themselves and appearances. What it does show is that such a relation cannot be explicated in terms of the characteristics of whatever forms of intuition we have.

The fact is, then, that the dilemma facing the Affection Condition is instructively fraudulent. It serves only to underscore the inadequacies of both the *TDT* and *TWT* accounts of the distinction between things in themselves and appearances. Both accounts assume the ontological interpretation of transcendental ideality. The *TWT* assumes it because a condition of its viability is that the forms of our intuition be characteristics of our modes of intuition rather than the things we perceive under those modes. There would otherwise be two *worlds* and not two *descriptions* of one and the same world. The *TDT* assumes it because it assumes that we know that what we perceive has some modes of intuition or other. And that assumption makes it impossible to account for the notion of affection without making it into something that it is not. It cannot be explained by first saying that it is the relation something has to our modes of intuition and then making those modes themselves possible objects of experience. Nor can it be explained by saying that affection obtains whenever an object stands in a relation to but is not a part of the content of our perceptual experience. This serves only to show that affection cannot be assimilated to a spatial or temporal relation. It does not show that there is no such relation as affection at all.

None of this follows if you substitute the epistemic for the ontological interpretation of transcendental ideality. This requires only that our acquaintance with a content of intuition be dependent upon our acquaintance with space and time. We are required here to bracket the question of whether the forms of our intuition are also characteristics of things that may exist independently of our experience. And this does not require us to make the fact of perceptual dependence into the relation between the content of an intuition and the subjective characteristics by which we are unable to stand in an immediate epistemic relation to that content.

A theory that uses the notion of transcendental ideality promiscuously in both an epistemic and an ontological sense suffers disastrously. It gives the affection relation an undeservedly bad name. The object that, according to the theory, affects our sensibility both has and lacks the properties of the modes of sensibility. It has them because these properties are epistemically ideal. It lacks them because those same properties are ontologically ideal. We are left, then, either with one object that affects our sensibility and quite another that serves as the immediate object of intuition or with the obliteration of the distinction between things in themselves and appearances.

We are left with the conclusion that the tradition goes wrong, both in its reconstruction and its criticism, about the distinction between things in themselves and appearances. Insofar as an object can affect our sensibility in the required way, it cannot have spatial or temporal characteristics. And insofar as it can have such properties, it cannot affect our sensibility. This mistaken alternative generates the equally mistaken alternatives offered by the *TWT* and *TDT* accounts of the distinction between things in themselves and appearances. The difficulty lies, not with the notion of affection, but rather in the explication visited by both theories on that notion. The dilemma facing affection arises only because it has been wrongly assimilated to a kind of relation that it is not. And the assimilation has served only to obscure the real character of the distinction between things in themselves and appearances.

What I have tried to show so far is the real nature of the distinction between things in themselves and appearances by attacking the major historical alternatives. We have seen that the nature of that distinction depends upon a theory about the nature of the relation of affection. We have also seen how that relation has been traditionally construed as a kind of causation. And, finally, we have learned that the traditional construction has made it impossible to give a coherent account of the distinction between things in themselves and appearances. The *TDT* tries to escape this problem by appealing to the same object under different descriptions. But the same problem of assimilating affection to causation cannot be removed by removing it from one set of circumstances that we declare to be actual to another that we proclaim to be possible.

What, then, are we to make of the distinction between things in themselves and appearances once we have disentangled the affection from the causation relation? We have learned that we must say that affection is a relation that is logically independent of our forms of intuition. Thus the alternatives offered by the ontological and the epistemic interpretations of these or any other forms of intuition do not alter the Affection Condition. Secondly, we now know that a thing in itself is anything that is known apart from the causal conditions required for the affection relation to obtain. This is not a matter of our being given something, actual or possible, independently of our modes of intuition. What we are given is something which is present to us under such forms but which is not given to us independently of any such forms at all.[22]

3. Things in Themselves (II)

WHAT HAS come down to us as a theory of double affection is false because it distorts Kant's notion of affection in that it wrongly conflates that notion with the quite different notion of causation. The source of this problem and the inspiration of the major attempt to solve it is the ambiguity about what, on Kant's theory, affects our sensibility when we are perceptually aware of something. If things in themselves affect our sensibility, then we have to explain how something that is not subject to causal action can nonetheless act causally on us. If we try to avoid this consequence by claiming that what Kant calls phenomenal substance really affects our sensibility whenever we perceive something, we are pushed back to the original problem. For part of what it means to be aware of a phenomenal object is that it is the result of something affecting us in certain ways. As we now know, the relation of causation might obtain between a mental act and things in themselves or appearances. In either case, such a relation assumes a logically prior relation of affection if a successful Kantian account of causation is to be given. For in order for something to cause me to be aware of its presence, it must also be able to affect me.

Neither alternative is philosophically acceptable or textually vindi-
cated. Both of them derive from the common and false assumption
that affection is logically equivalent to causation. But the two notions
are logically quite distinct. This distinction undermines the alleged
fact of double affection. And it enables us to avoid the otherwise disastrous consequences of having to choose between things in themselves
and appearances when we ask what affects our sensibility.

The distinction between causation and affection faces even more
fundamental difficulties. That distinction assumes, as we have seen,
the distinction between things in themselves according to its traditional interpretation and appearances. But that distinction assumes, in
turn, things that satisfy what I have called the Cognitivity Condition
and the Affection Condition. These conditions must be concomitantly
satisfiable if we are to preserve the distinction in some sense between
appearances and things in themselves. But insofar as something satisfies the Cognitivity Condition, it cannot be a thing in itself. Things in
themselves are not possible objects of experience in the sense required
by Kant's theory: They can never be presented to us independently of
some form of intuition. And insofar as it satisfies the Affection Condition, it cannot be an appearance. We explain how something gets to
be an appearance by appealing to the relation of affection between
our forms of intuition and something that is not an appearance. If we
were to say, *horribile dictu*, that appearances in turn stand in the relation of affection to our perceptual acts, the result would merely generate a vicious infinite regress of affection relations. And this is not
only contrary to Kant's theory but is also philosophically objectionable. Contrary to Kant's theory, because that theory stands or falls on
the fact that only things in themselves can affect us. Philosophically
objectionable, because any attempt to construe affection as a relation
between appearances is flatly inconsistent with the very task that such
a relation purports to perform. We have already witnessed the anomo-
lous situation in which both conditions must be jointly satisfied by the
same things but in which joint satisfaction of the type required results
in the collapse of the distinction between things in themselves and appearances. And, as we have seen, if different kinds of entities satisfy
each of the two conditions, they remove the impossibility of satisfying
them only to abolish the very distinction for which the conditions are
supposed to be the joint criterion.

Neither of the two received theories of the distinction between
things in themselves and appearances, superficial textual evidence to

the contrary, is either textually or philosophically defensible. The *TWT* fails to satisfy the Affection Condition. And the *TDT* founders on the false assumption that one and the same object can simultaneously satisfy both the Affection and the Cognitivity Conditions. The former rests on the illegitimate assimilation of things in themselves to noumena. And the latter merely postpones the problem of distinguishing things in themselves from appearances by transporting it to other, possible, worlds.

This problem dissolves once we see that the distinction between things in themselves and appearances requires neither the *TWT* nor the *TDT* but can be rescued by distinguishing two states of enlightenment about one and the same object in this world. The two criteria for the distinction between a thing in itself and an appearance can be joined and consistently satisfied once we remember the difference between the relations of causation and affection. They are two relations in which one and the same object can stand to us. But the relational facts that result from the difference of those relations circumvent the contradiction that the joint satisfaction of the two conditions would otherwise generate.

But this does not exhaust the issues surrounding the distinction between things in themselves and appearances. The problem that the joint satisfiability of the Affection and Cognitivity Conditions creates arises all over again in the context of the relation between a self and whatever it is that self knows when it is said to have self-knowledge. Kant distinguishes between appearances and things in themselves for material objects. But he also applies that distinction to selves. I have previously argued that the distinction as applied to material objects is different from what the tradition tells us it is. The traditional views are, I hope to show, dispensable for selves. That we can do without the traditional distinction for selves is not, however, an immediate consequence of the arguments that permit us to reject it when it is applied to material objects. There are peculiarities of self-knowledge that demand an independent demonstration of this general thesis when it is made to include self-knowledge.

Let me review the conditions that a thing in itself must meet and my reason for rejecting that notion when it is applied to material objects. Two conditions are required. There is, first, the Affection Condition: A thing in itself must stand in some epistemic relation to an act of perceiving by affecting what Kant calls our modes of intuition. To say that somebody is perceptually aware of something in intuition is, on this condition, just to say that a thing in itself affects his sensibility. The thing in itself is not the content of that act. It is, rather, something that brings about what we do perceive by acting in a certain way on our modes of intuition.

There is, secondly, the Cognitivity Condition: A thing in itself, though it acts on our modes of intuition, cannot itself be a part of a content that those modes give us. The reason for this is, simply, that to assume the opposite is to bring about the collapse of the distinction between things in themselves and the phenomenal items that can occur in the content of acts of perceptual awareness. Once a thing in itself could be intuited, then there would be no difference between such a thing and the phenomenal items which we see as a result of being affected by things in themselves. There would, in other words, be no relation of affection. For there would not be two relata—one a thing we do not perceive and the other something we do perceive—that could satisfy the description of that relation. Recall my previous argument. The basis of the distinction between things in themselves and appearances is the existence of what Kant calls the relation of affection. The distinction between two relata one of which is something we perceive while the other brings about the content of that perception by affecting us is the basis of that relation. Without the Cognitivity Condition, there would be no affection. For we would lack the requisite number of things between which that relation holds. The distinction between things in itself and appearance would deliquesce.

This is not all. That distinction as it has come down to us would collapse without the Affection Condition. In order to see this, we have only to suppose that there are things that cannot belong to any content of our perceptual acts. This, for Kant, is tantamount to supposing that there are things that lack spatial or temporal properties. If there were such entities, they would satisfy the Cognitivity Condition. They would, however, not qualify as things in themselves. It would be impossible for them to appear to us. And this would violate the Affection Condition, for it would prevent the entities in question from standing in any epistemic relation to the modes of our apprehension—which would be to say that they cannot affect us. Both conditions are necessary to the viability of the distinction between a thing in itself and an appearance.[1] The Affection Condition, because there must be an object present to our modes of intuition. The Cognitivity Condition, because we must be unable to perceive what affects us independently of some forms of intuition or other.

But the distinction as we have become accustomed to understanding it breaks down. Both conditions are conjointly necessary but cannot be conjointly fulfilled. Let me review how, according to my previous argument, such a difficulty arises.[2] Kant accounts for what it is to be in a state of immediate perceptual awareness of something by saying that an object affects our modes of intuition.[3] To affect our modes of intuition is, on Kant's theory, to bring about the existence of a phenomenal content of perception.[4] Yet what is supposed to bring about such a content need not do this despite the fact that we cannot perceive it. If we need not perceive what affects us, then it need not stand in any relevant epistemic relation to what Kant calls our modes of apprehension. A mode of apprehension is for Kant the way in which we perceive an object.[5] And if we need not perceive the object that allegedly affects us, the relation of affection cannot possibly hold between a thing in itself and our modes of apprehension. We cannot be affected by something that we cannot perceive under any description at all. This is the traditional scenario.

This impasse cannot, moreover, be argued out of existence by saying that what we perceive is an object qualified by characteristics that really belong to us and not to the objects. All this accomplishes is a brief postponement of the original difficulty. This can be shown as follows. Suppose that we perceive objects to have spatio-temporal characteristics but that such characteristics are really only properties of our perceptual mechanism. We are still as far away as ever from explaining how affection can take place without assuming that we perceive the object that affects us.

Let us grant for the sake of argument that some of the characteristics we presume an object to have are really characteristics, not of the object, but rather of our perceptual apparatus. We must still explain how it is that we perceive the spatio-temporal part of what we intuit. As soon as we make our modes of perception into components of our perceptual content as distinct from our perceptual act, then the affection relation must apply by parity of argument to them as well as to whatever else is presented to us. But the affection relation can obtain only so long as we are allowed to distinguish between things in themselves and the modes of our apprehension. To claim that those modes are perceptual components of what we apprehend merely serves to place them under the same restrictions that bind anything else that we might apprehend. It applies the initial problem about the conjoint applicability of the two conditions to the modes of apprehension themselves. So far from giving us a solution to the problem, the foregoing maneuver provides at best a new example of the kind of situation that raises the problem in the first place.

This accounts for the collapse of the standard, received, interpretations of the distinction between things in themselves and appearances. We are told that Kant uses that distinction to explain how something can appear to us by relying on the relation of affection that holds between a thing we cannot and something we can see. But insofar as the thing affecting us cannot be perceived, it cannot affect us. And insofar as it can affect us, we must be able to perceive it without the mechanism of the affection relation. The collapse of this account undercuts the distinction between things in themselves and appearances.

The argument I have just reviewed, however, is not completely general. It may prove as a consequence of the traditional explication that the distinction between things in themselves and appearances cannot be applied to the material objects we perceive. But cases of self-awareness escape the foregoing argument while offering instances of the distinction between something as it is in itself and as it appears to us. Consider a case in which a self is introspectively aware of itself. Here the content of the act of awareness must be the same as the act itself. This enables cases of self-awareness to evade the difficulty facing the distinction between things in themselves and appearances when it is applied to material objects.

The dilemma besetting the distinction when it is applied to material objects is this: How can something other than an act of awareness appear to that act and remain nonetheless essentially unknowable? This problem disappears in the case of self-awareness. Here an act and the content of that act are *ex hypothesi* one and the same. The fact of self-awareness removes the incompatibility of the Affection and Cognitivity Conditions. This follows from Kant's claim that time is a form or mode of our apprehension of things but is not itself a characteristic of what we apprehend.[6] The relevant difference between awareness of material objects and self-awareness is this. When we make the distinction between appearances and things in themselves of material objects, we assume that a thing in itself cannot be given to us on any occasion of perceptual awareness. When we make the same distinction for acts of awareness, we assume that the act of which we can be aware on one occasion can be the same act of which we are aware on a different occasion. In the case of material objects, the object present to us on one occasion may be the same as the object presented to us on another occasion. The basis for making the distinction between something in itself and an appearance shifts here. In the case of a mental act, we call it an entity in itself when it focuses on something else and call it an appearance when it in turn becomes the content of another mental act. The self can affect itself by being present to another mental act in the same mental history at a later time. The self at two different times is nonetheless numerically identical. Thus the Affection Condition is satisfied. But the self that is the content of awareness is in the past; hence, the Cognitivity Condition is satisfied.

Place this alongside the requirement, peculiar to acts of self-awareness, that the content and the act are the same and the two conditions are compatible. The self is in time because it is characterized by the mode in virtue of which it apprehends other objects. The acts of the self are, accordingly, also in time. And since the content of those acts in cases of self-awareness is the same as the subject of these acts, neither act nor content lacks the temporal property essential to its being apprehended. Whatever other difficulties remain, then, the self can, on Kant's theory, affect itself without being affected by something that cannot in principle form part of the content of an act of apprehension. What preserves the Cognitivity Condition here is that the self that affects itself in self-awareness cannot in principle be known at the same time as it is aware of itself. Thus the Affection and Cognitivity Conditions can be reconciled in the case of self-awareness, whereas they cannot be conjointly satisfied when they are applied to an awareness of a material object. The incompatibility between the two conditions, for which I have argued elsewhere, is not, then, generally applicable. And in escaping this difficulty, the existence of self-awareness would seem to undercut the main support for the dispensability of things in themselves.

But showing that the Cognitivity and Affection Conditions are *compatible* when they are applied to cases of self-awareness is one thing. It is quite another to show that self-awareness *demands* the distinction. Kant argues by implication that the existence of such acts requires the applicability of the distinction. The basis of this argument is what I shall call the Paradox of Self-Knowledge. But that paradox cannot be removed by introducing the distinction between what a self is in itself and what it is as it appears to itself. The alleged capability of that distinction to solve the paradox cannot, then, be used as independent evidence for the existence of the distinction. And, finally, what prevents its use here is, once again, the apparently insuperable difficulties facing the traditional accounts of Kant's doctrine of affection.[7]

1. The Paradox of Self-Knowledge

Kant uses the fact that we are aware of ourselves to support the distinction between two selves. The fact is this: Whatever else is given to me when I am aware of myself, it is some content that is in time alone or, as Kant puts it, in inner sense. Kant accepts this as a fact that generates a contradiction:

> [T]his sense represents to consciousness even our own selves only
> as we appear to ourselves, not as we are in ourselves. For we in-
> tuit ourselves only as we are inwardly *affected*, and this would
> seem to be contradictory, since we should then have to be in a
> passive relation [of active affection] to ourselves. It is to avoid
> this contradiction that in systems of psychology *inner sense*,
> which we have carefully distinguished from the faculty of *apper-
> ception*, is commonly regarded as being identical to it.[8]

Kant seeks to recognize the fact without accepting the contradiction generated by the distinction between inner sense and apperception. Writing of inner sense, he says that "we must also recognize, as regards inner sense, that by means of it we intuit ourselves only as we are inwardly affected *by ourselves*; in other words, that, so far as inner intuition is concerned, we know our own subject only as appearance, not as it is in itself."[9]

The paradox, then, is no sooner stated than it is dissolved. What generates the paradox is how a self can be both an act of consciousness and the content of that act. The notion of a content assumes the existence of something which is conscious of it. But if the content is the very act of consciousness itself, it cannot be what it is supposed to be. For the act that is the content would only assume the existence of another, numerically distinct, act in order to be a content at all. An appeal to a further act would only alter the fact to be explained. What the paradox requires us to explain is how one and the same act can be a content for itself. We are not being asked to explain the very different fact that one act can be the content for itself. We are not being asked to explain the very different fact that one act can be the content of another act.

Kant's solution has two steps. One: What is called an act in cases of self-awareness is the self as it is apart from all modes of intuition.[10] The content of that act is an appearance. This is supposed to show how there is no contradiction in saying that we can be aware of ourselves. If act and content in self-awareness are, respectively, the self as it is apart from our modes of apprehension and the self as it appears to those modes, then the contradiction disappears. Two: The fact remains, however, that both of the foregoing descriptions must designate one self. The relation of affection is the only thing in Kant's theory that could show how both descriptions could designate one and the same self while still designating them differently.[11]

Kant seeks to make good the second part of his theory by changing the sense of "affection." The Paradox of Self-Knowledge is stated in terms of a sense of "affection" that is introduced in the Aesthetic.[12] We are asked to explain how it is possible that the self can be its own content. And the answer seems impossible so long as "content" is construed as an entity immediately available to consciousness in an act of intuition. It would, in other words, be impossible so long as Kant retained the notion of affection that figures in the Aesthetic. There he proceeds as follows. He first introduces the notion of intuition as "that through which it [a mode of knowledge] is in immediate relation to them [objects]."[13] Having said that intuition is possible only insofar as an object can be given to us "only . . insofar as the mind is affected in a certain way."[14]

The notion of affection is introduced in terms of an object's acting upon our modes of apprehension. If the Paradox of Self-Knowledge were to be stated in these terms, there would be no way out of the contradiction that Kant finds in an otherwise indisputable fact. For we would have to say that an object can be given to a self that is numerically the same as the self to which it is given. No appeal to the fact that what we are given is phenomenal and not a thing in itself would help resolve this contradiction. The very notion of phenomenality here would assume the numerical diversity of what affects the self and the self that it affects—an assumption that solves the paradox only at the cost of falsely stating it.[15]

The fact of self-knowledge neither supports nor is supported by the *TWT* or the traditional interpretation of the *TDT*. Suppose we construe the relation of the self as it is in itself and the self as an appearance in the idiom of the *TWT*. Self-knowledge would not be a *prima facie* contradiction, for the self as an appearance would be numerically distinct from the self as it is in itself. But an appeal to the *TWT* would falsify the Paradox of Self-Knowledge. If the empirical or phenomenal self and the self in itself were numerically diverse, we would not be given a fact of self-knowledge. There would be no logical distinction between claiming that I am aware of *my* self and the quite different claim that I am aware of *a* self that is not mine. The appeal to the *TWT* as a solution of the Paradox of Self-Knowledge would violate the ownership condition implicit in the statement of the Paradox of Self-Knowledge.

The *TDT* in its traditional acceptation fares no better. Let us say that the ego in itself and the empirical ego are one and the same particular that satisfies different descriptions. One of these descriptions is satisfied by the ego in our world. The other is satisfiable in another, possible, world. According to the *TDT*, the empirical ego satisfies a description in our world. The ego in itself satisfies other descriptions in other, possible, worlds. This move breaks down on two stubborn facts. First, if we are to solve the Paradox of Self-Knowledge, we must be able to supply descriptions that are satisfied by the ego in the actual world. Secondly, to say that the ego in itself is the same ego in other, possible, worlds once again transports the problem raised by the Paradox of Self-Knowledge from one world to another. Even though the ego is the same from one world to another, it does not follow that the ego in any of these worlds can affect itself in another world even though one and the same ego can be a constituent of both worlds.

This is not, however, the only way in which the notion of affection is used to solve the Paradox of Self-Knowledge. Contrast how Kant introduces the notion in the Analytic:

> What determines inner sense is the understanding and its original power of combining the manifold of intuition, that is, of bringing it under an apperception, upon which the possibility of understanding itself rests. . . . The understanding, that is to say, in respect of the manifold which may be given to it in accordance with the form of sensible intuition, is able to determine sensibility inwardly.[16]

Kant concludes in the following paragraph that "[t]he understanding does not, therefore, find in inner sense such a combination of the manifold, but *produces* it, in that it *affects* that sense."[17] The sense of "affection" has been completely inverted. The notion previously denoted the action of an object on our forms of apprehension. It now denotes the action of an intellectual capacity on a series of intuitions. The kind of action involved in each case is very different. To affect a mode of sensibility is, on the one hand, to bring about an appearance, which, as Kant explicitly recognizes in the Aesthetic, is "[t]he *undetermined* object of an empirical intuition."[18] But to affect such a mode is, on the other hand, to order a series of perceptions in a certain way.[19]

The consequences of this shift in the sense of "affection" for the Paradox of Self-Knowledge are these. The second sense of "affection," unlike the first, requires that the self I introspect be a sequence of mental events that I can assign to my mental history rather than to the history of things that can exist outside my history. Inner sense gives me a sequence of contents that can be ascribed to myself or to whatever exists independently of me. To have self-knowledge is to have an *ability* and not introspectively to intuit any kind of *entity*. We are aware of ourselves, on this version of Kant's theory, just insofar as we have a way of distinguishing sequences of contents belonging to ourselves from those which do not. Both what is revealed to us in inner sense and what orders the sequence thus given are the same self. But it is given to us in different ways. The self we intuit is a sequence of mental contents. To be aware of the self that intuits these contents is to have the ability to ascribe the latter to one's own mental history. They are the same self given in two different ways—once as an introspected content and once as the awareness of our possession of the ability of self-ascription.

2.   The Perils of Affection

The fact remains, however, that neither conception of affection successfully dissolves the Paradox of Self-Knowledge. Consider them again, beginning with the notion of affection prominent in the Aesthetic.[20] Suppose an introspective act S' intuits a content S''. If this is to describe a case of self-awareness, both S' and S'' must be the same item. And if it is to provide for the distinction between an act and its object, S'' must be what Kant calls a phenomenal self; S', the self as it is in itself. But this conflicts irreconcilably with the traditional statement of the distinction between a thing in itself and an appearance. To be a thing in itself is to lack the characteristics that belong only to modes of apprehension characterizing the self.[21] S' is the self; hence, it must have those very modes in virtue of which anything can be an object of apprehension.

But this is not all. There is another reason why the self, according to Kant's theory, must have these modes. If S' and S'' are really the same thing, then S'' must have all the characteristics that S' has. Otherwise one could not be said to be the same as the other. The difficulty facing the theory, then, is this: S' must both have and lack the characteristics of S''. It must have temporal properties as a condition of being appeared to by anything else. Yet it cannot have any such properties because S' must, according to the theory, affect the self and thereby generate a content of phenomenal awareness that is in time.

The point can be generalized. If self-affection is to be possible at all, two incompatible requirements must be fulfilled. S' must be in time if S'' is to be a faithful reproduction of the S' it mirrors. Yet S' cannot be in time if it is to affect itself. For affection requires that something lacking the characteristics of our modes of apprehension stand in relation to those modes. If what is said to affect us itself has the characteristics that belong to our modes of apprehension, then affection could not take place. For the Cognitivity Condition would be violated. If both S' and S'', say, were in time, it would seem that there would be no way to distinguish, as Kant's theory requires, between the self as it is in itself and the self as it appears. Kant's view of affection in the Aesthetic cannot solve the Paradox of Self-Knowledge. But it remains to be seen whether this is the only possible interpretation of that view.

Someone might argue against this conclusion. Suppose we distinguish between having temporal properties and being a thing in itself. Something can be a thing in itself just insofar as it cannot be a content of an act of apprehension. And something can be a thing in itself insofar as it lacks spatial or temporal properties. It might be argued that something can be a thing in itself although it still has, say, temporal properties, because something can have such characteristics and still be incapable of forming part of the content of an act of apprehension. Self-knowledge provides a prima facie example of this. Suppose I am introspectively aware of myself at time t. The act of awareness in such a case is not itself part of the content of awareness at time t. And, what is more, it cannot be part of a subsequent act of memorial awareness. This is merely an immediate consequence of the notion of memorial awareness.

In order to remember something, I must first have been aware of it at a time prior to my remembering it. If this were not the case, then there would be no distinction between remembering something and being aware of it in the present. This fact about memory, so the argument might go, demonstrates that acts of awareness can be in time without being part of any content of awareness. That S', for example, is in time is compatible with its being a thing in itself. The relation of affection can, according to this objection, still obtain between S' and S'' without entailing the collapse of the distinction between things in themselves and appearances.

The foregoing objection is significant, not because it is cogent, but rather because it shows the irrelevance of the doctrine of affection to the Paradox of Self-Knowledge. In the first place, it is not cogent. So far from providing independent support of the distinction between things in themselves and appearances, it entails the collapse of that distinction as many Kantians have felt bound to expound it. Grant for the sake of the argument that acts of introspective awareness can be temporal without being capable of forming the content of any act. Such an act and the self that is given in the content of an act of introspective awareness cannot be related by affection, since one of the requirements of affection is that something that is not a mode of apprehension stand in relation to such a mode. But since time is just such a mode, one temporal entity cannot affect another. So whatever the problem about the introspective availability of acts of self-awareness, the appeal to perceptually unavailable temporal items prevents a thing in itself from relating in the relevant way to an appearance. But since the distinction between a thing in itself and an appearance depends essentially upon their being related by means of affection, the collapse of affection is also the collapse of the distinction.

Yet the objection is nonetheless instructive. For it shows that the Paradox of Self-Knowledge arises even if you distinguish between two senses of "thing in itself." Suppose that there can be things in themselves that are temporal. What makes self-knowledge paradoxical is that one and the same self must but cannot be simultaneously an act of introspective awareness and the object of that act. To distinguish between a temporal but perceptually unavailable mental act and a temporal content merely permits that paradox to arise all over again. The self I perceive cannot be the act by which I perceive it. But it must be that act if I am to be introspectively acquainted with myself. The distinction between two kinds of temporal items does not, then, solve the paradox so much as it provides another example of it. The use made of affection in the Aesthetic provides no way out of the paradox.

This leaves us with the theory of affection that Kant gives us in the

Analytic. To affect inner sense is, on this account, for the transcendental unity of apperception to order a series of representations according to a rule.[22] Inner sense consists of groups of intuitions that are exclusively temporal. And the self affects inner sense when it orders these groups so as to ascribe them to the mental history of that self. We do not, however, have an intuition of the self that affects inner sense. We have only a *thought* of the activity by which the combination takes place.[23] The self does not, strictly speaking, intuit itself when it is acquainted with itself. To be acquainted with one's self is to be able to ascribe elements of the manifold in inner sense to one's own mental history. What we thereby ascribe is how the self appears. The self that affects the manifold of inner sense in this way is just another designation for our ability to perform acts of self-ascription. We are acquainted with this self only by grasping the thought of what it is to have this capacity.[24]

The first step in an assessment of this theory is to remove an irrelevancy from it. To say that we are acquainted with the *thought* of a self having the ability to combine the elements of a manifold when we are acquainted with the self that appears under the forms of apprehension is true but seriously misleading. Suppose such a thought were the content of an act of self awareness. The paradox would break out all over again: My awareness of myself in introspection is one thing; an awareness of the thought of myself is quite another. The self performing the introspective act would not, therefore, be the same self that is part of the content of that act. The self that introspects is not imaginary but real; hence, an appeal to a thought inevitably founders.

There is an even worse difficulty facing the use of "affection" in the Analytic. The account of that notion in the Analytic assumes and does not replace the sense of "affection" used in the Aesthetic. Consider how this comes about. If affection is the ordering of elements in a manifold, each one of the elements must still stand in some relation to something that acts on our sensibility. For the ordering can take place only on the condition that it be given something to order. Ordering assumes, then, a manifold that it cannot produce. What is given to us in inner sense cannot, therefore, be supplied by whatever ordering rules we have. Yet the problem raised by the Paradox of Self-Knowledge is how to relate those elements to the objects that act on our sensibility. And this is a problem that the doctrine of affection in the Analytic cannot solve. The doctrine of affection assumes a prior solution to that problem in virtue of the fact that it assumes a given manifold as a necessary condition of applying ordering rules at all. The Analytic solution of the paradox is not, accordingly, independent of the Aesthetic solution. It must stand or fall as a solution of the paradox with the Aesthetic doctrine of affection. And this, in turn, means that it must share the fate of that solution.

We cannot, I conclude, apply the distinction between things in themselves and appearances to the self. The applicability of that distinction depends upon Kant's doctrine of affection. The notion of an appearance assumes a relation between a self that is appeared to in a certain way and a self that generates the appearance by standing in some relation to the former self. Without this relation there would be no difference between the self we introspectively apprehend and the self that somehow generates the self we apprehend. Yet the attempt to invoke this relation only proves to be its undoing. It requires that the self that is affected be the same as the self that does the affecting. And this is what undermines the notion of affection when it is applied to cases of self-awareness. The affecting self cannot have the characteristics that Kant describes as the forms of intuition. If it did have them, then it could not *generate* an appearance for it would already *be* an appearance. Nor, indeed, can the affecting self lack such properties, for the theory as it is applied to the self requires that the affecting self be the same as the self that is affected. And the latter does have the characteristics which are the forms of intuition. In both cases, then, the doctrine of affection breaks down. Without the doctrine of affection, there can be no distinction between things in themselves and appearances. The Paradox of Self-Knowledge cannot provide independent evidence for the existence of a distinction between things in themselves and appearances. And what is responsible for this difficulty is the inadequacy of the doctrine of affection.

3. Resolving the Paradox

The breakdown of the doctrine of affection seriously threatens Kant's theory of perceptual awareness. He must, on the one hand, solve the Paradox of Self-Knowledge if he is to maintain his theory of synthesis. The self, like any other object, is apprehended only successively in a manifold of perceptions. The self that apprehends such a manifold must, however, itself be apprehended in some other way. Otherwise we would be unable to identify any manifold as a series of perceptions belonging to our experience. Yet, on the other hand, the means by which he chooses to solve that paradox are irrelevant to it.

Consider first what makes the resolution of the paradox indispensable to Kant's theory of synthesis. Kant's statement of the doctrine is familiar:

> It must be possible for the 'I think' to accompany all my representations; for otherwise something would be represented in me which could not be thought at all, and that is equivalent to saying that the representation would be impossible, or at least would be nothing to me.[25]

The claim is that I must be capable of being aware of the fact that what I combine in a series of perceptions belongs to one and the same consciousness. Kant concludes:

> Only in so far, therefore, as I can unite a manifold of given representations in *one consciousness*, it is possible for me to represent to myself the *identity of the consciousness in* [i.e., throughout] *these representations.*[26]

But there is a problem here. Our knowledge of objects depends on the continuity of the self through time. This is just a consequence of the relation of that knowledge to synthesis. We perceive objects through a period of time. Yet if we are not aware that these acts of perceiving are part of our mental histories, no such perception could ever take place. This requires not merely that there be a continuous self, but that there be a consciousness that the series of perceptual awareness belong to one self. The Paradox of Self-Knowledge would seem to forbid such a conclusion. If, as I have argued, the distinction between things in themselves and appearances does not apply to selves, then it would seem to follow that I would never be able to ascribe perceptual awareness to my mental history.

The first step in a resolution of this difficulty is to dispose of the Paradox of Self-Knowledge. Kant's statement of that paradox makes it impossible to resolve even if we abstract that paradox from the context of the theory of affection. We are asked how an act of perceiving can be the simultaneous content of that act. The requirement on which this question implicitly rests is that one entity function as two. And what makes it impossible to satisfy this requirement is that it conflicts with the nature of the distinction between an act and the content of that act. The latter demands a diversity of elements. The former forbids it.

But this is not the only sense in which we can be said to have self-awareness. Kant in fact supplies us with another that implies another solution to the Paradox of Self-Knowledge. There is what I shall call the self-ascriptive sense of self-awareness. I am aware of myself whenever I can exhibit an ability to ascribe a series of perceptions to my mental history.[27] A typical example of this sense of the notion emerges in the *B* version of the Transcendental Deduction when Kant says that "only insofar as I can grasp the manifold of representations in one consciousness, do I call them one and all *mine*."[28] Self-awareness is not, on this account, an act of awareness of a special kind of object but rather an ability to ascribe the objects of which we are aware to our respective mental histories. To have the ability to identify the contents we have as belonging to our respective mental histories does not require us to say that a self can be both an act and a content simultaneously of perception. For what we are, on the self-ascriptive account, saying is that we have an awareness of a content that is not the act by which we are aware of it standing in a certain relation to the self that is aware of it. What we see, then, in self-awareness is not, say, an act that is its own content but a content different from the act that stands in a unique relation to that act. Self-knowledge is, therefore, a paradox only because, on one statement of the problem, one condition of its solution is wrongly imposed on it.

We must still reconcile the foregoing solution of the paradox with an apparent demand on Kant's theory of synthesis. We are told that our knowledge of any object requires an ability to combine or synthesize the temporally ordered parts of that manifold in what Kant calls a unified experience.[29] Yet this would seem to require the existence of a self that is numerically one through time. Self-ascription would seem to rely on the existence of an ego that, though it is numerically one through time, cannot be perceived. What we perceive is the fact that certain contents of perception belong to our mental histories. But this does not allow us to claim that we can be acquainted with the self to which those contents stand in this unique relation.

But if the ego has temporal qualities, it must be perceivable, for it would then stand under a mode of apprehension. Thus as soon as it is admitted that the ego perceives a series of contents that it relates to its mental history, Kant's problem would seem to arise all over again, albeit in a different place. The distinction between a self and a content that is ascribed to the self may serve to remove the paradox by providing a content that is not the act by which that content is perceived. But the self is continuous through time. And this requires it to be perceptually available to itself just because it admittedly exhibits a form of intuition.

The foregoing objection requires us to be aware of the self. But it does not require such an acquaintance to be simultaneous with every act of perceiving. This is why the Paradox of Self-Knowledge does not arise all over again. I can remember that I was in a certain state with respect to a mental content at a time subsequent to my having been in that state. This does not require that either my former or present act of awareness be *simultaneously* act and content with respect to itself. What I remember is the relation in which a certain event in my mental history stands to other events; hence, that the self is in time does not, after all, conflict with our inability to be aware of it at the same time that it is aware of a content in the present.

There remains another argument that Kant deploys against rational psychology and that might easily be used to discredit the reconstruction I have given of his theory of self-awareness. The ego that is temporally continuous and the foundation of our ability to synthesize any manifold cannot, Kant argues, be an object of intuition. I summarize his argument in the following steps:

(1) In order to know myself, I must be aware of myself by applying categories to a manifold in intuition.[30]

(2) But the self (the transcendental unity of apperception) is "itself the ground of the possibility of the categories."[31]

(3) Therefore, the self "does *not know itself through categories*, but knows the categories, and through them all objects, in the absolute unity of apperception, and so through itself."[32]

(4) "I cannot know as an object that which I must presuppose in order to know any object."[33]

(5) Therefore, "there is nothing more natural and misleading than the illusion which leads us to regard the unity in the synthesis of thoughts as a perceived unity in the subject of these thoughts."[34]

The transition from (2) to (3) is the crucial step in this argument. It tells us that we must be able to have some cognitive access to the self as a condition of our ability to apply categories to the manifold of perceptual awareness. We must be able to combine a series of discrete perceptual contents as at least belonging to our respective mental histories. This is just another statement of the fact that we can put together a series of separate perceptual units and know that they are all members of one series even if it is only the series constituting our various private histories. Without this fundamental ability, we would not be able to apply any of Kant's categories at all because there are so many ways in which we perform acts of synthesis. Without the notion of synthesis in general, then, we cannot understand what it is to perform any specific kind of synthesis. The logical priority of the former over the latter is the basis of the Kantian claim that the self is the ground of the categories.

The sense of "ground" here may be justifiable, but it is not adequate to support the conclusion that is supposed to follow from it. A category is still a variety of a concept. Whatever else Kant may mean by the notion of a concept, the notion of a rule of synthesis for a manifold in intuition is basic to his theory of synthesis.[35] And a rule for combining a manifold given to us in intuition is for Kant a characteristic of mental activity by which we come to know an object that is given to us.[36] This makes the self the ground of the possibility of the categories in the sense that it is the subject to which we ascribe certain capacities of organizing what is given to us by intuition: What grounds the categories is the subject of which they are predicated.

This leaves the move from (2) to (3) enigmatic only if we conflate acts of combination with acts of synthesis. To show that the categories are logically dependent upon the existence of a self is one thing. To infer from such a fact that the categories cannot be applied to the self is something else that does not follow from any claim about existential dependency. Step (4) seems, wrongly, to bolster the move from (2) to (3). The claim amounts to this: Whatever I must use in order to know something as an object cannot without circularity be an object for me.

But the claim that step (4) formulates is seriously endangered. It is true that we cannot know the act of awareness by which we are aware of a state of the self at the same time as we are aware of the state. But this fact does not imply that we are unable to be aware of the self that perceives these states at a different time from which the original act of perception takes place. Step (4) formulates a difficulty that can be solved by recalling a distinction between a subject and a state of that subject. What is presupposed in order to know an object is something that can be called an act of awareness. It does not follow that every act of awareness presupposes the applicability of the categories to what is the object of awareness. You can be acquainted, say, with such concepts as substance and causality without having to subsume those objects under the concepts of substance and causality. The categories are not, therefore, presuppositions of knowing any object whatsoever. They are, at most, presupposed in knowing *perceptual* objects.

The same point can be put in a different but equivalent way. The fact that the transcendental unity of apperception is the capacity we have for synthesis in general makes it the logically necessary condition of any particular kind of synthesis. But this binds it only to rule-governed acts of synthesis. And this excludes synthetic acts that are mere combinations (*Verbindungen*) without the governance of rules. The distinction between synthesis and combination of manifolds makes it possible for the self to be the object of combination but not of synthesis. The claim that the self can be made into a synthetic object of consciousness *is* circular because we are unsuccessfully trying in such instances to explain how we are acquainted with something by appealing to the application of the very characteristics of what we want to know as conditions of our knowing it. The circularity that undermines the notion of synthesis in this kind of context does not, however, infect the self understood as a capacity to perform acts of combination. We can invoke that capacity to explain the fact of self-knowledge without circularity. What is circular here arises from the claim to know the self as a categorially determined object and not as an object that is a combination of a series of perceptual acts belonging to somebody's continuous mental history. We can, accordingly, have self-knowledge without applying Kantian categories to the self. The argument Kant gives us does not show the impossibility of self-knowledge. It shows only the impossibility of *categorial* self-knowledge.

It is no answer to this to argue that the self must be made into a perceptual object in order for us to have knowledge of it. All that need be claimed is that we can relate perceptual items to the mental history each of us has without having to claim that we can intuit the self as an isolable object or that we can perceive the self as being continuous through time. Kant's argument against rational psychology does not, therefore, show the impossibility of the continuity of self through time. Step (4) is ambiguous. If we interpret "object" as "the set of perceptual contents combined according to a rule," then that step dramatizes what Kant asserts to be the circularity in the claim that I can know the self as an object. But if "object" is interpreted as "whatever can be ascribed to one's own mental history," then the putative circularity is avoided because the self is not an object of categorial attention. Step (5), therefore, must be dismissed as an irrelevant conclusion from the premises. We need not regard the unity in the synthesis of thoughts as a perceived unity in the subject of these thoughts in order to say that there is a continuity of the self through time constituting the basis of our ability to combine any elements into a manifold.

4. The Reduction of Egos

Kant's problems begin with his distinction between empirical, noumenal, and transcendental egos. The distinction between a noumenal and an empirical ego requires the distinction between something as it is in itself and something as it appears to our forms of sensibility. This distinction depends on the viability of the notion of affection. Yet this notion can neither be applied to cases of self-knowledge nor derive independent support from an appeal to the fate of self-knowledge. It cannot be applied to any case of self-knowledge because it requires an ego that affects the ego that intuits something that affects it Nor can it derive independent support from the fact of self-knowledge because that fact is not an instance of affection. The requirement of affection cannot be met by one and the same ego, for one and the same ego cannot appear to itself in the way in which a material object appears to us in perception.

We have now seen how the distinction between things in themselves and appearances generates two different problems when it is placed in the context of the Paradox of Self-Knowledge. There is, first of all, the problem of explaining how an act can be its own object. This problem arises independently of the issues surrounding the distinction between things in themselves and appearances. Neither of the traditional alternative interpretations of the nature of that distinction can resolve the paradox. They only reproduce it. There is, however, a quite different problem that is associated with but different from the Paradox of Self-Knowledge. This turns on whether we can make the distinction between things in themselves and appearances for selves just as we have done for things that are not selves.

The solution of the Paradox of Self-Knowledge can be provided once we understand that the paradox must be stated differently. To ask how I can know myself is not to ask—an impossible question—how two things can be one. It is, rather, to ask about the basis of my ability to ascribe events to my own mental history. Part of that basis is the continuity of the ego through time. Another part is my ability to combine temporally discrete parts of the manifold given to that continuous ego. The Paradox of Self-Knowledge becomes irresolubly troublesome only if we accept it to be a proper description of the phenomenon to be explained. The strategy by which it can be resolved is not the acceptance of the original description and the subsequent importation of the distinction between things in themselves and appearances but rather the demonstration that the paradox gives us a faulty statement of what is to be explained.

The Paradox of Self-Knowledge does not, then, supply independent evidence for distinguishing between what Kant calls an empirical ego and an ego that is a thing in itself. It does, however, give evidence for the existence of the quite different distinction between an ego to which the distinction between things in themselves and appearances does not apply and a noumenal ego. The solution that results in the paradox does not depend on the notion of affection. That notion makes sense in the context of the distinction between things in themselves and appearances. It is out of place in the context of a distinction between our idea or thought of an ego and the events in our experience that we ascribe to ourselves as parts of our mental history. None of the difficulties that beset the notion of affection when it is transferred to facts of self-knowledge shows that the notion of affection is philosophically defective. They merely demonstrate that the solution of the Paradox of Self-Knowledge does not require a relation between two egos.

Let us take stock. Placed in the context of the fact of self-knowledge, the viability of the relation between things in themselves and appearances faces two ostensibly major difficulties. First of all, that context requires an explanation of how an act of awareness can stand in the relation of affection to itself without violating the condition of the successs of the very description of what is to be explained by the fact of self-knowledge, namely, that the self that affects itself is not the same entity as what is presented to that act in such a situation. If this description of the fact is true, then it would seem that cases of self-knowledge could not be explained in terms of the distinction between things in themselves and appearances because such an attempt at explanation would violate the Affection Condition. This condition requires that we stand in an epistemic relation to what affects us. But in cases of self-knowledge, it would seem that the condition cannot be satisfied without contradiction just because what we claim to be aware of does not constitute part of a perceptual content.

Secondly, however, even if cases of self-knowledge could somehow satisfy the Affection Condition, they would accomplish this only at the cost of failing to satisfy the Cognitivity Condition. If an act of awareness were to be its own object of awareness, it would have to be the same act of awareness as the act in which it stands in the required relation. But this would involve our standing in the relation of affection to an appearance and not a thing in itself. All of the problems already recorded about the results of claiming that the relation of affection can hold between an act of awareness and an appearance rather than a thing in itself properly understood arise all over again. Things in themselves, not appearances, stand in the relation of affection to forms of intuition.

Neither of these problems is genuine. The notion of affection does not apply to the theory of self-knowledge contained in the Transcendental Analytic. Nor does it apply, as traditionally understood, to that theory in the context of the Transcendental Aesthetic. The proper understanding of how the notion of affection does not apply requires the distinction between causation and affection as well as the appeal to the revised version of the *TDT* of the distinction between things in themselves and appearances. In the Analytic, the solution of the problem of self-knowledge concerns our ability to ascribe events in our experience to our respective mental histories. But the problem of exercising an ability to ascribe ownership of experiences to ourselves ultimately assumes the solution of the problem of self-knowledge at a deeper level. The notion of synthesis, so important to the theory of self-knowledge in the Analytic, rests on an explanation of what it is to be perceptually aware of the individual members of any synthetically combined series.

If we accept the revised version of the *TDT*, both of the problems facing the Kantian account of self-awareness can be resolved. According to that version of the distinction between things in themselves and appearances, the particular in a Kantian appearance is numerically the same particular in what, according to the theory, is a thing in itself. What distinguishes an appearance from a thing in itself is our state of enlightenment about the range of descriptions that the particular in question might satisfy. And what follows from the identity of the particular in an appearance with the particular in a thing in itself is that one and the same particular can occur simultaneously in two different states of affairs.

The main impediment to accepting this as a solution of the problem of self-affection as it is stated in the Transcendental Aesthetic is the implied argument that affection is a case of causation, that the causal relation demands two numerically diverse terms, and that there can, accordingly, be no explanation of self-affection. But since the relation of affection cannot be assimilated to the relation of causation, the Kantian theory of self-affection need not be burdened by the necessity of assuming that the affection relation must have two numerically diverse terms. We are forced into such a conclusion by assuming that the relation of affection cannot be structurally similar to, say, the relation of identity, going on by attempting to locate the numerically diverse terms in the relation of self-affection, and then concluding from the first two stages in this line of argument that one of these particulars both can and cannot occur simultaneously with the other. The result of the argument is a philosophical disaster. But it is harmless because the steps on which the conclusion is based are demonstrably wrong.

4. Things in Themselves: The Historical Lessons

*W*E HAVE thus far seen that Kant's epistemological theory does not require the theory of double affection but only a combination of the logically distinct concepts of causation and affection. This distinction has also enabled us to dispense with the notion of a thing in itself as it has been traditionally conceived. The distinction between causation and affection enables us to separate sense from nonsense in what we have been told to think about the distinction between things in themselves and appearances. Both the *TWT* and the *TDT*, traditional hermeneutical and philosophical rivals for understanding Kant's distinction, had to be rejected because neither one of them could jointly satisfy what I have identified as the Cognitivity Condition and the Affection Condition. This problem can be traced along with the theory of double affection to the illegitimate conflation of affection with causation. But Kant's distinction between things in themselves and appearances has not been traditionally viewed in any of these ways. It has faced objections that move from very different premises to the conclusion, not that the distinction has been falsified, but that there is no basis for the distinction at all.

Kant's theory of things in themselves has been unfortunate in its treatment by most of its critics. They do not state the theory properly because they assimilate it to something it is not. They then succeed in refuting one or another theory that Kant does not hold but that misleadingly goes under the name of the theory he does hold. All of these efforts have succeeded only in obscuring what I shall identify as the genuine issue facing Kant's theory of things in themselves. None of the critics, other hermeneutical misgivings apart, has recognized a crucial ambiguity in Kant's use of the notion of transcendental ideality.

1. Jacobi

Friedrich Heinrich Jacobi begins the philosophical disaffection with things in themselves by giving it a slogan: "[W]ithout that presupposition [I] could not enter that system . . . and could not remain there with that presupposition."[1] He reasons this way. Objects make impressions (*Eindrücke*) on our sensory apparatus. What makes these impressions Kant calls the transcendental object.[2] But this object is not itself an impression and therefore can "never be an object of experience; but appearance and that this or that affection of sensibility is in me constitutes no relation of these representations to an object."[3] Jacobi concludes that "[w]here this cause might be and what kind of relationship it might have on the effect remain concealed in the deepest darkness."[4]

Jacobi's polemic can be cast in this argument form:

(1) Objects (*Gegenstände*) make impressions (*Eindrücke*) on our sensory receptors. [Assumption]

(2) Objects stand in causal relations to those receptors. [Assumption]

(3) The causal object cannot be an impression. [From steps (1) and (2) by the lemma that the immediate content of every sensory awareness is the causal result of an object, making it impossible for anything to be both an object and an impression simultaneously.]

(4) Therefore, that any impression is present to my consciousness does not imply that the impression stands in any relation to an object. [From (3) with the lemma that whatever cannot stand in any relation to consciousness cannot be an object.]

(5) Therefore, there are no things in themselves. [From step (4) with the lemma that what cannot stand in relation to consciousness cannot exist.]

The argument is a failure. The notion of thing in itself cannot be discredited by saying, as Jacobi does, that it stands in a causal relation to our sensory receptors. Nor can it be discredited by saying, as Jacobi also does, that we lack an impression of a thing in itself.

Jacobi's argument feeds on two confusions about the distinction between a thing in itself and an appearance. It is one thing to say, as Jacobi does, that a thing in itself causes the impressions we have. It is, however, quite another to claim that objects outside us cause whatever impressions we have. The presiding assumption of the confusion is that whatever is a thing outside us is a thing in itself. A sensation can be caused by something outside us which itself is a phenomenal object.

The second confusion is that what causes an impression cannot itself be an impression. Here the argument slides from one to another deceptively similar proposition that makes step (3) in the argument fatally ambiguous. We can say that an object cannot be an impression when it causes an impression. But this is compatible with saying that an object cannot be an impression on *any* perceptual occasion. And this leaves open an alternative that discredits step (3) and undermines Jacobi's attempt to show the indemonstrability of the existence of things in themselves: An object that causes us to have certain impressions on one perceptual occasion can itself be an impression on another such occasion. Jacobi's argument does not exclude this possibility; hence, his argument does not show what it purports to show.

The same conclusion can be reached from a somewhat different interpretation of Jacobi's argument. We can say that phenomenal objects cause us to have impressions by acting on our receptors. Jacobi sanctions this conclusion because he does not distinguish clearly between a thing in itself and whatever stands in a causal relation to our forms of intuition. For all the argument shows, a thing in itself is initially introduced as any object that causes impressions to occur in us subject to our forms of intuition. But this does not license the conclusion that we cannot be directly aware of phenomenal objects that cause the impressions we have. Both of them are subject to the forms of our intuition. An object of direct perceptual awareness can stand simultaneously in the relations of affection and causation to acts of perceptual awareness.

The foregoing conclusion emerges immediately from the revised version of the *TDT*. If a thing in itself is a particular that cannot satisfy certain kinds of description in our world, then there is no contradiction in saying that an object can simultaneously stand in the relation of affection and causation to us. Thus Jacobi's argument is cogent only if we first interpret what it is to be a thing in itself according either to the *TWT* or the traditional version of the TDT, then endow a thing in itself thus interpreted with causal properties, and finally conclude—rightly, on these contraband premises—that we can never be aware of the causes of what we directly perceive. This chain of reasoning explicates Jacobi's claim that he cannot enter Kant's system without assuming that there are things in themselves but that, with such an assumption, he cannot remain there. But it also exposes the tenuous evidence he has for it.

But Jacobi's argument is only superficially shabby. It conceals a serious threat to the viability of things in themselves. The notion of a thing in itself is apparently incompatible with both Kant's notion of an object and a cause. These alleged incompatibilities supposedly enable Jacobi to move from step (3) to (4) of his argument. Take them in turn.

Kant repeatedly tells us that what he calls an object is a synthesis of representations that we refer to something according to a rule.[5] Yet "we know the object when we have caused [*bewirkt*] synthetic unity in the manifold of intuition; and the concept of this unity is the representation of the object=x."[6] But if an object is a cluster of representations there is nothing in the world to distinguish the occurrence of one cluster from any other cluster; hence, Kant's account of what an object is cannot distinguish the *concept* of an object from the object itself. And this only goes to strengthen step (4) of Jacobi's argument against things in themselves.[7]

Suppose that what functions as an object on one perceptual occasion can function as an impression on another such occasion. We still cannot have an impression of whatever functions as an object causing impressions in us because we cannot perceive what we do as an *object* but only as an impression. And so long as we cannot perceive objects under their proper descriptions, we cannot perceive objects that cause impressions to occur in us even if we were presented with them and not the impressions they caused on a previous occasion. The reason for this is that we would still be forced to describe what we see as one impression among others. And this, according to Jacobi's argument, yields us only the concept of an object that cannot be perceived under the description of an object.

Worse is to come. A thing in itself is supposed to cause impressions in us by acting in the appropriate ways on our sensory receptors. Jacobi's gloss is that "they [perceptual objects] make impressions on the senses and in this way generate representations [*Vorstellungen*]."[8] But this contradicts the Second Analogy, according to which something is caused to happen whenever it follows something else necessarily according to a rule (cf. A139=B232). And it implies that a thing in itself cannot cause an impression just because the impression cannot follow upon the occurrence of a thing in itself in time according to a rule. So long as a cause is merely a rule for the combination of impressions, then things in themselves cannot cause these impressions to occur in us. Even if we interpret the sense of the Second Analogy more liberally and allow, not necessary succession according to a rule, but rather simultaneous occurrence according to a rule to count as a case of causation, the relation of a thing in itself to the impressions it is supposed to generate in us fares no better. The impression that occurs in us simultaneously with the activity of the thing in itself on our senses may be caused by that activity. But this only makes a thing in itself an object among other objects in time, requiring an explanation of the relation in which it stands to the thing in itself that is causally responsible for the existence of that object as part of our possible or actual experience.

This, then, is the historical sense of Jacobi's sibylline claim that he cannot enter Kant's system without the notion of a thing in itself and with that notion cannot stay within that system. Kant needs an object rather than a *concept* of an object in order to account for the existence of the impressions that occur in us. But the concept of a causal object is one thing; the object properly so called is another. Kant requires the latter but gives only the former. The Kantian distinction between things in themselves and appearances allegedly collapses on one or the other of two mutually exclusive assumptions. Assume that a thing in itself is the cause of an appearance, and all you produce is another appearance. Assume that there is a distinction between an appearance and something causing it but which is not itself an appearance, and you merely reproduce the original problem of causally relating the appearance to the thing in itself because the thing in itself becomes another appearance under a misleading name; for what can be a thing in itself on one perceptual occasion can be an appearance on another.

Jacobi's attack leaves us with an empty concept or a fraudently named object.

But I do not think it does. What Kant supplies in the Transcendental Analytic is not, as Jacobi's objections intimate, the concept of an object but rather the different concept of what it is to *know* an object. Kant's account requires both. We need a concept of what it is to be an object in order to account for what it is that we must synthesize according to a rule. But we also need an account of what a concept is without which we cannot explain how we go about knowing the objects that are given to us. Moreover, Kant's problem about relating things in themselves to our forms of intuition rests on the dilemma suggested by Jacobi's argument only if we assume either the *TWT* or the *TDT* in its received version as an account of the relation between things in themselves and appearances. Once again, Jacobi's complaint is ironically instructive. It exposes, not the faulty character of Kant's distinction between things in themselves and appearances, but rather the incapacity of traditional ways of explicating that distinction to account for the facts for which they are meant as an explanation.

2.   Fichte

Fichte takes up where Jacobi leaves off. This is the outline of Fichte's argument in the *Erste Einleitung in die Wissenschaftslehre* of 1797:

(1) We have immediate awareness of all of our representations [*Vorstellungen*].[9] [Definition]

(2) I can be immediately aware of the production of certain determinations [*Bestimmungen*] in me.[10] [Assertion of fact]

(3) These determinations are in me only insofar as I perceive them.[11] [Assumption]

(4) Therefore, the description of an object implies the possibility of our perceiving it.[12] [From steps (1) through (3)]

(5) Therefore; the description of an object that is impossible to perceive is a contradiction in terms. [From step (5)]

(6) Therefore, the notion of a thing in itself is internally contradictory. [From steps (1) through (5)]

The startling gaps in this argument do not presently concern me. They are obvious enough. For one thing, the move from step (3) to step (4) begs the question. It may be the case that what Fichte calls a determination exists only insofar as I perceive it. But this does not imply that determinations are the *only* things I perceive. Nor does it imply that perceptual objects are either themselves determinations or constituted of determinations. For another, it does not follow from this version of Fichte's argument about the perceptual objects of our experience—whether they are determinations, clusters of determinations, or whether they exist only insofar as I perceive them—that there are no things in themselves.

So much for the gaps. My interest here is to understand the relevance of a suitably reconstructed argument to Kant's theory of things in themselves based on what Fichte says in his 1797 introduction to the *Wissenschaftslehre*. Fichte's argument does not imply the internal incoherence of concepts of things that cannot be objects of possible experience. So his argument must be restricted to *perceptual* objects and step (3) must be replaced by

(3') No perceptual object can have determinations that are not themselves objects of possible experience.

Step (3), unlike its replacement, conflates two very different philosophical issues. There is, first, the problem of whether objects can exist only so long as they are perceived. And, secondly, there is the quite different issue of whether objects can have determinations that cannot be perceived even though the objects can exist only so long as they are perceived. The former issue is irrelevant to the tenability of Kant's theory of things in themselves: It is possible for objects to exist that go out of existence when they are not perceived and still have the properties while they are being perceived that cannot themselves be objects of perception. Hence the need for (3'): No perceptual object, whether or not it goes out of existence when it is not perceived, can have properties (i.e., determinations) that are not perceived.

But Fichte's 1797 argument must be supplemented in another way. We must allow him the assumption (call it the Equivalence Postulate) that "representation" and "determination" have the same meaning. Denying him the Equivalence Postulate would make it possible for us to be aware of representations that are not determinations of my self and would, therefore, render the 1797 argument against the possibility of Kantian things in themselves completely innocuous. For the rejection of the postulate would allow us to raise, as Kant did, the ques-

tion about the relation of a representation to what produces it all over
again. This question cannot be raised with respect to Fichtean determinations just because we are said to be aware, not only of the
determination that is produced in consciousness, but also of the activity by which they are produced. And if this is true, the distinction
between things we cannot perceive that produce those we can perceive
by affecting our sensory apparatus simply collapses. The Equivalence
Postulate is, therefore, not only implicit in but indispensable to the
success of Fichte's 1797 argument.

Fichte's *Die Bestimmung des Menschen* (1800) moves against things
in themselves in another way.[13] Let me introduce three initial caveats.
First: My examination of the argument is an attempt to assess not
primarily its soundness but rather its relevance to Kant's problem of
things in themselves and only then to ask whether Fichte's attack on
the existence of things in themselves solves that problem. Second: The
1800 refutation must be seen in the broader context of Fichte's claim
that we can know nothing but our own mental states. This approach is
necessary because it is essential for my present purpose to discover
whether in relating our knowledge of our own mental states to the objects of what we take to be the external world Fichte confuses the problem of relating what he calls sensations (*Empfindungen*) to external
objects with the logically independent problem of relating things in
themselves to appearances (*Erscheinungen*)." External objects cause
us to have sensations. They do not for this reason, however, consist of
sensations. Nor does this fact prevent us from perceiving the objects
that cause the sensations we have. The relation between things in themselves and appearances can, therefore, be raised independently of the
relation between sensations and their causes. For appearances can
cause us to have sensations, but we can still ask about the relation between those appearances and what they are appearances of. Third: I
distinguish between a proof that all I can ever *know* is my sensations
from the proof of the very different claim that all that *exists* is my sensations. The former allows the problem about the relation between
things in themselves and appearances to be raised all over again within
the context of the extent of my knowledge. The latter, however, abolishes the distinction between things in themselves and appearances altogether and, if successful, solves Kant's problem.

I divide Fichte's argument into two distinct stages. The first purports to show that all we can ever know is states of our ego; the second, that the notion of a thing in itself, though logically coherent, is a

misnomer for what must be an object that is the content of possible experience. The first stage runs as follows:

(1) My sensory apparatus tells me that there are objects that exist external to me [*außer mir*].[14] [Assumption]

(2) I know immediately that and what I am doing when I engage in an *act* of sensing.[15] [Assumption]

(3) Therefore, I am directly conscious of "a particular determination or modification of [my]self."[16] [From step (2) with the lemma Fichte introduces earlier that every modification or attribute of a substance has "a something to support these attributes—a *substratum* for them."][17]

(4) Therefore, you are directly conscious of "a particular modification of *yourself*."[18] [From steps (2) and (3)]

(5) Therefore, we are not conscious of external objects: "*In all perception you perceive only your own condition*."[19] [From step (4) with the lemma: "What you do not perceive *immediately*, you do not perceive at all."][20]

I deliberately leave the argument skeletal in order to identify and exclude those strands in it that are irrelevant to Fichte's principal objection to things in themselves. His general strategy is to show that a substratum or a bearer of properties can be an object of awareness (the thrust of step 3); that such a substratum cannot be perceptually abstracted from its properties (the burden of step 2 and the lemma needed for step 3); and, finally, that the ontological distinction between a substratum and its properties collapses, leaving only the self and its sensations (the import of steps 4 and 5).

The gaps in the strategy are evident but irrelevant. Whether every perceptual property is a modification or state of the self is logically independent of whether there are things in themselves: The same problem arises for selves as well as external objects. Whether substrata are perceptually indistinguishable from their properties is equally irrelevant: Even if we grant perceptual indistinguishability, we can still ask whether we must distinguish between things in themselves and appearances with respect to a substratum that happens to be perceptually indistinguishable from its properties. The distinction between things in themselves and appearances is also logically independent of the realism-idealism issue. But for Fichte it is not distinguishable from the quite different issue of whether all substrata are objects of possible experience. We can raise the issue about the relation between things in themselves and appearances even if we assume that everything that exists is either a mental act or a property of a mental act. For the distinction between a substratum or bearer of properties and the properties it bears can be applied to mental entities just as it is applicable to those entities in the world none of whose parts is mental. In each case Fichte's problem is the same. If we are always presented with a property that we perceive together with the substratum that has it, we allegedly cannot perceptually distinguish between the two. This is the issue on which the background of Fichte's attack on the existence of things in themselves ultimately rests. This is the second stage of the argument.

(1) There is nothing more to an object than its attributes because they are always perceived as spread over the surface of what we commonsensically take to be the substance or substratum in which they inhere.[21] [Assertion of fact]

(2) To sense, say, a surface of a perceptual object is always to be immediately aware of, e.g., smoothness, redness, shape, and size. [Assertion of fact]

(3) Therefore, there is no sensation of a substance or substratum that is supposed to have the attributes of which we are immediately conscious. [From step (2)] [22]

(4) Space itself is the only remaining candidate for a thing in itself, and you perceive it, not as a property of an external thing, but as an affection of your own being." [From steps (2) and (3)] [23]

(5) Therefore, there are no things in themselves. [From steps (1) through (4)]

The background and the foreground of Fichte's attack on things in themselves reinforce each other. The first stage of Fichte's 1800 refutation begins with two innocent stipulations from which he seeks to extrapolate a dramatic philosophical conclusion in the second stage. We acquire our knowledge of the external world primarily by immediate awareness of the objects around us. And whatever these objects may be, they share the characteristic of being sensations. All of this is innocuous legislation so long as "sensation" is understood to mean merely "content of sensory awareness": This leaves it open whether that content is mental or physical, a property of a mind or a property of a material object.

But the innocence ends here. The distinction between a substratum and a property, attribute, or characteristic that inheres in it is epistemologically irrelevant. In Fichte, we cannot distinguish an attribute from what has it because both are epistemologically on the same footing. Phenomenologically, they are both sensations; hence, the distinction between a substance (i.e., substratum) and an attribute cannot be made for Fichte by inspecting the contents of immediate awareness; hence, there is no substratum underlying the attributes we perceive. And there is, therefore, no thing in itself.

We can say the same thing in an instructively paradoxical way. Whether there are things in themselves is independent of the issue of whether there is a distinction between a substratum and the attributes that inhere in it. We can say either that there is no substratum-attribute distinction. Or we can say that there is such a distinction but that no substratum can be a thing in itself. Both of these conclusions are compatible with Fichte's strategy. If we say that there is a substratum-attribute distinction, then the substratum we claim to distinguish from the attribute is as phenomenologically available to us as the attribute that inheres in it, for every element of experience that we call a substratum is really only a surface of a content of consciousness. And surfaces are on the same experiential if not ontological footing as their characteristics. If we take Fichte's argument of 1800 to show that there is no substratum-attribute distinction, all we succeed in doing, according to that argument, is to demonstrate that no thing in itself can be a substratum. This supplies independent if circuitous confirmation of conclusions that have already been reached. Fichte's argument of 1800 succeeds in showing that the distinction between things in themselves and appearances cannot be explained by either of the traditional alternative interpretations of that distinction.

The historical case against Kant's arguments for the existence of things in themselves has begun to assume a pattern. There is, as Jacobi argues, no impression of a thing in itself; hence, there is nothing in our experience that can justify us in assigning a representation to the history of one perceptual object rather than another. And, what is even worse, even if there were an impression of a thing in itself, it would only reproduce the very problem it was supposed to solve—the problem, namely, of justifying the ascription of an impression to one object rather than another. In this respect all impressions share the same fate: Impressions suffer from a definitional vow of silence about which object to which they belong. And producing an impression of a thing in itself merely makes it impossible to do what the theory requires it to do, for it only reproduces the original problem.

The Kant of the first *Kritik* gives us a *concept* of an object that lacks the characteristics of our forms of sensibility. And this is as fatal to the doctrine as the ascriptional difficulty that precedes it. If all that Kant gives us is a concept, idea, or notion of what it is to be a thing in itself, his theory must still account for how impressions or representations occur to us irrespective of our ability to assign any given impression to the family of temporally sequential impressions to which it belongs. Even though there is only one instantaneous impression, Kant still has the problem of relating it to whatever acts on our sensibility in order to generate it. The concept of something that does not conform to the forms of our sensibility cannot do the job of an *object* that, though it may lack the characteristics of our forms of sensibility, still acts upon them.

3. Schopenhauer

Schopenhauer multiplies the entries in this bill of particulars. A Kantian thing in itself is either a misnomer or a self-contradiction. We are free to dismiss the entire doctrine as a self-contradiction, which can be exhibited by unpacking the very notion of a thing in itself. If what we call a thing in itself is supposed to be a thing, it is a possible object of experience, for it must stand under the category of causation and must have at least the characteristics of spatiality and temporality in order to count as a thing in the first place.[24] But this is logically incompatible with saying that the thing exists in and for itself (*an und für sich*)— which is just to say that it is not knowable because it lacks the characteristics of our forms of sensibility and cannot be causally active.

But if a thing in itself is not a downright self-contradiction, then for Schopenhauer it is at least a misnomer for a material object. And a material object is an appearance. Schopenhauer argues himself into this position as follows. Kant's object of representation (*Gegenstand der Vorstellung*) is a composite of what Schopenhauer claims is partly taken from representation and partly from a thing in itself. The object of representation is partly characterized by causal activity just in vir-

tue of its being a material thing.[25] Material things cause the sensations
we have and must therefore be temporal entities just because they fall
under the category of causation. Thus Kant is faced with a dilemma. If
things in themselves cause us to have the sensations we do, then we
apply the category of causation to those objects for the conditions of
our sensibility and what was a thing in itself turns out to be just one
material object acting causally on others, namely, our sensory receptors. If things in themselves have no such causal properties, then all
that Kant's argument gives us is the concept of a thing that lacks the
characteristics of our sensibility or is incapable of having any characteristics of any possible sensibility—in which case we are given a concept that by its very nature prevents it from having any object falling
under it. In either case, so Schopenhauer's conclusion goes, the thing
in itself is inherently unstable. Emphasize its relation to material
things and their causation of sensations, and you make it indistinguishable from a material object. Emphasize its lack of causal relations to the material things of our world, and its lack of spatial or temporal characteristics, and you have transformed what was supposed to
be an object into an empty concept. In either case there are no Kantian
things in themselves.[26] Thus Schopenhauer.

Consider, first, the claim that the Kantian object of representation
is what Schopenhauer calls a composite. It is a material object because
it causes sensation. But it is a thing in itself because the category of
causation does not apply to it. This kind of composite is, to be sure,
unstable. But the overriding assumption of Schopenhauer's objection
is that one and the same subject of predication—what he calls the object of representation—must both have and lack causal properties.
But the composite character of the object of representation has been
incorrectly described. That kind of object is composite only in the
sense that one and the same *particular* can be part of different *states of
affairs*. The object of representation is, accordingly, a composite of a
particular together with one or more properties. This kind of composition is not philosophically objectionable. The state of affairs can
be causally efficacious while the particular in it is not.

The objèction seems to be sound only because it illicitly trades on
the distinction between "object" as "particular" and "object" as "state
of affairs." Taken in the former sense, we are given Schopenhauer's pe-
jorative sense of "object of representation." Taken in the latter sense,
however, it gives us the philosophically honorific sense of the sameness
of particulars with the difference of the states of affairs in which they

are or can be a part. Causation resides in a property that a particular has and not properly in the particular that has the property. That a particular may be a part of a state of affairs that is not actual shows this. The particular as such does not have causal characteristics. The ambiguity in the notion of an object of representation does, as Schopenhauer says, expose the instability of an object of representation. But it does not vitiate the notion of a thing in itself. It merely emphasizes the distinction between particulars and states of affairs in the explication of the distinction between things in themselves and appearances. It is, in fact, indirect confirmation of what I have called the *TDT* in its revised version.

4. Hegel

Hegel exhausts the fundamental themes of the historical attacks on Kantian things in themselves. The greater *Logik* and the *Phänomenologie des Geistes* are the main sources of the theme.[27] Consider the *Logik* first. We are told that "the thing in itself is what exists as present, essential immediacy through sublated [*aufgehoben*] mediation."[28] Hegel glosses this as follows. What we call a thing in itself has two sides. One is unmediated: It is given to us directly and not by inference from something else that is given to us. The other is mediated: It is given to us only insofar as we infer to its existence from something that is given to us directly. A thing in itself exists only insofar as it stands in a causal relation to various sensory organs. What makes it a thing in itself is that it has causal properties that enable it to act on our sensory receptors and thereby make it an object of possible human experience.

This is Hegel's attempt to combine what can and what cannot be present to our sensory apparatus. A thing in itself is something that causes us to perceive the things we do but that cannot itself be perceived in the absence of these properties. It exists, but it does so only in relation to something else.[29] The contrary assumption generates contradictions. If a thing in itself existed only in relation to something else, then it ceases to be a thing in itself. But if it existed in the absence of any such relations, then it loses its identity even as a thing just because part of that identity resides in its being the repository of properties that can act on our sensory receptors.

The strategy needs to be disentangled. The distinction between what is mediated and immediate as Hegel applies it to things in themselves masks three different distinctions. There is, first, the distinction between the cause of what we perceive and the effect of that cause on our sensory apparatus. The latter is immediate; the former is mediated by our acquaintance with sensory effects. We distinguish, secondly, a particular and its properties. Our acquaintance with the particular can sometimes be inferred and thus mediated by our acquaintance with one or the other of its properties. And, finally, we can try to individuate the particulars of our perceptual experience by claiming that they are at least partially analyzable into their properties. Each of these distinctions marks a shift in the sense of "mediation." But the shifts have a common theme: A thing in itself cannot be perceived in isolation from something else. Hegel concludes that we do perceive things in themselves but never under that description because we cannot perceptually separate a thing from its properties. This is how Hegel can claim there are things in themselves and then go on to assimilate them to appearances without contradiction.

Hegel continues this theme in the section entitled *Force and Understanding (Kraft und Verstand)* in the *Phänomenologie des Geistes*.[30] This follows upon his chronicle of the collapse of other attempts to account for the object of perceptual awareness. We can say, as we are told in the section of the *Phänomenologie* concerning the designation "Sense Certainty," (*die sinnliche Gewissheit*) that the immediate object of perceptual awareness is the particular without any properties or without any relations to any other particular.[31] But, if Hegel is right, we cannot isolate such an entity in our perceptual awareness. No indexical like "this" or whatever other linguistic expression is intended to do duty for a rigorous designator can make the particular we intend to designate perceptually available to us—and all for the same reason: The vehicle we use in order to isolate particulars can be used on different occasions to isolate numerically different particulars. But this is what makes indexicals or any other pretender to the title of "rigorous designator" a universal term in disguise.[32] Whatever designates many cannot uniquely designate.

The opposite extreme fares no better. Suppose, as Hegel asks us to do, that what we perceive is a bundle of common properties.[33] When we claim to perceive something that is a particular, the object of our perceptual awareness is not a mere something devoid of properties and relations. What we perceive is a bundle of properties. But, as Hegel tells us, bundles of properties are the ontological mirror images of particulars without any properties at all. Both are merely two illustrations of the same defect described differently. One bundle of common properties is no better off than one particular without any properties. For one thing, the same strictures that vitiate our use of designators of propertyless particulars apply with undiminished force to bundles of common properties: A "this" that should but fails to single out one particular from another repeats that failure when it applies to bundles of properties. There is nothing in one bundle of common properties that distinguishes it from another such bundle just because both bundles can contain numerically and qualitatively the same properties. What masks as theoretical adequacy is, once again, demonstrable fakery.

The bundle theory breaks down: It cannot account for the numerical diversity of different bundles of common properties.[34] The Theory of Force and Understanding (*Kraft und Verstand*) is supposed to repair all of this.[35] Suppose we think of what we call the properties of perceptual objects as so many expressions of a force acting on our sensory receptors. Perceptual properties are contained in what Hegel calls a medium that, unlike the referent of a bare "this," can be singled out in experience as numerically distinct from other media and that, unlike a mere bundle of properties, can be used to distinguish one bundle of common properties from another.

Hegel is quick to point out that the theory collapses of its own weight. The notion of a force is merely a verbal camouflage for whatever appears to perceptual consciousness but that cannot itself be just one appearance among others without repeating the errors of its dialectical predecessors. *A force must but cannot be logically both the medium that is different from what is present to perceptual consciousness and identical with the properties that are its ostensible expressions.* The notion of a medium just pushes the problem back one step further. We begin by asking about the relation of particulars and common properties in the content of perception. We provisionally end by introducing a notion that merely reproduces the problem.

The attempts at remedy go on. The section in the *Phänomenologie* described as a theory of the medium is another such attempt.[36] The medium functions as the individuator of particulars and at the same time as the property or properties that are available to perceptual consciousness. But the notion of a medium is inherently unstable: It camouflages the problem it is expected to solve. "Medium" like "force" is really shorthand for what is behind the appearances and for what appears to us: it is both the repository of the forces that is other than the expressions of those forces and the expression of the forces of which it is the repository. The philosophical economy, as Hegel points out, is illusory, for there are really, not one, but two forces in every property. There is the force that is called the medium. And there is the phenomenally given force that is different from the medium. The problem of the relation between particulars and their properties in perceptual experience has merely been thinly concealed. The medium cannot be both what has the property and the expression of the property it allegedly has at the same time: They are two and not one.

The Law of Force attempts to pick up the pieces of the theories that Hegel records.[37] We are asked to suppose that what we call a thing is a set of appearances and that what binds them together is not a medium or a thing that is perceptually unavailable to us but nonetheless acts on our sensory apparatus but rather a law or rule according to which we combine these appearances through time. The law is not a thing. It is a guide for the activity by which we combine appearances; hence, the problem of relating a thing to its appearances, our ability to designate bare particulars, and the self-destructive character of a medium containing forces would seem to evaporate. For all of them are so many faulty statements of what in fact happens when we perceive an object. What really happens is that we combine appearances according to a rule. And it is the rule that gives what would otherwise be a jumble of unrelated temporal occurrences the unity necessary for it to be a genuine thing.

Hegel rejects this whole enterprise. Substituting laws for forces gives a new name to an old problem. Hegel distinguishes between what he calls the notion of a law in general and the specific laws that are supposed to guide our acts of ordering appearances.[38] The same problem recurs when we try to relate the notion of a law in general to the plethora of specific laws. Hegel puts it this way:

> Insofar however as it is not *law* in general but *a* law, it has the character of definiteness; and thereby there are indefinitely *many* laws present. This multitude is, however, a defect; for it contradicts the principle of the understanding which, as consciousness of what is simply internal, is the truth of what is in itself universal *unity*.[39]

In a law of forces there are really two distinguishable aspects. There is a description of phenomena or appearances. There is the concept of lawfulness as such. But this lawfulness must somehow be related to the description of the appearances. And this fails for two reasons.

For one, the problem about relating specific laws to what Hegel calls lawfulness as such is logically no different from the problem of relating a thing to its properties or a medium to the forces through which it acts. What Hegel calls lawfulness as such must stand in some relation to the specific laws that govern our knowledge of specific laws. And this raises once again all of the problems about how we are to relate specific instances of something to whatever appears through instances. For another, the notion of a law as an explanation that merely describes the phenomena it is supposed to explain can only beg the question it should answer. The problem facing the relation between an appearance and what appears cannot be solved without begging the question if we introduce a description of the order of appearances and call it an explanation of what it is to be a thing that appears. A rule for combining appearances is either an evasive description of the problem about the relation of a thing to its appearances or, what is worse, an illegitimate substitution of an epistemological for an ontological issue.

Suppose we say provisionally that what we ordinarily call a material thing is really a temporally ordered collection of appearances that we combine according to certain rules. This may tell us how we come to know such an object. But it leaves us none the wiser about the relation of any one of those appearances that we combine according to a rule that appears to us. The former is an epistemological account of what an object for us must be if we are to experience it; the latter is an ontological account of what it is to be an object irrespective of the rules we must follow if we are successfully to combine the sequence of appearances in our experience. Both descriptions of the perceptual situation are mutually compatible. They are merely solutions to two distinct problems. The fact remains, however, that the relation between an object and any one of its appearances is different from the relation between one appearance and another. And the solution of the epistemological problem cannot do duty for the solution of the ontological problem because we can adequately solve the former without raising the latter.

This evidence that Hegel is attacking the Kantian or any other notion of a thing in itself is superficially shaky and thus runs the risk of being dismissed as historically irrelevant to such an issue. Everything that Hegel says in the *Phänomenologie* about perceptual consciousness and repeats elsewhere in different versions applies to perceptual objects as much as it does to things in themselves. Thus arises our alleged inability to locate propertyless particulars in perception, the collapse of the bundle theory of particularity, and the fact that the notions of a medium and force merely reproduce the problem they are introduced to solve. This is as much a problem for what we commonsensically call appearances as it is for things in themselves; hence, we might conclude that Hegel's arguments, so far from showing that the notion of a thing in itself is philosophically disreputable, really succeed in showing that the notice of an appearance is no less disreputable.

The objection does not, however, disqualify the arguments in the *Phänomenologie* from being a concentrated attack on the notion of a thing in itself. The arguments concerning perceptual consciousness are reproduced in both the *Enzyklopädie* and the *Logik* with specific reference to the notion of a thing in itself.[40] The parallel is too striking to be dismissed. And we can dispel the suspicion of irrelevancy by a closer examination of the more general assumption on which the objection rests.[41] It is this. What Hegel says in the *Phänomenologie* running from Sense Certainty through the section on the Supersensible World admittedly applies to both things in themselves and appearances. But this does not imply the incoherence of perceptual knowledge of appearances even though the problems that Hegel raises are applicable to appearances and things in themselves alike. His arguments may apply equally to things in themselves and appearances, but Hegel directs his arguments against *theories* of perceptual consciousness and not the fact of such consciousness. It remains an open question whether any theory of perceptual consciousness can meet the objections of the *Phänomenologie*. But my present purpose requires only that the arguments there cut against things in themselves no matter what else may be included in their scope.

The Hegelian pattern should by now be clear. It depends upon the viability of the inference from the fact that something is dependent upon the existence of something else in order for us to know it to the conclusion that it cannot be a Kantian thing in itself because it cannot be known independently of our knowledge of something else. If a thing in itself is the cause of what we perceive, then we cannot know it because all we can know, according to Hegel's argument, is the effect of its action on us. If it is a particular, we cannot know it because we cannot perceive it independently of the properties it has. Nor can we claim to perceive a particular if we reduce it to a set or collection of properties, whether they are forces or the merger of a medium with its expressions, because such a reduction makes us unable to distinguish one collection from another. It is logically possible for both sets to consist of the same properties.

Hegel gives us further confirmation of a claim that we have already defended. That there is a causal relation between one object and another does not threaten the Kantian distinction between things in themselves and appearances. That relation holds between properties and not particulars. Thus we can be immediately acquainted with particulars without having to rely on our acquaintance with the properties in the states of affairs of which they are parts. We can use an indexical expression or whatever can serve as a linguistic vehicle to pick out objects uniquely on many numerically different occasions of use. This does not, however, show that such expressions, although they can be used on different occasions to make successful identifying references, fail to do so on any given occasion. The Hegelian pattern does show that Kant's theory of individuation cannot be successfully explicated in terms of the theories that Hegel reviews only to reject them. But it does not demonstrate the inadequacy of the distinction between things in themselves and appearances as it is set forth within the context of the revised version of *TDT*.

5. Error and Indictment

This, then, is the historical case against the existence of Kantian things in themselves. The arguments constituting that case are different, yet they share a common flaw: *None of them correctly states Kant's theory because each assimilates that theory to other Kantian distinctions that are logically independent of his distinction between things in themselves and appearances.* Let me begin by provisionally sketching the issues that the tradition has almost hopelessly confused. The claim that the concept of a Kantian thing in itself is internally incoherent is a confusion, probably initiated by Jacobi but surely perpetuated by Fichte; it is a confusion of that notion with the quite different notion of a transcendental object. Identify them and, as I shall show, you will generate a contradiction. But they are distinct notions and, on both textual and philosophical grounds, cannot be identified.

The second historical error, contributed by Fichte, is no less serious than its predecessor. It succeeds only on the assumption that there are things in our world called things in themselves that cannot be objects of possible experience. It is one thing to say, as Kant does, that the objects that present themselves in our world to our forms of sensibility can be perceived under other such forms. It is quite another to say, as Kant does not, that there are things in our world that cannot present themselves to *any* form of sensibility. These claims are not equivalent and, what is even more telling, the latter does not follow from the former.

The third strand in the historical tradition of criticism, for which Hegel is mainly responsible although Fichte helps to perpetuate it, is based on an obstinate blindness to Kant's text. It confuses the distinction between what Kant calls a thing in itself and an appearance with the very different distinction between a perceptual thing and its properties. We are told that a thing cannot be presented to us apart from its properties. And we are asked to conclude that there is really no genuine distinction between a thing in itself and a perceptual thing because such a distinction is just a misnomer for the relation that a perceptual thing has to its properties. We cannot perceive a perceptual thing without perceiving some or other of its properties. But this does not make it impossible to perceive a perceptual thing at all. It merely implies that we cannot perceive it without doing so under some description or other.

The fourth and most pervasive strand in the polemical tradition remains. Despite the differences in the other arguments against Kant, they all claim that the relation between a thing in itself and an appearance functions in Kant's argument as the relation between cause and effect. They begin by pointing out that things in themselves affect our sensibility, go on to point out that "affection" is really only a verbal disguise for the relation of cause to effect, and conclude that there can be no relation between things in themselves and appearances because the category of causation cannot apply to things in themselves without generating a contradiction or assimilating a thing in itself to a phenomenal substance. The conclusion is the rejection of Kantian things in themselves. But the conclusion falsely assumes that the concept of a thing in itself does duty for concepts that are logically distinct from it and that it cannot exist because the concept cannot do that duty.

Begin with the historical theme that the Kantian notion of a thing in itself is internally incoherent. Jacobi's argument for this conclusion is deceptively simple. What Kant calls the transcendental object is not itself a part of the manifold to which we ascribe our impressions. It is only the unity of the manifold insofar as it stands in a relation to an object. The transcendental object is not itself an object but only the concept of an object to which we assign the parts of our sensuous manifold. The concept of such an object assumes and therefore cannot account for what it is that makes the impressions on our sensory manifold that we then assign to the transcendental object.

An unsympathetic critic might object to this gloss. I might be told that we can schematize concepts but that it makes no sense to say, as I have just done, that we can schematize objects in any way—let alone objects answering to the description Kant gives of things in themselves. A schema is a way in which we apply a concept to an object; hence, to talk about a schema of an object is at best a semantical slip and at worst a contradiction in terms.

The critic is helpfully wrong—helpful, because he unwittingly spots the fundamental ambiguity in Kant's notion of schematism, wrong, because he clutches to one and only one sense of that notion. A Kantian schema is a mark in the object in virtue of which we can tell that such an object corresponds to an element that we think in the concept of that kind of object. If we insist that only a concept can be a Kantian schema, we invite the hopeless problem of specifying just how the concept that we call a schema is to be applied to objects. And this merely gives us our original problem of applying concepts to objects all over again. If we are to avoid attributing this consequence to Kant's theory, we must recognize that a schema must ultimately be a characteristic of things that has its counterpart in our concepts of those things. The narrow view of schematism invites a problem it cannot solve. A recognition of the ambiguity of Kant's use of that notion remedies it.

This sharply conflicts with Kant's argument.[42] The transcendental object is an epistemic place marker for the particular empirical object to which I assign the experiences that I have of it when I perceive it. To say, as Kant does, that the transcendental object is unknown is not, then, to say that it is an entity that we cannot know. The notion of a transcendental object stands for a range of objects that we *can* know without specifying any particular object. But this requires explication.

What Kant calls a transcendental object cannot be a thing in itself just because we refer the parts of our sensuous manifold to the transcendental object; but this implies that the transcendental object is a temporal and hence phenomenal object. Yet the transcendental object cannot be a member of the sensuous manifold and for this reason cannot be an object of possible experience. But a thing in itself cannot be an object of experience, either. The transcendental object and a thing in itself have experiential inaccessibility in common. But that commonality is misleading. A thing in itself cannot be an object of possible experience because it is a particular that cannot be given independently of our own or any other forms of intuition. The transcendental object, on the other hand, cannot be an object of possible experience because the expression "transcendental object" stands for any object to which we refer any part of a manifold of perceptions by means of which we experience any phenomenal object. The transcendental object is not just one more—albeit peculiar—particular among others. The notion specifies phenomenal objects indifferently. The relation between a phenomenal object and thing in itself cannot, then, be the same kind of relation that obtains between a phenomenal and a transcendental object. The difference between the two kinds of relation vitiates Jacobi's objection. Consider how this comes about.

Neither the transcendental object nor things in themselves are objects of possible experience. But the reasons for their respective unknowability are important since they undercut Jacobi's objection to the distinction between appearances and things in themselves. The transcendental object cannot be a member of the manifold of sensuous intuitions; therefore, it is not an object of possible experience. Assume for the sake of the argument that what Kant calls the transcendental object is one among other members of the manifold that we synthesize when we perceive an object. This assumption would require that we refer the transcendental object to yet another object of which it is an appearance. And this only generates an infinite regress that must terminate in the admission that what Kant calls the transcendental object cannot be a member of the manifold the parts of which must be referred to an object that we perceive successively. And this also shows why the transcendental object cannot be conflated with a thing in itself.

The issue facing the distinction between Kantian things in themselves and appearances can be raised for every member of the manifold. But it cannot be raised with respect to the transcendental object, for the distinction between an appearance and a thing in itself cannot be made with respect to it. That there is an object that we perceive serially but that cannot itself be a member of the series is to say that it cannot be given to us in one fell perceptual swoop. It is not to say that it cannot be given to us at all. It is unknowable as a member of the series in our sensuous manifold. Things in themselves are unknowable because they cannot be given to us in any series. The transcendental object and a thing in itself cannot be run together, as Jacobi does, so that the sense in which the one is unknowable is assimilated to the sense in which the other is unknowable.[43]

The problem about the relation between things in themselves and appearances arises only with respect to the specific objects that collectively constitute the range of what Kant calls the transcendental object; therefore, the transcendental object cannot be identified with a thing in itself. Jacobi is, accordingly, right for the wrong reasons. We cannot have an *impression* of a transcendental object.

The transcendental object is not, however, to be identified with a thing in itself. Both of them are admittedly unknowable: Things in themselves are as inaccessible to us as the transcendental object. But they are inaccessible to us in different ways. A thing in itself cannot be given to us because we are limited to our forms of intuition. The transcendental object cannot be given to us because it does not designate any kind of object. The term stands for a general characteristic of any object that is given to our forms of intuition. It does not designate an object that might but somehow cannot be presented to us. The term tells us something about the characteristics of our way of experiencing the objects that are given to us. And this information contains nothing about a kind of object. Jacobi's objection is decisive against the transcendental object, then, only on the false assumption that it is a thing in itself. But the identity is illusory.

The philosophical incoherence surrounding this problem perpetuated itself. History passed the distinction between the transcendental object and a thing in itself on to Fichte, who holds that the notion of a perceptual object that is not a possible object of experience is logically inconsistent. Every description of such an object implicitly specifies the characteristics that make it perceptually available to us; therefore, to describe a thing in itself is to transform it into what it is not.

But the argument fails. It confuses the description of an object that appears to us under our forms of intuition with the description of that object as it might appear to us under other forms of intuition. Fichte's argument succeeds once we admit that any description of a thing in itself must assume the possibility of our experiencing it. But the objection collapses once we distinguish between descriptions that are governed by our forms of sensibility and those governed by other possible forms of sensibility. Any description of an object of Kantian intuition assumes that the properties involved are possible objects of experience. But this does not assume that the description of such an object

must contain only those characteristics governed by our forms of intuition. There is, therefore, no internal contradiction in saying that we
can describe sensuous objects that are not objects of our possible experience and still claim that they are Kantian intuitions. The contradictions arise only if we assume that our forms of sensibility are the
only logically possible forms under which sensuous objects can be
given.

This, however, is only the most conspicuous problem with Fichte's
assessment of things in themselves. It serves at most to cloud the real
historical lesson that Fichte's discussion should teach us, for he has
misrepresented the issue that he addresses. He argues that no object of
sensuous intuition can be described and then declared to be impossible
to experience without contradiction. The argument fails. But grant its
conclusion provisionally in order to uncover the underlying error in
Fichte's attack. Even if we hold that no sensuous object can be described without automatically becoming an object of possible experience, we still have not done away with the problem of Kantian things
in themselves. For whatever problems that arise with respect to a thing
that appears to us within our own forms of sensibility arise all over
again with respect to the subject of that description under other forms
of sensibility.

The problem does not go away. Fichte's attack is completely silent
about the subject of a description. It applies at most to the characteristics that appear to us under our forms of intuition. It does not apply to
the objects that can satisfy those descriptions. It would be logically
possible to give an exhaustive description of what appears to us under
our forms of intuition and still consistently hold that the object that
has these properties in our perceptual world could have properties in
another possible world perceptually incompatible with those it has in
our world; and this raises the issue of things in themselves once again.
Kant's distinction between things in themselves and appearances in
our perceptual world can be made all over again for a world in which
the forms of intuition are totally different from ours. Fichte has not
failed in his attempt to show that things in themselves do not exist. He
has merely given us a false statement of the problem.

The alleged contradiction endemic to any attempt to describe a
thing in itself occurs under the false assumption that the notion of a
thing in itself is identifiable with the notion of a thing that can be perceived under different forms of intuition. Fichte is right: We cannot
describe without contradiction the perceptual characteristics of some-

thing that is supposed to exist independently of any forms of intuition at all. But we can give self-consistent descriptions of things that are perceived under forms of intuition different from ours. None of this implies that the notion of a thing in itself is inherently self-contradictory. It tells us only that a thing in itself cannot be described without reference to possible forms of intuition. And this condition is completely silent about whether such a restriction makes it impossible to distinguish between things in themselves and appearances. It informs us only that any attempt to describe a thing in itself inevitably involves reference to other forms of intuition. The conclusion is obvious but not, as Fichte claims, self-contradictory. Yes, any attempt to describe a thing in itself involves implicit reference to some sort of form of intuition or other. But it does not involve an implicit reference to *our* forms of intuition. The former is self-consistent. The latter is not. But they are two and not one.

Schopenhauer's attack on things in themselves provides another reminder of what should be avoided in stating that problem. The complaint is familiar. Things in themselves allegedly cause whatever representations that are the constituents of our sensuous manifold. But if things in themselves are causes of what we perceive, Kant applies his category of causation to things that, on his own showing, cannot be given to our forms of intuition; therefore, to say that a thing in itself is a cause makes it an object that must have the properties of our sensibility. And this confronts Kant with an intolerable choice. Either what he calls a thing in itself is really a phenomenal object in disguise or the very idea of a thing in itself is self-contradictory because it must both have and lack the characteristics of our sensibility and consequently must but cannot stand under the categories. In either case, it is an ontological myth.

This objection goes the way of its predecessors. It breaks down on Kant's distinction between causation and affection. For Kant, a cause "makes strict demand that something, *A*, should be such that something else, *B*, follows from it *necessarily and in accordance with an absolutely universal rule.*" [44] Kant introduces the notion of affection in this way: "The effect of an object upon the faculty of representation, so far as we are affected by it, is *sensation.*" [45] Two differences between the two notions are important for my present purpose. In the first place, Kant formulates the principle of causation in terms of relations between temporal events and not between those events and material objects. It demands a kind of relation between phenomenal items.

Kantian affection makes no such demand. Secondly, Kant's routine statement of the affection relation admittedly says that objects cause occurrences in our sensibility. He does not, however, say that causal action is the *same* as affection but only that the relation of affection is a *necessary* condition for the occurrence of causal relations between phenomenal items.[46] Thus something can affect us in one mode or another without acting causally on us.

An argument that Kant's use of the affection-causation distinction requires but that he does not explicitly elaborate independently supports such a distinction. Suppose that the affection of one or another of our sensory receptors can be described as a causal chain the last member of which is to be designated by one or more of the appropriate substitutes for the generic notion of an act of awareness. If the relation between the act and the object of such an act were simply causal, it would be impossible for us to be aware of anything. The perceptual situation is supposed to be the effect of a cause. But the object of which we are aware cannot be the cause of what we are aware of. Otherwise it would merely generate an infinite regress of causes whose objects would never be perceptually available to us, for they would have to function as causes of what we do perceive. And this would disqualify them from counting as an object of perception for the situations in which they function as causes. If we are to avoid irreparable damage to Kant's text, then, we must distinguish, as Schopenhauer does not, between affection and causation.

The affection-causation distinction circumvents Schopenhauer's objection. Perceptual objects can cause appearances in our experience. But the distinction between things in themselves and appearances can still consistently be drawn between the first link in that causal chain and the appearance we directly perceive without forcing the extension of the category of causation to things in themselves. And this is just an immediate consequence of the distinction between affection and causation. It would be useless to object here that the affection-causation distinction merely generates a vicious infinite regress that leaves Schopenhauer's objection intact. Somebody might argue as follows: To say that we must distinguish between a thing in itself and an appearance even with respect to the first element in the causal chain that generates an effect in the appearances we experience gives us a vicious infinite regress, reproduces the original problem, and only postpones the inevitable conclusion that things in themselves are causes of appearances.

ances. The question we ask about the final link in the chain of causes arises all over again with respect to the initial link in the chain.

The objection to the tenability of the causation-affection distinction collapses on the fact that there are two kinds of infinite regress, one of which is vicious and the other philosophically harmless. The object of awareness in the perceptual situation I have described cannot be the cause of that object without generating a regress in which we must have the first link of the chain as a necessary condition of our having the final link in that chain. But a necessary condition of having the final link in the chain is our possession of the first link. If the perceptual situation must be described as the last link in a causal chain, such a regress arises. The perceptual object is supposed to be the cause of what we perceive. Yet it is perpetually condemned to being the effect of the object we perceive. What we perceive is one step behind what we are supposed to perceive on the causal account of the relation between a thing in itself and an appearance. Thus the viciousness of the infinite regress occurs.

This must be strictly separated from the regress that is generated by the claim we can make that the distinction between a thing in itself and an appearance for every link in a perceptual series even if it is described as causal. Assume for the sake of the argument that what Kant calls affection is merely an alternative expression for causation. Schopenhauer's argument assumes this, but the abolition of the distinction between things in themselves is not a consequence of the argument or its principal assumption. For there is no point in a potentially infinite series of perceptual situations where we cannot make that distinction. The regress may be infinite. But in this case we can assume the existence of the first link in that series without having to assume that the series has a final link necessary for the existence of the first link, thus making the regress harmless. What is not harmless about this regress is that any attempt to substitute the causal relation for the relation of affection is doomed to defeat because the relation between a thing in itself and an appearance can be made for every link in the series; hence, the grounds on which the affection relation is to be accepted cannot be causal. To say, then, that we must distinguish between a thing in itself and an appearance with respect to the initial link in the causal series strengthens Schopenhauer's objection.

But does it? I think not. The distinction between appearances and things in themselves arises for every link in the chain of causes leading from the original material object to the appearances of which we are aware; hence, there is a potentially infinite regress from the first to the last link in the causal chain. But since causal connections are not the same as those between appearances and things in themselves, the regress from cause to effect may be infinite—an issue irrelevant to the present problem—but it is not viciously infinite. For no link in that series each member of which can be analyzed into the relation between an appearance and a thing in itself assumes, as Schopenhauer's argument requires, that what is called a thing in itself is really a phenomenal entity. The relation of cause to effect is transitive. The relation of affection is not; hence, the claim that Kant must make the distinction between things in themselves and appearances for every member of a causal series implies the irrelevance of Schopenhauer's criticism of Kant's claim. It does not imply that the claim generates a vicious infinite regress.

Hegel introduces the fourth and final dominant strand in the tradition of the criticism. Discovering what is new in his criticism requires, however, considerable pruning of what he associates and at time confuses with it. I omit assessment of his claim that things in themselves exist only because they are really phenomenal objects. Fichte both propounds and exhausts the arguments for that claim. I also pass over Hegel's assimilation of a thing in itself to something that causes appearances to occur to our sensibility. Schopenhauer states the claim more clearly and succeeds in making a better case for it than Hegel in either stating or refuting that contention. The novelty of Hegel's criticism is the argument that a thing in itself cannot exist independently of some properties or other and that this relation of dependence of a thing on its properties is the proper statement of what Kant wrongly believes to be the relation between a thing in itself and its appearance.

Hegel is right. The distinction between a thing and its properties is logically distinct from the relation between a thing in itself and an appearance. But he does not succeed in showing that Kant attempted to substitute the one distinction for the other. Whatever the difficulty with the theories of the thing-property distinction that Hegel reviews in the *Phänomenologie*, they do show that what Hegel calls a thing or a law governing appearances is a philosophical cryptogram for the notion of a thing in itself. The arguments there demonstrate at most that the *theories* about what a perceptual particular is and its relation to its properties are philosophically defective.

There is independent support for this. The distinction between a thing and its properties can be made for both things in themselves and appearances. Things in themselves can have properties that are not objects of possible experience. We can distinguish for an intuition between something that has a property and the property it has. Hegel does not state the issue correctly. For we can know the nature of a thing as well as its relation to the properties it has and still remain ignorant of a thing in itself and the relation in which it stands to an appearance. Thus the alleged congenital dependence of a property on the thing that has it and our consequent inability to perceive a thing that has no properties at all cannot explicate Kant's distinction. And objections against theories of the thing-property distinction cannot qualify ex officio as arguments against the distinction between an appearance and a thing in itself.

By now some of the darkest clouds enshrouding things in themselves should have vanished. If we take a thing in itself to be the transcendental object, we can succeed in showing that there are no things in themselves. But the success of the attempt, as we have seen, is illusory. The transcendental object is a designation for any object to which we refer the members of the manifold of any appearance.[47] And this is compatible with there being no things in themselves at all. But it does not demonstrate that there are no things in themselves.

Nor can you say, as Fichte does, that the notion of a thing in itself is inherently self-contradictory because every description you offer of such a thing automatically makes it an object of possible experience and for that reason contradicts the notion of a thing the very definition of which prevents it from being an object of possible experience. We have seen how this is true but irrelevant. The contradiction that Fichte finds is not the contradiction he needs. The description of a thing in itself may require that it be an object of possible experience. But such a description need not require that it be an object of *our* possible experience. It requires only that the object can be experienced under some form of sensibility or another, none of which need be ours.

Finally, as we have also seen, what Kant calls a thing in itself cannot be transformed into a phenomenal object because the affection relation is said to be really only another form of the causal relation. The relation of affection requires only that an object be present to our forms of sensibility. And this does not imply that the object is causally related to those forms. And, as I have argued, once we assume that

Kantian affection is a case of causation, we do not destroy the distinction between things in themselves and appearances but only set out on a vicious infinite regress.

6. The Rebuttal

The confusions of the tradition are instructive. They help us to disentangle what is a genuine problem in distinguishing things in themselves and appearances from the pseudoproblems that have been historically associated with it. What remains is this. Kant introduces the distinction by means of the relation of what he calls affection and the argument in the Aesthetic of the first *Kritik* according to which space and time are transcendentally ideal.[48] We intuit objects that affect our sensibility. The forms of that sensibility are transcendentally ideal. All of this is familiar. What has been less than familiar to the tradition is that the result of the argument of the Aesthetic confronts Kant's theory with a major difficulty. Let me explain.

The distinction between things in themselves and appearances must be made with respect to our world. No appeal to alternative forms of sensibility can explain how something in our world can affect our forms of sensibility. The objects that appear to us as spatial and temporal may appear under other forms of sensibility in other possible worlds. But the question about what affects our sensibility and its relation to what we call the objects of our sensible intuition arises in every one of these possible worlds. Unless we can answer that question for our world, all we do by appealing to how an object might appear to us or others in different possible worlds merely perpetuates the problem without solving it.

This restriction generates a dilemma confronting Kant's distinction that the history of the debate about its viability has completely obscured. We must assume that what affects our sensibility is either a phenomenal object or a thing in itself. The former assumption produces a vicious infinite regress. A phenomenal object is supposed to be the outcome of a relation between a thing in itself and the forms of our sensibility. To say that it initiates such a relation is to make it a thing in itself by another name and to raise the problem of the relation between things in themselves and phenomenal objects all over again. The latter assumption would entail that we can know what characteristics things in themselves must have in this world. This in turn implies that things in themselves, though they may have characteristics in other possible worlds that they do not have in our world, at least genuinely have them in our world. And this makes a thing in itself perceptually available to us. In either case, the dilemma makes Kant's distinction spurious.

But does it? Emphatically not. The dilemma reveals what really faces Kant's distinction. The structural root of this lies in a pervasive ambiguity in the use of "transcendental ideality." Distinguish an epistemic and an ontological interpretation of the phrase. To say, as Kant does, that space and time are necessary conditions of our ability to intuit things can mean that all the objects we can perceive really have spatial or temporal properties. Call this the ontological interpretation of transcendental ideality. It implies our ability to know that these characteristics define what is to count as an object of possible experience. And this, furthermore, implies that we can know what properties an object of our experience has or lacks independently of being an object of possible experience. The epistemic interpretation of "transcendental ideality" is ontologically neutral. It implies only that we cannot know what an object is like independently of possible experience—the consequence of which is that an object of possible experience is defined independently of the forms of our sensibility.

If we say that we know the characteristics of an object of possible experience are what it appears to have under our forms of intuition, this leaves open the possibility that the object lacks these same characteristics apart from appearing to have them under our forms of intuition. But it also leaves it open whether the same object can have the characteristics of our forms of intuition independently of possible experience. To verify the claim would require us to be acquainted with the same object under our forms of intuition apart from any forms of intuition at all. We cannot do this on Kant's theory; hence, we cannot say that objects independent of our forms of intuition lack the characteristics of those forms without illegitimately claiming an impossible ability. But the same epistemic impossibility applies also to the claim that we can know those objects do have such characteristics independently of our forms of intuition. For this would imply that we could perform the very task that we cannot perform when we say that objects governed by our forms of intuition lack the characteristics of those forms.

This is a fact that has two important consequences for the interpretation of Kant's distinction between things in themselves and appearances. One consequence is that the particulars in phenomenal states of affairs can be numerically identical from one set of forms of intuition to another. If it is possible for the same particular either to have or to lack the characteristics it has independently of any specific form of intuition, then that particular is only contingently and not necessarily connected to those characteristics. It also implies that the connection between the object that affects us subject to our modes of intuition and those modes is logically distinct from the characteristics that it exhibits under them. Both consequences combine to corroborate the adequacy of the revised version of the *TDT* and to undermine the credibility of both the traditional version of that theory as well as the *TWT*.

The epistemic-ontological distinction is allowed by Kant's text, has been largely overlooked by the tradition, and is the philosophical root of an historical debate that has been ignorant of it.[49] In the first place, Kant's text sanctions the distinction, for it allows us to define what is to be an object of possible experience independently of the notions of space and time. The conclusion of the Aesthetic of the first *Kritik* is that we cannot conceive of objects without conceiving of them as spatial or temporal. It does not say that objects cannot be spatial or temporal independently of our capacity to conceive of them. This is the textual source of the dilemma.

If you interpret Kant's argument epistemically, then the relation of affection holds between phenomenal objects and our forms of sensibility. And there is no problem about circularity in the definition of "affection." All we are asked to believe is that we cannot compare what an object is like for our forms of sensibility with what it might be apart from those forms. This is impossible just because we would have to assume that we can compare what an object of possible experience is for us with what it might be independently of any forms of sensibility. But such an assumption requires us *per impossibile* to be able to compare what an object of possible experience is like when it is not an object of possible, experience. And this conclusion is reached independently of the issue whether the objects we perceive as spatial or temporal have those properties independently of being objects of possible experience; hence, the distinction between things in themselves and appearances can be preserved without the disastrous consequences of the first horn of the original dilemma.

There is, then, a distinction between things in themselves and appearances for our world. But that distinction must be defended on epistemic and not on ontological grounds. Kant's problem arises because of an ambiguity that is not resolved in the Aesthetic of the first *Kritik*. The philosophical issue is whether "being an object of possible experience" must be defined in terms of "having the characteristics of our sensibility" or whether that notion can be defined independently of such a claim. If the former, then we will have said that the object we perceive genuinely has those characteristics. And we would then be prevented from distinguishing between things in themselves and appearances. If the latter, we will have to distinguish between what it is for something to function as a form of intuition and what it is to be a characteristic of whatever we perceive under such a form. That is the philosophical problem that has been obscured by layers of historical misinterpretation.

Let us return now to the focus of this chapter and my contention that what may seem to be nothing more than a random series of criticisms is really an exegetical structure illustrating a common theme with two variations. The Ariadne's thread conducting us through these variations is the persistent claim that the very idea of a thing in itself is internally incoherent. Jacobi provides the first variation on this theme when he says that a thing in itself is causally responsible for the existence of the objects we perceive but that it cannot itself be an object of perception. For insofar as a thing in itself is the cause of what we perceive, it cannot be the cause of what we perceive. Fichte continues this variation when he says that the description of any perceptual object implies the possibility of our perceiving it and concludes that the very idea of a thing in itself is therefore self-contradictory. Once this restriction is placed on the notion of an object, the notion of a thing in itself as an object must include a specification of forms of intuition. And this make it an ex officio object of possible experience.

Fichte's attack on the viability of the substratum-attribute distinction merely confirms the existence of what I have called a common theme in the traditional criticism of Kant's theory of things in themselves. He rejects substrata, as we have seen, because they cannot be perceived in isolation from the properties they have. But this is nothing more than a variation on the theme that Jacobi begins; the theme, namely, is that the notion of a thing in itself is inherently self-contradictory. For once we describe a thing in itself, we must describe it under *some description or other*. And once we do this, the description we give of such an object must include by implication the conditions under which it can be a possible object of experience. The theme lingers on: Whenever you describe an object of possible perception, say that it cannot be an object of possible experience, and yet add to that claim of description of some of the characteristics it must have in order to be an object, then you have contradicted yourself.

Schopenhauer merely dramatizes the problem all over again, albeit with a new twist. Here the contradiction is supposedly generated by the fact that a thing in itself acts as a cause of what we perceive. Once that happens, it ceases to be a thing in itself just because it becomes part of the world that is subordinated to the forms of our or somebody else's forms of intuition. And insofar as this does not happen, what we choose to call a thing in itself can only be something that lacks any relation to our forms of intuition—which frees the notion of such an object from self-contradiction only at the fatal cost of making it irrelevant to the perceptual problem it is supposed to solve. Once again, the same theme: Whenever you describe a perceptual object and then say that it cannot—logically cannot—be an object of possible experience, you have succeeded only in contradicting yourself.

The theme lingers on. Hegel initiates what I have identified as the second variation. We cannot perceptually isolate a thing from its properties. He rightly infers that we cannot perceive a thing in itself but wrongly concludes that a thing in itself is not a possible object of experience just because a subject of properties cannot be perceptually isolated from those properties. And no matter how many times the Hegel of the *Phenomenology* or *Logic* wrings the changes on this theme, it does not change: A thing in itself cannot be given in isolation from its properties; ergo, we cannot describe a situation in which we might be able to perceive a thing in itself with contradiction.

Despite the succession of forms in the *Phenomenology*, what Hegel tells us is thematically no different from what Jacobi tells us. What we cannot perceive apart from the properties it has cannot be an object of perception. And what cannot be an object of possible perception cannot be an object at all. Why? Because to say that anything is an object in the relevant sense is just to say, according to the critical tradition, that it satisfies some description or other. And to say this is to imply that it must, after all, be either an object of possible experience or no object at all. This theme cuts across all of the regional peculiarities of the Jacobi-Fichte-Schopenhauer-Hegel connection. For all parties to this connection tell us that, however we describe an object in the relevant sense, we must implicitly specify the conditions under which the object satisfying them can be perceived. Thus whether you confuse a thing in itself with the transcendental object, with things in our world that can be perceived under other forms of intuition, with whatever bears the properties that we perceive in our world, or even with the causes of what we perceive, the mistake is the same.

But there is, as we have also seen, a philosophical lesson to be learned from this self-perpetuating theme in the criticism of Kant's theory. In the first place, what vitiates the tradition is its illegitimate identification of the transcendental object with the very different notion of a thing in itself. There is, secondly, a confusion of a thing in itself with a noumenon. The objects that we perceive in our world are presented to us under certain forms of intuition. And, for all we know, there may be denizens of that same world that cannot be presented under any forms of intuition at all. But this distinction does not entail any internally inconsistent description. Thirdly, we may not be able to perceive a substance or substratum in complete isolation of any properties at all. But this does not make a thing in itself into a phenomenal substance. It shows at most that we never perceive a substance, phenomenal or otherwise, without some property or other. But since this requirement applies both to things in themselves and appearances alike, it cannot be pressed into the service of an attempt to show that the very notion of a thing in itself is self-contradictory. Fourthly and finally, the relation between a thing in itself and an appearance cannot be construed causally. To say, as Kant does, that things in themselves affect our sensibility does not imply that they are causally related to what we perceive; hence, the description of the relation between a thing in itself and our sensibility need not be described in such a way as to make that description inherently self-contradictory.

The antidote to all of these philosophical confusions that are at the bottom of the hermeneutical record is the exegetical distinction between an ontological and an epistemic interpretation of Kant's undeservedly maligned doctrine of things in themselves. If we interpret things in themselves epistemically and not ontologically, as I urged here and argued elsewhere, it is possible both to make the distinction between things in themselves and appearances for this world and not to box Kant into the hopeless alternative of claiming that a thing in itself is really perceivable or that it is really a phenomenal substance in transparent disguise. For that distinction can be taken to hold between two ways of conceiving what can be one and the same object—in which case what we understand as a thing in itself is merely what we perceive in our world that can present itself to us under other forms of sensory intuition if only we were endowed with them. The history of the misguided polemics surrounding this doctrine should recommend such an interpretation.

5. Kant's First Antinomy

*T*HE DISTINCTION between causation and affection has enabled us to break through the impasse generated by the claims of the *TWT* and the *TDT* accounts of the relation between things in themselves and appearances. We have already seen that both of these alternatives are plausible because some textual evidence supports each of them. The *TWT* exploits Kant's claim that things in themselves can exist independently of our forms of intuition. The *TDT* appeals to Kant's characterization of things in themselves as objects capable of being described in different ways. But the two theories are mutually incompatible. We cannot consistently say both that a thing in itself cannot be given under any form of intuition and that it is an object that can be given under forms of intuition that are different from ours.

The two theories are both distortions of what Kant's general theory requires the distinction between things in themselves and appearances to be. A Kantian thing in itself must, on any theory, be an object that cannot be given separately in any possible experience and must nonetheless stand in some relation to every object of possible experience.

Neither of the received theories is viable because both of them rest on a false assumption. They both assimilate affection to causation. The *TWT* transforms objects that are not in space or time into causes of those that are spatial or temporal. The *TDT* makes a thing in itself into something that acts on our sensibility but that might satisfy descriptions applicable under other forms of intuition. The objects so described, however, are still causes of what we perceive.

Neither theory works because both assume that things in themselves cause appearances. And both are doomed to a swift demise because they do not allow us to distinguish between the fact that an object affects our sensibility from the quite different fact that one object causes another. Something can simultaneously function as the cause of something else and yet affect our sensibility. The difference in relational situations enables one and the same object to function as a cause and to affect our sensibility. It assumes causation because the theory gives us two numerically diverse subjects of interpretation. Those particulars must conform to the Affection Condition, according to which we must be immediately aware of whatever we intuit. But once we substitute one particular for another in the account we give of affection, the only other alternative available to Kant is a causal relation between the particular that is part of the thing in itself and the particular that is part of what, on the *TWT*, is the appearance. The initial incompatibility of the two traditional theories of the distinction between things in themselves and appearances disappears. An object affects in that it is or can be present to our perceptual consciousness. It causes in that it does or can initiate a series of events all of whose members are possible objects of our experience because all of them are in time. Something can be both an effect and a cause at the same time without forcing the admission that something that is not spatial or temporal can cause something that is.

That is the philosophical mandate. The historical response to that mandate has, however, exhibited only a series of attempts to forget that mandate. They present us with this unacceptable alternative: Either what Kant calls a thing in itself is to be unavoidably identified with what Kant calls a noumenon or it is to be assimilated to what Kant calls an appearance. If we opt for the former, then we cannot explain the relation between a thing in itself and an appearance. But if we opt for the latter, there is no need for us to ask for any explanation. Both options are unacceptable. And both of them, different though they may seem, are rooted in a confusion of affection with causation.

The argument that Kant uses to resolve the First Antinomy is a test case. That resolution purports to show that the thesis and the antithesis of that antinomy falsely assume that the world is a thing in itself. Kant's argument here demands what I have called an epistemic as opposed to an ontological interpretation of the distinction between things in themselves and appearances. Kant admittedly does not clearly make that distinction in his argument. But the argument will, as we are to see, not work without imputing such a distinction to Kant. The ontological interpretation disastrously assimilates affection to causation. The epistemic interpretation as it has come down to us claims unsuccessfully to separate the two notions. We are told that relation between a thing in itself and an appearance is that between an object as it is truly described in our (actual) world and the same object as it is described in another (possible) world. The object in question, however, is numerically the same from one world to another. According to the traditional version of the epistemic interpretation, the relation of the object in our world to our sensory apparatus is causal. The same object acts on the sensory apparatus of members of other worlds in some other, unspecified way. This way out of the problem is illusory. The same problem that confronts us in this world would be merely duplicated in a possible world we do not inhabit. For the change from the actual to a possible world may serve only to change the characteristics of the sensory apparatus of the inhabitants. It does not, however, change the fact that there is some sort of sensory apparatus in both worlds. Thus affection is not only assimilated to causation in this world. The problem facing this attempt at assimilation breaks out all over again in other worlds. The epistemic interpretation as I have revised it avoids this difficulty. This enables Kant to resolve the antinomy. But it also requires him to assume that the relation between a thing in itself and an appearance is affection and not causation.

In the First Antinomy of the *Critique of Pure Reason*, Kant draws two conclusions from the argument he gives. First, Kant takes his argument to show that the referent of the concept of "world" does not exist as a thing in itself. At B532 he says:

If we regard the two propositions, that the world is infinite in magnitude and that it is finite in magnitude, as contradictory opposites, we are assuming that the world, the complete series of appearances, is a thing in itself that remains even if I suspend the infinite or the finite regress in the series of its appearances. If, however, I reject this assumption, or rather this accompanying transcendental illusion, and deny that the world is a thing in itself, the contradictory opposition of the two assertions is converted into a merely dialectical opposition. Since the world does not exist in itself, independently of the regressive series of my representations, it exists *in itself* neither as an *infinite* nor as a *finite* whole.

Kant also thinks that the same argument establishes yet another conclusion; he holds that the argument of the First Antinomy gives an independent proof of the transcendental ideality of time and space. This is set forth at B534:

> It affords indirect proof of the transcendental ideality of appearances—a proof which ought to convince any who might not be satisfied by the direct proof given in the Transcendental Aesthetic. This proof would consist in the following dilemma. If the world is a whole existing in itself, it is therefore also false that the world (the sum of all appearances) is a whole existing in itself. From this it then follows that appearances in general are nothing outside our representations—which is just what is meant by their transcendental ideality.

The two inferences Kant makes here, then, are these:

(1) If the complete series of appearances is a thing in itself, then it must be either finitely or infinitely large. It is neither of these; therefore, the complete series of appearances does not exist as a thing in itself.

(2) If the complete series of appearances is neither finitely nor infinitely large, then all appearances are transcendentally ideal. The complete series of appearances is neither; therefore, all appearances are transcendentally ideal.

Now I believe that neither (1) nor (2) is a valid inference. In what follows I shall undertake three things: to establish the invalidity of (1) and (2); to ask whether Kant's arguments can be reconstructed to prove what he wanted them to prove; and to assess some recent objections to Kant's argument in the First Antinomy.

1.   The Argument of the Antinomy

As Kant sets it out, the argument of the First Antinomy runs as follows.[1] The thesis asserts that the world has a beginning in time and is limited spatially. Proponents of this view argue for it by assuming the opposite view and reducing it to absurdity. We begin, accordingly, by assuming that the world has no beginning in time. And this assumption is taken to be logically equivalent to the claim that infinitely many intervals of time have elapsed. But an infinite number of moments cannot have elapsed simply because we cannot complete an actual infinity of moments by successively synthesizing them. An actual infinity of moments cannot, therefore, have existed—from which it is inferred that the world cannot be temporally infinite.

A second claim is made by the proponents of the thesis; the claim, namely, that the world is limited spatially.[2] Here we are first asked to assume that the world is unlimited in spatial extension. It is then pointed out that we could not completely synthesize the parts of such a world. And it is inferred that the world cannot be spatially infinite. The conclusions of both of the foregoing arguments are then conjoined to derive the further conclusion that the world is both spatially and temporally finite.

The contention of the antithesis is twofold: That the world has no beginning in time (being therefore temporally infinite) and that the world is spatially unlimited (being therefore spatially infinite). We are asked to assume that the world did have a beginning in time. On this assumption, the time at which the world began would have been preceded by a time at which the world did not exist. But the moment prior to the moment at which the world came into existence would then be an empty time. But if time is empty, no coming into existence could take place. Why? Because no part of that empty time "possesses, as compared with any other, a distinguishing condition of existence rather than nonexistence."[3] Thus the world cannot have had a beginning in time.

The second part of the antithesis—that the world is not spatially limited—is defended on the ground that the world, as a limited spatial whole, would have to be related to empty space that borders it. Empty space cannot, however, be related to the world as a whole, for a relation to empty space would be a relation to nothing and hence not a relation at all. But since the world cannot be spatially and temporally finite, then the only other conclusion open to us is that it is infinite in both respects. *Tertium non datur.*

The general conclusion that Kant draws from the arguments of thesis and antithesis here is familiar: Each is right in what it denies but wrong in what it affirms. Thus the thesis is right in denying that the world is infinite but wrong in affirming that the world must therefore be finite. The antithesis is right in denying that the world is finite but wrong in inferring that it must therefore be infinite. What Kant takes the arguments to show is rather that the world is neither finite or infinite.[4]

2. What the First Antinomy Does Not Prove

For the moment I do not want to ask whether Kant has succeeded in showing that the world as a whole is neither finite nor infinite. I propose to grant him that conclusion for the sake of argument and ask whether he has shown either that the world does not exist as a thing in itself or that appearances are transcendentally ideal.

Consider first the alleged conclusion that the world does not exist as a thing in itself. This has not been demonstrated by the argument as it stands. To see this, we need only examine what Kant means by "thing in itself." There are two senses of the term in Kant's text. I shall call the first the ontological conception of the term. This is found in the Transcendental Aesthetic, embedded in Kant's discussion of time:

> Time is not something which exists in itself, or which inheres in things as an objective determination, and it does not, therefore, remain when abstraction is made of all subjective conditions of its intuition.[5]

The same point is made for space when Kant says the following:

> [S]pace does not represent any determination that attaches to the objects themselves, and which remains even when abstraction has been made of all the subjective conditions of experience.[6]

The argument for this conclusion is instructive because it shows the criterion according to which Kant will count anything as a thing in itself. At A33 he argues that space and time cannot be things in themselves because, on such an assumption, we would have to say that they are actual while not being actual objects. Nor can they be relational properties of substances because, on that assumption, they could not precede objects as a condition of their being objects for us. The conclusion is drawn from this when Kant says at A43 that space and time are "conditions which are originally inherent in subject." The pattern of this argument works itself out as follows: If something can be neither a substance nor an accident of substance when separated from space and time, then it cannot be a thing in itself. A thing in itself is, then, either a substance or a property when separated from space and time. What is important for our purposes is that Kant talks of a thing in itself as a kind of object. It is the kind of object that remains when we abstract from the conditions under which that object is given to us.

There is, however, a quite different conception of what a thing in itself is running parallel to the ontological conception. This, too, is present in his discussion of time. For at A31 he says that time is merely "a necessary representation that underlies all intuitions." And the same point is made for space when, at A24, he says that space is an intuition that underlies all outer intuitions. To speak of things as they are in themselves is to speak of them apart from the relation they have to our means of representing them. But here what is to count as a thing in itself has changed. For here when we talk about an object as a thing in itself, we mean only to talk about it as it is apart from possible human experience. *But we do not say that such an object is nonspatial and nontemporal.* On this second view (which I shall call the epistemic conception) all that is implied is that we do not *know* whether things as they are in themselves are nonspatial and nontemporal. On the ontological view, however, what is being claimed is that things in themselves are necessarily nonspatial and nontemporal. That view is the main assumption governing the argument in which Kant says that space and time do not remain when "abstraction has been made of all the subjective conditions of experience." But this claim should nonetheless be strictly separated from the other, weaker, claim according to which space and time are necessary representations that underlie all our intuitions. This latter claim is completely neutral about the ontological issue of whether space and time do in fact exist apart from possible human experience. And the neutrality of the claim about this issue gives a second view of what is to count as a thing in itself.[7]

Return to the conclusion of the First Antinomy. Does that conclusion show that the world cannot exist as a thing in itself in either of the two senses I have distinguished? Take the ontological conception of the thing in itself first. Does the argument of the antinomy show the world does not exist as a nonspatial and nontemporal whole? I think not. What Kant tries to show in the antinomy is that the world is neither finite nor infinite with respect to time and space. And this is not enough to show that the world is neither finite nor infinite apart from space and time. Both the thesis and the antithesis of the antinomy assume that the world is the totality of all *appearances*.[8] And both the thesis and the antithesis assume that only the notion of a spatial and temporal world is being considered. But to show that something is or is not true of such a world is to be completely silent about whether the same things might be true of a nonspatial and nontemporal world. So Kant has not shown that the world of phenomena cannot exist as a thing in itself.

But perhaps the argument of the antinomy works when we interpret the notion of the thing in itself epistemically. Perhaps Kant has succeeded in showing that the world cannot exist as a thing in itself if we interpret him to be saying that we cannot *know* whether the world as a whole is finite or infinite. This interpretation, unlike its ontological counterpart, does make sense of Kant's argument. True, we know that the world is neither finite or infinite. True, we know that "world" understood as "complete series of appearances" lacks a referent, finite or infinite. We cannot, however, infer from the fact that a member of a series of appearances appears to us under our forms of intuition that the set of which these appearances are members, be it finite or infinite, also can have these characteristics. We cannot know the characteristics of the set independently of the forms of our intuition. For we cannot generate an infinite set by synthesizing a series of appearances. And we cannot know whether a finite set of appearances constitutes the world because we can never reach the last member of a finite series about which we can say that it is absolutely the last member of the series of appearances. And we cannot know this because such knowledge would involve an acquaintance with something, finite or infinite, that exists independently of our forms of intuition.

Kant's second conclusion is that his argument gives an independent proof of the transcendental ideality of space and time. The argument for this conclusion that he gives in the Aesthetic is already familiar: Space and time cannot be substances, for they would have to be actual without being actual objects. They cannot be relations, for then they would not be conditions of our being presented with objects.[9] Kant's conclusion: Space and time are properties of our sensibility. They are, therefore, transcendentally ideal.[10] We know that space and time are the conditions under which any object must be presented to us; therefore, space and time cannot be properties of the things that they present but are rather forms of our apprehension of things and are therefore transcendentally ideal. The argument here, with whose validity I am not at present concerned, yields three characteristics of transcendental ideality: (1) Something is transcendentally ideal if it is a property of human sensibility; (2) Something is transcendentally ideal if it is a universal condition of our being presented with objects; (3) Something is transcendentally ideal if it is neither a substance nor an accident of a substance. (1) is the definition Kant himself gives of the notion. (2) and (3) are both exclusive descriptions of the notion that emerge from the argument Kant gives in the Transcendental Aesthetic.[11]

How does the First Antinomy give us a demonstration that space and time are transcendentally ideal independent of the one offered in the Transcendental Aesthetic? Let us grant for the sake of argument that the world is neither finite nor infinite. It does not, however, follow that space and time are properties of human sensibility, or that they are universal conditions of our being presented with objects, or yet that they are neither substances nor accidents of substances. There are three arguments to support this conclusion.

This is the first argument. Whether space and time are properties of things or merely forms of our apprehension of things is quite independent of whether the totality of phenomena is finite or infinite. The argument that we cannot apply either of two mutually exclusive predicates to a collection depends upon certain characteristics possessed by the collection as a whole. That space and time are forms of our apprehension does not depend upon properties of the collection collectively but rather on the properties the collection has when taken distributively. To show that the collection as a whole is neither finite nor infinite tells us nothing about whether the parts of the collection are in fact properties of things as they are in themselves. To say that the collection of all men is not itself a man does not permit us to infer that no number of that collection is a man. Similarly, to say that the collection of all spaces and times is neither finite nor infinite does not permit us to infer the same about specific moments of time and specific moments of space. Hence, we cannot use this conclusion to ground the further inference that space and time are merely forms of our apprehension of things.

Why should Kant have thought that he could make the inference that I have just questioned? He apparently reasoned as follows. If it could be shown that there are some things in the world that are neither finite nor infinite, then they cannot be objects. This is the case with space and time, for they are included in the world as a whole. And from this it is inferred that space and time cannot be properties of things by means of the auxiliary premiss that anything that is neither finite nor infinite must be mental. Kant does not, to be sure, explicitly defend this premiss. And my reason for attributing it to him is that only by means of it can he successfully move from the conclusion that the world as a whole is neither finite nor infinite to the further conclusion that space and time are transcendentally ideal. But even if this auxiliary premiss is admitted, the argument still suffers from the same defect: Kant has not shown that space and time are mental properties by showing that the totality of space and time is neither finite nor infinite.

There is a second argument that shows that the First Antinomy does not give us an independent proof of the transcendental ideality of space and time. Kant holds that the antinomy does give us such a proof because it could arise only on the assumption that space and time are transcendentally real.[12] His reason for saying this follows from his discussion of the distinction between dialectical and contradictory opposition.[13] We are tempted, he says, to take the thesis and the antithesis of the antinomy to be mutually exclusive and exhaustive alternatives. But this can be so only on the assumption that space and time are something in themselves: To say that they are things in themselves is to imply that they must have one of two contradictory predicates. The fact that neither of two contradictory predicates applies to them shows that the opposition between these predicates is dialectical and that there is a third alternative, namely, that space and time are just forms of our sensibility. On this assumption, what appeared to be a pair of contradictory propositions now becomes a pair of contraries, both of which are false.

But does the antinomy really assume that space and time are transcendentally real? I think not. Kant in fact assumes the very opposite in the argument he gives. The argument for the thesis assumes, for example, that space and time are appearances. For it is only on this assumption that one of the crucial moves in the argument is intelligible. The move is this. Kant rejects the possibility that the world could be infinite because of the fact that "the infinity of a series consists in the fact that it can never be completed through successive synthesis."[14] Kant moves here from "cannot be synthesized by us" to "cannot be in itself infinite." And this move in the argument can be explained only on the assumption that Kant is assuming the world to be the totality of appearances and not the totality of things as they are in themselves.[15] For if the world is the totality of appearances, then showing that we cannot synthesize all of these appearances is equivalent to showing that the totality itself cannot be infinite. To say that there is an appearance that we could not synthesize would be to say what is self-contradictory—that there is an appearance that cannot appear. But the assumption that the world is the sum total of appearances runs counter to Kant's claim that the antinomy assumes space and time to be transcendentally real. It cannot, therefore, be the case that the antinomy can be removed by assuming space and time to be transcendentally ideal. That assumption is already present in the antinomy as Kant states it.

The third argument, showing that the antinomy does not give an independent proof of transcendental idealism, is a variant of the second argument and runs as follows. Even if we do assume that space and time are forms of our sensibility, we may not infer that they are neither finite nor infinite. We could in fact hold that space and time are merely subjective forms and still hold that they are infinite. We could say, in other words, that they are infinite just in the sense that neither the temporal nor spatial series has a last member. And this would not be precluded by the fact that they are subjective forms. The totality of these series would not be exhibited in intuition. But this is not to say that there is any member of the series that could not be so exhibited. There would be no element in the series that would not be capable of being presented in possible human experience. And this is enough to fulfill the requirement implicit in saying that space and time are forms of apprehension. To say this is in part to say that they are possible objects of human experience. And both space and time could be infinite. They could not, of course, be exhibited synoptically. But this is not to say that no part of each series cannot be presented in intuition and thus be a possible object of human experience. What I have said does not *prove* that there are infinitely many spaces and times. It shows only that the assertion that there are such things does not violate the condition implicit in saying that space and time are nothing beyond possible human experience.[16] My conclusion, then, is that there is no connection between saying that space and time are subjective forms of apprehension and saying that they are neither finite nor infinite.

3. What the First Antinomy Does Prove

What I have been arguing so far is that the two main conclusions that Kant draws from the First Antinomy do not in fact follow from it. But can this argument be reconstructed to yield these two conclusions? I believe that the first conclusion—that the world does not exist as a thing in itself—can be made to follow from an argument that Kant gives. But, as I hope to show, although this conclusion can be established, the argument is powerless to establish the second conclusion.

I propose the following reconstruction of Kant's argument for the conclusion that the world does not exist as a thing in itself. When Kant says that the world as the totality of appearances does not exist as a thing in itself, this can be made to follow from the more general conclusion that the definite description, "the sum of all appearances," has no referent. But how exactly can Kant's argument be made to prove this? The totality of appearances, if it exists, must be either finite or infinite. Consider each alternative in turn. It cannot be finite. Kant tries to prove this in two ways. He holds that the world cannot be finite because such a world would have to be preceded by an empty time that lacks "as compared with any other, a distinguishing condition of existence rather than non-existence."[17] I interpret him to be arguing that the world cannot be finite just because such a world would lack the causally sufficient conditions for coming into being.

But this is not all. Kant's second argument against the finitude of the world runs like this: A world that is finite must be related in some way to empty space. And this for Kant is a relation to nothing. The argument is, as it stands, confusing. For "world" here means "totality of appearances," and space and time are both appearances. Thus even a world that is finite logically cannot stand in relation to empty space. But Kant's argument can perhaps be reformulated as follows. The assumption that the world is finite can be said to entail a contradiction. Saying that it is finite implies, on the one hand, that it be related to what it does not include; otherwise such a world would not be the totality of appearances. The contradiction, then, is that a finite world must both have and lack a spatial relation to what it does not include.

If the preceding arguments are sound, then "the sum of all appearances" cannot have a referent that is finite. The only other alternative, accordingly, is to supply it with a referent that is actually infinite. But this alternative is as unsuccessful as its predecessor. The totality of appearances cannot be actually infinite. Here two quite distinct arguments for this conclusion must be disentangled. The first consists in a definition of an infinite series that Kant introduces at B544, when he says that "the infinity of a series consists in the fact that it can never be completed through successive synthesis."

The argument is inconclusive as it stands. It might be true that *we* cannot complete the series although the series itself is, in fact, infinite. But there is another argument, occurring at B459, where Kant says that "no multiplicity is the greatest, since one or more units can always be added to it. Consequently, an infinite given magnitude, and therefore an infinite world (infinite as regards the elapsed series or as regards extension) is impossible." The argument here does not depend upon any assumption that refers only to *our* ability to synthesize the successive parts of an infinite series. The reason we cannot complete an infinite series is the result of a property about the series itself—namely, that, for any given unit you reach in the series, it is always possible to add a further unit. And if it is always possible to do this, then the notion of a last member of the series is self-contradictory. And this tells us something crucial about a series with a final member. Either such a series is not infinite or the member chosen is not the last member. From this it follows that the totality of appearances cannot be actually infinite.

The reason Kant rejects an actually infinite magnitude is that such a notion contains, strictly speaking, a contradiction. It implies a number such that it must but cannot be the last member of the series. My evidence for attributing this position to Kant lies in what he means when he says that an actual infinity is "a quantity which is greater than any number." [18] If we combine this definition of infinity with Kant's statement that an infinite series is such that it can never be completed by successive synthesis, we can more readily see how the contradiction in the notion of an actually infinite magnitude arises. The claim that we can synthesize such a magnitude entails a contradiction, for it entails that we can assign a number to such a magnitude as its measure. In such a case, the magnitude alleged to be infinite would both possess a number and lack it. This is the source of the contradiction.

This interpretation of Kant's argument has, however, been disputed

principally by Kemp Smith, who says it is "all-important to observe that Kant does not, either in the *Critique* or in any other of
his writings, assert that the concept of the actual infinite is self-
contradictory." [19] But this is an over-simplification of Kant's position.
Kant holds that the concept of what he calls an infinite *multiplicity*
does not contain a contradiction. But this is to be distinguished from
the very different concept of an infinite *magnitude* that figures in the
argument of the First Antinomy. [20] The former concept does not entail
a contradiction because it is merely the concept of a collection that
cannot be numbered. The latter concept does entail a contradiction
just because it entails that the collection in question can be assigned a
number. And it is this latter concept that is being discussed in the
antinomy.

But if Kant does make the distinction I have just pointed out, it
might be asked why he appears to reject this method of disproving the
existence of an actually infinite magnitude at A430. Kant says that he
might have sought to disprove the existence of the actual infinite by
saying that "a magnitude is infinite if a greater than itself, as determined by the multiplicity of given units which it contains, is not possible." [21] Kant could then have pointed out that there is no greatest
multiplicity "since one or more units can always be added to it." [22] For
this reason an infinite given magnitude is impossible. Now Kant rejects
this proof because it is based on what he considers to be a defective
concept of infinity. But what exactly is defective about the concept of
infinity? The definition is defective because it purports to tell us how
great the infinite collection is and gives us the concept of a maximum.
And this is not, according to Kant, what we think in the concept of
infinity.

Can we take this as evidence for the conclusion that Kant does not
hold the concept of an actual infinity to contain a contradiction? What
this passage says is that we cannot define infinity as a magnitude since
we then imply that we can say how great the magnitude is; i.e., are
able to assign it a number. The passage does not say, however, that the
concept of an actually infinite *magnitude* is free from contradiction.
And the way in which Kant disproves the contention that world is
temporally infinite rests on the assumption that such a concept must
be assumed by those asserting the temporal infinity of the world and
that such a concept does contain a contradiction. For anyone holding
that an infinite collection of temporal intervals can be synthesized
must assume that it is possible to assign a number to an infinite collection, which is just to assume that an infinite magnitude has a last mem-

ber. And this assumption does contain a contradiction because it rests on a misunderstanding of what an infinite collection is. Hence, the argument Kant gives against the possibility of a temporally infinite world does assume that one kind of concept of an actual infinity contains a contradiction.

The referent of "the totality of appearances" cannot, then, be infinite. This exhausts the alternatives. From this it follows that the referent is nonexistent. Now, if this is the real structure of Kant's argument, then he has proved that the totality of appearances does not exist as a thing in itself; for he has established that it does not exist at all, and *a fortiori* it does not exist as a thing in itself. But this conclusion has nothing to do with the characteristics peculiar to things in themselves. Nor does it turn on the notion of transcendental ideality. It is an immediate inference from the conclusion—which Kant's argument does establish—that the object called the totality of appearances does not exist at all. I admit, of course, that Kant wanted to move from showing that the totality of appearances does not exist as an object to the conclusion that the totality of appearances exists as a form for apprehending objects. But I have already argued that the move is not supported; and the conclusion that I have drawn from Kant's reconstructed argument is, I believe, the only conclusion that the argument will support.

Thus Kant's argument will yield the conclusion that the world does not exist as a thing in itself. Will it also support the conclusion that space and time are transcendentally ideal? Kant's argument, even as reconstructed, will not license such an inference. Nothing follows about whether space and time are merely properties of human sensibility from showing that there is no such object as the totality of phenomena.

4. Recent Criticisms of the First Antinomy

The purport and success of Kant's antinomy have been persistently assailed. And Kant has generally been unfortunate in his critics. The standard objections to his argument are unsound. Russell has, for example, raised several objections that have since become legion. The first runs like this:

[W]hen Kant says that an infinite series can "never" be completed by successive synthesis, all that he has even conceivably a right to say is that it cannot be completed *in a finite time*. Thus what he really proves is, at most, that if the world has no beginning, it must have already existed for an infinite time. This, however, is a very poor conclusion, by no means suitable for his purposes.[23]

This objection rests on a confusion of the two arguments Kant gives for the nonexistence of actually infinite magnitudes. It confuses the argument according to which we cannot synthesize a magnitude that is infinite with the quite different argument according to which there are no such magnitudes. Russell's argument holds against the former. We cannot synthesize an infinite series unless we had an infinite amount of time. But it does not hold against the latter. Russell is significantly silent about the possibility of an actual infinity.

Russell is silent in the present passage about the existence of infinite sets. But we need not guess about his position on the issue. He has argued that there are infinite sets and that it is a mistake to deny their existence. And lest this be thought an objection to Kant's view about infinite magnitudes, I propose to show that Russell's point does not affect Kant's argument. Russell is concerned to argue against those who think that the notion of an infinite number is self-contradictory. He holds that there are numbers that obey different rules from finite numbers and that the notion of such a number does not entail a contradiction. He argues as follows. There are series that have the properties of reflexiveness and noninductiveness. A number is reflexive when it is not increased by adding one to it.[24] A number is noninductive when it lacks at least one inductive property, one such property being that a noninductive number has no immediate predecessor.[25] The conclusion of Russell's argument is that there are numbers that are both reflexive and noninductive, that they are infinite numbers, and that the concept of such a number contains no contradiction.

Does this invalidate Kant's argument that there is no actual infinity? It does not. What Russell has established is that there can be numbers that are infinite in the sense that they have certain properties other kinds of numbers lack. But to establish that there are infinite numbers is not to establish that there are infinitely many numbers. When Kant denies that there can be a last member of an infinite series, what he is denying is presumably what Russell rejects when he denies the existence of a greatest finite number. Notice that, on Russell's account of a noninductive property, we begin the infinite numbers by postulating that the first such number has no predecessor. There is, accordingly, no way to count from finite to infinite numbers. And this is precisely what Kant is claiming when he says that you cannot start a series of finite numbers and generate an infinite series. Russell's demonstration of the existence of infinite numbers cannot be used as an argument against Kant's view that there is not an actually infinite magnitude.

But Russell adduces another argument that he believes to be fatal to Kant's view about the impossibility of a synthesis of infinitely many units. Russell argues the following:

> As we see from the word "synthesis," he [Kant] imagined a mind trying to grasp these successively, *in the reverse order* to that in which they had occurred, i.e., going from the present backwards. *This* series is obviously one which has no end. But the series of events up to the present has an end, since it ends with the present. Owing to the inveterate subjectivism of his mental habits, he failed to notice that he had reversed the sense of the series by substituting backward synthesis for forward happening, and thus supposed that it was necessary to identify the mental series, which had an end, with the physical series, which had an end but no beginning.[26]

There are two points that vitiate this objection to Kant's argument. First, even if we do make the distinction between the two kinds of series that Russell mentions, it has not been shown that Kant has confounded them, for it has not been shown that by "beginning" Kant meant or must have meant "beginning for us." Secondly, to say that one of these series—namely, the series terminating in the present—has an end is not to say that it is actually infinite. An independent proof must be given of this; and, as it stands, it is completely neutral concerning whether the series terminating in the present in fact can be actually infinite.

There remain three arguments that purport to uncover serious errors in Kant's argument. The first is to be found in Norman Kemp Smith's *Commentary* and has been recently pressed by Benardete.[27] Both claim that Kant's argument against an infinite series breaks down on a simple non sequitur. For, it is asked, does Kant not move from the impossibility of our *thinking* the world as infinite to the conclusion that the world *is* not infinite.[28] And if he does this, it need only be pointed out that the world's de facto infinity is quite compatible with our inability to conceive of it as infinite. The objection fails. And it fails because both Benardete and Kemp Smith confound the two arguments that are to be found in Kant against the possibility of an infinite series. Against the weaker argument the objection holds. But this leaves the stronger one completely intact.

The second and third objections to Kant's argument are ones that others have added to the budget. Benardete has tried to show that Kant's arguments against the infinity of an elapsed series collapse because an actually infinite magnitude is logically possible. One such argument is the following:

(1) It is necessary that either a finite or an infinite number of stars exist.
(2) It is not logically necessary that the number of stars be finite.
(3) Therefore, it is logically possible that the number of stars is infinite.[29]

This is offered by Benardete as a proof that actually infinite magnitudes are at least logically possible. Benardete concludes:

> To conceive of an infinite world does not require, as Kant seems to suppose, some special mental act of prodigious scope. It is not at all a matter of racking one's brains. One has only to recognize two tautologies as tautologies and then to perform a simple logical inference.[30]

The argument, then, amounts to the introduction of (1) and (2) as tautologies and the claim that (3) follows from them. There is, however, one fatal difficulty with this argument: It begs the question. Premise (2) assumes that it is not logically impossible that there be infinitely many stars—which is precisely the point at issue. Now it is, of course, true that the particular finite number assigned to the collection of stars is not logically necessary. But that the number be finite is, on Kant's position, necessary. Hence Benardete derives the conclusion he wants only at the price of circularity.

Benardete also attempts to argue to the same conclusion by a somewhat different argument. There are two parts to the argument: a reconstruction of Kant's position and a demonstration that the empirical use of the concept of finitude entails the metaphysical use of the concept of the actually infinite. Consider, first, how Benardete reconstructs Kant's position:

(1) The world as a whole is no possible object of experience; (2) Only what is a possible object of experience may be rationally supposed to exist; *ergo* (3) The world as a whole may not be rationally supposed to exist.[31]

So much for the reconstruction. Now Benardete holds that Kant's proof of premiss (1) is vitiated by the ability Kant grants us meaningfully to apply the concepts of the finite to objects in our experience. Benardete argues as follows:

We may say that the correlative terms finite and infinite are peculiar in that one of the terms denotes an empirical, whereas the other denotes a metaphysical, concept. If we contrast the hard empirical thesis that *this* wall before me is finite and the clearly metaphysical thesis that the universe is infinite, it follows that the denial or falsity of the empirical thesis logically entails the truth of the metaphysical thesis. . . . Finite and infinite being correlative concepts, the empirical is seen to be unintelligible apart from the cosmological.[32]

There is one interpretation that Benardete's words will bear that can be dismissed immediately. If it is false that this wall before me is finite, then it will be true that it is infinite. But this does not show that the empirical use of the concept of finitude entails its metaphysical meaningfulness. All that has been shown is that, if any entity is not finite, it is infinite—which is tautologically true. Thus on this interpretation Benardete has not shown the logical possibility of one actual infinity.

What Benardete is saying can also be interpreted as follows. He could be saying that, when we say that a particular object is finite, we are committed to saying that it is at least meaningful to entertain the possibility that it is infinite. But if this is so, then the proof that Kant offers to show that the world as a whole cannot be a possible object of experience is vitiated. For that proof assumes that the concept of an actual infinity is self-contradictory. And if the concept of an actual infinity can be meaningfully, though falsely, applied to particular objects in experience, then Kant cannot hold that the concept is logically impossible. In this sense, then, the empirical employment of the concept of the finite might be said to presuppose the meaningfulness of the concept of the actually infinite.

But does the empirical employment of the concept of the finite really commit Kant to hold that actually infinite collections are logically possible? I do not think it does. What the empirical employment of the concept implies is this: To say of a given object in experience that it is not infinite is meaningful only in the sense that it is always false to make such an assertion. Thus such an assertion is meaningful in that it is formulated in a well-formed expression and its denial generates a logically necessary truth. But this does not imply that the concept of an actual infinity is free from contradiction. What vitiates Benardete's argument is an equivocation on the notion of meaningfulness according to which he moves from "meaningful" understood as "either true or false" to "meaningful" understood as "logically possible." That something in our experience is actually infinite can be meaningfully denied without our being forced to say that the concept whose applicability is denied is free from contradiction. A concept that entails a contradiction is at least meaningful, for the negation of that concept is logically necessary. Thus when Kant permits the empirical employment of the concept of the finite, he is not forced to grant that the concept of an actual infinity is one whit less impossible than it is.

5. Kant's Resolution of the Antinomy: The Moral

The distinction between an epistemic and an ontological interpretation of the difference between things in themselves and appearances is, as we have seen, indispensable to the successs of Kant's resolution of the First Antinomy. He takes the problem of that antinomy to show that expressions containing the definite description "the world as a whole" have no reference. But the debate about the antinomy might still seem to have nothing to do with the distinction between things in themselves and appearances. The discussion of the issues raised by that antinomy centers on the existence of an actual infinite. And this dispute can be described and resolved irrespective of whether the members of such a set are appearances or things in themselves. The character and viability of the distinction between a thing in itself and an appearance must be raised and resolved with respect to each member of the set and is, therefore, independent of whatever view you have of the ontological status of actually infinite sets.

The resolution is plausible but wrong. To show why the world conceived as the sum total of appearances cannot be a substance enables him to show that the expression "the world" has no reference. And this is just to show that a thing in itself is not an entity that lacks spatial or temporal characteristics. This is what indirectly disqualifies the *TWT* of the distinction between things in themselves and appearances. If a thing in itself is not a substance, then it cannot be identified with something that can be a subject of predication but lacks spatial or temporal characteristics. Kant's resolution of the First Antinomy also glaringly highlights the deficiencies of the *TDT* of the distinction between things in themselves and appearances. If what I have called the epistemic interpretation of that distinction does while the ontological interpretation does not resolve the antinomy, then what is to count as a thing in itself is not, as proponents of the *TDT* would have us believe, an object that can but does not satisfy certain kinds of description in our world, for there is no such object that has this capacity. We are left with a view of a thing in itself as an object that may or may not satisfy some descriptions, not in another possible world, but in the actual world.

Kant's resolution of the First Antinomy serves, then, to show that the distinction between things in themselves and appearances cannot be reconstructed by an appeal to objects in this world that are neither spatial nor temporal any more than it can be salvaged by a flight to another, possible, world in which the objects of that world can take on characteristics they do not have in this world. This conclusion is part and parcel of the epistemic interpretation of the notion of a thing in itself. And it is an interpretation that not only resolves Kant's difficulty in the resolution of the First Antinomy but also preserves the integrity of the notion of a thing in itself.

Neither the *TWT* nor the traditional version of the *TDT* serves in understanding the structure and cogency of Kant's resolution of the First Antinomy. The *TWT* fails for at least two reasons. First, the problem arises with regard to the transcendental ideality of space and time for each member of the set of all appearances that arises for the set itself. Introducing the *TWT* of the distinction between things in themselves and appearances does not resolve the problem because it arises about the status of putative entities like the sum of all appearances. Nor does Kant's solution of the problem besetting such a notion provide independent evidence for it. Secondly, since there are, according to Kant's argument, no infinite sets of appearances, there is no need to postulate a further entity called a thing in itself to set in some relation to a set, infinite or otherwise.

The *TDT* as it has come down to us must also be disallowed. Here, again, the resolution of the First Antinomy neither supports such a theory nor does it assume the truth of such a theory. That version of the theory relates a thing in itself to an appearance by invoking the notion of a possible world governed by other forms of intuition which instantiate other characteristics epistemically unavailable to us in this world. But the distinction between things in themselves and appearances must be defined for this world. Removing it to a possible world only brings about the very real difficulty that faces the theory in this world. The problem generating the First Antinomy exists for our world and the forms of intuition by which we are given the constituents of that world. Nor is this all that is wrong with the *TDT* when it is linked to Kant's resolution of the First Antinomy. The theory gives us at most a concept that has no object known to fall under it. For the concept of relation between things in themselves and appearances in a possible but epistemically unavailable world is a notion about which we do not know whether anything answers to it. But the success of Kant's proof in the First Antinomy depends upon his demonstration that the set of all appearances in our world is neither finite nor infinite. This is a claim that does not rest upon a possibility but establishes a fact about our world and our knowledge of it.

This leaves us with the *TDT* in its revised version. The argument of the First Antinomy does show something about the nature of space and time understood, not as characteristics of things in themselves, but rather as forms of our intuition of those things. This is only to show that the things in our world may have the characteristics of our forms of intuition independently of possible experience but that we cannot put ourselves into a position to know whether or not those characteristics actually inhere in things apart from any forms of intuition. We can know that the set of all appearances is neither finite or infinite because the discussion turns on sets of appearances and not sets composed of things in themselves. Thus the only version of the distinction between things in themselves and appearances that the argument of the First Antinomy might either support or imply is the *TDT* in its revised form.

There is further evidence for the conclusion that the revised version of the *TDT* is the only account of the distinction between things in themselves and appearances that is compatible with the results of Kant's resolution of the First Antinomy. The evidence is set forth in the Transcendental Aesthetic; but it figures implicitly in Kant's resolution of the dispute constituting the First Antinomy. We are told that neither space nor time can be substances or accidents of substances. Assume the former, and you wrongly imply that space and time are actual objects. But in showing that there is no such entity as the sum of all appearances, Kant concludes that neither space nor time can be objects of perceptual awareness. This is what is added in his resolution of the First Antinomy. If you assume, further, that properties, relational or nonrelational, presuppose the existence of a substance to which they belong, you must conclude that neither space nor time can be the properties of a substance. The notion of property is logically dependent upon the notion of substance.

The argument is important for our understanding of the revised version of the *TDT* because it supplies further evidence that Kant believes what is given to us in immediate perceptual awareness is definable independently of the forms of intuition under which it stands. That a particular is a substance is independent of the fact that it has the characteristics of whatever forms of intuition we might have. This does not show that any such particular can be presented to us independently of some forms of intuition or other. But it does show that whatever intuitional characteristics belong to a particular are contingently related to it. The reason for this, first set forth in the Aesthetic and confirmed in the Dialectic, is that neither space nor time nor any other forms of intuition can be substances. An essential part of the viability of the revised version of the *TDT* is that whatever characteristics a perceptual object has when it is presented to us under the forms of our intuition are logically independent of whatever particulars that have them. And this enables us to distinguish the relation of affection in which those particulars stand to us and the very different relation of causation that is associated with but not reducible to it.

The lesson of the First Antinomy can be formulated in a different but equivalent way. Just as knowledge of whether the sum total of appearances is finite or infinite is denied to us, so likewise knowledge of the characteristics of any member of that set is denied us independently of possible experience. This is not a claim about the constitution of possible worlds. It concerns only the epistemic relation in which we stand to this (our) world. The conclusion of the First Antinomy implies that the distinction between things in themselves and appearance turns on the difference between our states of enlightenment about the constituents of this world and does not betoken a designation of two kinds of object in this or any other world. The basis of this move in the argument of the First Antinomy, then, is that what applies to the dialectic of the sum total of all appearances applies, mutatis mutandis, to every member of that set. What I have called the ontological interpretation of the argument cannot explain this fact because it assumes the existence of different kinds of objects. Kant's resolution of the antinomy specifically forbids such a conclusion.

The traditional version of the epistemic interpretation of the conclusion of the First Antinomy is also incapable of explaining the conclusion of Kant's argument. This interpretation, as we know, merely assumes the difference between two worlds in which the object of our perceptual acquaintance is placed. But his account of the resolution still must fall back on a distinction between objects and not between states of enlightenment. The conclusion of Kant's argument thus indirectly confirms the revised version of the epistemic interpretation.

6. The Duplication Problem

THE ARGUMENT of the First Antinomy gives us independent confirmation of what we have seen to be true on more general grounds. Both parties to the dispute falsely assume that expressions like "the world" understood as "the sum total of all appearances" have a reference. They also assume that the reference is a thing in itself. Whether the sum total of all appearances is an infinite or a finite set of things is irrelevant to the resolution of the antinomy. The underlying issue is, as we have seen, whether the members of that set, infinite or finite numerosity aside, are appearances or things in themselves.

Kant's statement of the First Antinomy obscures this, and this is reflected in the ambiguous way in which Kant states the relation between things in themselves and appearances. The success of Kant's resolution of that antinomy depends upon what I have called the epistemic as distinct from the ontological interpretation of the distinction between things in themselves and appearances. The latter interpretation of that distinction makes the antinomy turn on whether the world comprises an infinite or a finite set of appearances. And this supports the ontological interpretation of the nature of appearances and their relation to things in themselves. The original antinomy remains, however, whether we say that the members of the set of entities comprising the world are appearances or things in themselves. The epistemic interpretation of the distinction between things in themselves and appearances shifts the burden of the argument. This interpretation of the distinction is a claim, not about the number of members in a set, but rather about our capacity to combine the elements in a sensory manifold. Nothing is said about the number of members in the set of appearances comprising the reference of the expression "the world."

This is not, however, the only confirmation of the claims that affection and causation are logically independent concepts, that the traditional accounts of the distinction between things in themselves and appearances are fatally defective, that the received criticisms of that distinction are seriously misguided, and that the main argument in the Dialectic of the *Kritik* can be made to provide independent evidence for these conclusions. The Third Antinomy and Kant's resolution of it support all these conclusions. Here Kant undertakes to reconcile the claim that every event is caused by its relation to antecedent events with the claim that some events are not subject to the law of causation.

But this is a prima facie contradiction surrounded by serious problems all of which can be traced to the distinction between things in themselves and appearances. Kant appeals here as elsewhere in the Dialectic to the transcendental ideality of our forms of intuition as a way out of this dilemma. And once again, the distinction between what I have called an epistemic interpretation of the distinction between things in themselves and appearances runs counter to an ontological interpretation of that distinction.

The source of this alternative is the inherent instability of Kant's notion of affection. If affection is construed as causation, Kant's resolution generates a vicious infinite regress whether we attribute an ontological or an epistemic account of the distinction to Kant's resolution of the antinomy. The proper understanding of that resolution demands, as we shall presently see, a reconstruction of the relation between a thing in itself and an appearance in terms of an unschematized category and the possibility of various different way of schematizing it. And, as we shall also see, the problem is not confined to the first *Kritik*. It extends to the second *Kritik*, and the *Groundwork* attempts to resolve the perplexity that forms the problem of the Third Antinomy.

Let me begin with Kant's arguments for the transcendental ideality of the form of our intuition. Kant argues for the transcendental ideality of time in two ways. The Aesthetic of the first *Kritik* gives us the direct proof. Time is transcendentally ideal because we can think time independently of all appearances, but we cannot think appearances apart from time.[1] The Dialectic, however, tells a different story. Kant's solution of an antinomy of pure reason gives us "indirect proof of the transcendental ideality of appearances—which is just what is meant by their transcendental ideality."[2] We may refuse to believe that we can conceive of time without any appearances and hence refuse to believe that time is transcendentally ideal. But we cannot refuse to accept this conclusion from the transcendental idealty of time if we are to resolve the Third Antinomy.

The indirect proof for transcendental ideality, like its predecessor in the Aesthetic, allegedly implies the distinction between things as they are in themselves and things as they appear to us. This is Kant's proof of transcendental ideality in the Dialectic. Either what Kant calls an antinomy of pure reason cannot be resolved or time must be transcendentally ideal. If time is transcendentally ideal, then there must be a distinction between things in themselves and appearances. Thus the distinction between things in themselves and appearances, if the account of the Dialectic be accepted, is a necessary condition of the solution of an antinomy of pure reason.

The clarity of outline in Kant's resolution of the Third Antinomy disguises a problem that is different from the one Kant tells us that he confronts. And the distinction between things in themselves and appearances is powerless to resolve that problem. Kant's Third Antinomy does, I concede at the outset, confront us with a genuine problem. But here Kant mislocates a problem that he correctly identifies. The philosophical issue here can be schematically put in this way: The antinomy as Kant states and purports to resolve it suffers from a threefold crisis. One: Kant's claim that the issue of the transcendental reality or ideality of time is, as traditionally understood, logically independent of the problem presented to us by the Third Antinomy. Two: Kant also claims that the distinction between things in themselves and appearances proved directly in the Transcendental Aesthetic is indirectly established by its philosophical utility in the Transcendental Dialectic. But, again, these doctrines, so far from resolving the antinomy, merely duplicate the problem Kant introduces them to solve. Three: Kant describes the problem before him as an antinomy. The fact is, however, that what confronts Kant is not a genuine antinomy at all—and for reasons quite different from the one Kant adduces to solve the problem. But Kant has a genuine problem despite his difficulties in stating it. Let me first state the issue as Kant's text gives it to us.

1. The Third Antinomy: "*Crux Kantiana*"

The argument in the Third Antinomy is deceptively familiar. The claim of the thesis is that in order to explain what Kant calls the appearances of the world, "it is necessary to assume that there is another causality, that of freedom."[3] These are the steps of the argument:

(1) Assume that "everything which takes place presupposes a preceding state upon which it inevitably follows according to a rule."[4]

(2) Everything that *takes place (was geschieht)* "presupposes, in accordance with the law of nature, a preceding state and its causality, and this in similar manner a still earlier state."[5]

(3) But (1) and (2) contradict the very notion of a law of nature: "[N]othing takes place without a cause *sufficiently* determined *a priori*."[6]

(4) (3) implies "a causality through which something takes place, the cause of which is not itself determined, in accordance with natural laws, by another cause antecedent to it."[7]

(5) (1) implies the existence of a cause that does not stand as an effect to a prior cause.

This is the antithesis: "Everything in the world takes place solely in accordance with laws of nature."[8] And this is the accompanying argument:

(1) Assume "a power of absolutely beginning a state, and, therefore, also of absolutely beginning a series of consequences of that state."[9]

(2) (1) is incompatible with the truth of the law of causality.[10]

(3) But (1) "abrogates those rules through which alone a completely coherent experience is possible."[11]

(4) Therefore, (1) is false.

Kant has an ostensible problem. He says that he can demonstrate both that there are causes that cannot be the effects of prior causes and that there can be no such causes.

But Kant's problem is not what he claims it to be. There is one telling symptom of this: He has failed to produce a genuine antinomy. The argument of what Kant calls the Third Antinomy conflates an antinomy with the quite different discovery that one and the same subject of predication apparently satisfies two mutually incompatible predicates. In the idiom of his antinomy, Kant is saying that there are events that are not effects of prior causes and that every event must be the effect of a prior cause. This is admittedly a contradiction. It is not, however, an antinomy. Two reasons forbid the latter characterization.

For one thing, consider this rough but sufficiently adequate characterization of an antinomy. From the assumption, say, that P is the case, we can infer to the conclusion that $\sim P$ is the case and conversely. If we accept Kant's own account of what he is doing in the argument of the antinomy, we must conclude that we can deduce the antithesis of that antinomy from the thesis and then deduce the thesis from the antithesis. Suppose for the present that Kant successfully does this. His procedure violates at least one crucial condition for an argument involved in an antinomy: *The conclusion of the argument for the thesis and the antithesis of the antinomy must follow from the assumption of the first premiss alone without the introduction of any additional premisses that do not deductively follow from, say, the thesis alone or the antithesis alone.*

This restriction on the method of proof is essential. The addition of premisses in the argument for either the thesis or the antithesis of the antinomy that do not immediately follow from the first premiss of the argument may enable you to move from P to its negation. This shows, not that the thesis *implies* the antithesis, but only that the thesis is *logically incompatible* with one of the premisses imported to demonstrate the antithesis. And so long as this is true, all we learn from such a situation is that the thesis contradicts some other propositions. We do not learn that the assumption of the thesis implies the truth of the antithesis. Kant's statement of the antinomy does the former. It does not succeed in doing the latter. That everything taking place assumes a preceding state upon which it inevitably follows according to a rule contradicts the claim that there are causes that do not stand as effects to prior causes. But it assumes that nothing takes place without a cause sufficiently determined a priori. Now this may be true. But it does not follow from the initial premiss of the argument.

The same defect obscures Kant's argument for the antithesis. We can assume that there are powers in the world of absolutely beginning a state and therefore of beginning a series of consequences of that state (i.e., that there are causes that do not stand as effects to prior causes). But we cannot infer that everything in nature takes place solely in accordance with the laws of causality (i.e., that there is no event that can be a cause without standing as an effect to a prior cause) without importing another premiss. The first premiss of the argument for the antithesis is incompatible with what Kant takes to be the universal law of causation. This may be true. But it does not demonstrate the truth of the antithesis. It merely tells us that the truth of the first premiss of the argument is incompatible with the truth of the second premiss. And this does not generate the antithesis as the conclusion of the argument.

What Kant gives us, then, is a case of a state of affairs in which the subject apparently instantiates two incompatible properties. But no sooner than we have disentangled an antinomy from a contradiction, what I call the duplication problem stalks Kant's every effort to show that the contradiction he exhibits is not really there. Suppose that we distinguish two different subjects of predication, saying with Kant that the subject that can absolutely initiate a causal series is a thing in itself while the subject that must always stand as an effect to a prior cause is an appearance. Changing the subject only compounds the problem. If, as Kant insists, we are faced with a genuine antinomy, then the thesis will imply the antithesis and conversely no matter whether we say that the thesis is true of one domain of objects and the antithesis of another. If we are really faced with an antinomy, the implication of a contradiction would hold for things in themselves just as it holds for appearances. The mutual incompatibility of two properties does not generate an antinomy. That the application of one property to an object implies the application of another, albeit contradictory, property does yield an antinomy. But changing the subject of discourse does not remove the problem. It merely duplicates that problem at a different level. Things in themselves are no less immune than appearances to the argument of the Third Antinomy.

What I call the duplication problem arises in the following way. We begin by confronting the difficulty that one and the same temporal happening has two prima facie incompatible properties. The strategy for resolving this apparent contradiction is the introduction of the distinction between things in themselves and appearances. The received interpretations of that distinction, however, cannot remove the contradiction. Suppose we say, following the *TWT* interpretation of the distinction, that there are two numerically different particulars one of which is in time and the other nontemporal. This shows only that the relations of things in themselves one to another are not governed by our forms of intuition. It does not show that those relations are not causal at all but either that the unschematized category of ground and consequent applies to them or, what is equally troublesome, that they are governed by other forms of intuition. The problem confronting the original description of temporal occurrences is thus duplicated. And the duplication is not removed by an appeal from the *TWT* to the *TDT* as it has been usually expounded. That theory merely transfers the problem it is supposed to solve to a possible world in which all the circumstances that generated the problem in the first place are duplicated. In either case, then, the duplication problem arises despite the differences by which we might try to remedy it.

Kant's argument lacks the form of an antinomy. And changing the subject of discourse does not remove but, as we have seen, only reproduces Kant's initial problem. Let me examine the arguments in the Third Antinomy in greater detail. First, the argument for the thesis. Everything that takes place (*alles, was geschieht*) assumes a causal antecedent; hence, there must be an element in the series that does not stand as an effect to a prior cause. This conclusion does not follow from the premiss that supposedly generates it. Every effect, let us assume, must have a cause. This alone does not, however, imply that there must be an absolutely first cause in the series. So far from contradicting each other, the two claims are logically compatible.

The conclusion follows from the very definition of what it is to be a cause and what it is to be an effect. It is definitionally true on any theory of causation that every effect has a cause. A causeless effect is not an effect at all. But this is not the case with regard to cause that lacks a prior cause. A cause is not defined in terms of a prior cause. The attempt would merely presuppose the very notion—namely, that of a cause—that it must define. Nor is it to be defined in terms of standing in a relation to a prior cause. This, too, would make the attempted definition circular because it would assume the notion of what it is to be a cause in order to provide a definition of causation. A cause that is not an effect does not, therefore, imply that a cause is either absolute or conditioned by a prior cause. Or, again, every effect must, let us grant, have a cause. But it might also be the case that there is a cause that is not an effect of a prior cause. And this does not generate the contradiction that the argument for the thesis of the Third Antinomy requires if it is to be the kind of demonstration that Kant requires it to be.

Substitute the notion of what takes place (*alles, was geschieht*) for the notion of an effect in the argument for the thesis. It may be true that there can be causes that are not effects. But causes also take place. If the argument applies, not only to effects, but also to everything that takes place, then a cause without a prior cause would seem to be a contradiction in terms. This may be true. But it does not tell us how the thesis of the Third Antinomy generates its conclusion. Suppose everything that takes place assumes an antecedent just because "everything that takes place" means the same as "is the effect of a prior cause." Premiss (4) of the argument for the thesis of the Third Antinomy does not follow from this assumption. An infinite regress of temporally related causes does not imply the existence of causes that are not in the same series.

We get no further in understanding the character of the Third Antinomy if we say with Kant that every appearance necessarily stands as an effect to a prior cause but refuse to say this of a world populated solely by things in themselves. For one thing, the problem that arises about the impossibility of an infinite regress of causes returns all over again for the domain of things in themselves. We already know that the law of causation can be formulated, on Kant's own showing, independently of any reference to time. For another, the issue facing Kant is not how there can be entities that can be causes without standing as effects to other causes but the very different issue that concerns the explanation of how things that lack spatio-temporal characteristics can relate to those that have those characteristics. The problem lies with the possibility of the interaction of the members of the two domains and not with the possibility of explaining how something can be a cause that is not an effect of another cause in one domain but not in the other.

The argument for the thesis, nonetheless, produces a contradiction. Premisses (1) and (3) of the argument for the thesis do generate a contradiction. If we read the phrase "cause sufficiently determined a priori" as "causal set containing an absolutely first member," then a contradiction arises. If a sufficient cause must have an absolutely first member, then premiss (1) does assume the existence of an absolutely first cause. For it requires that every causal series contain at least one member such that it does not stand to a previous member as the effect of a prior cause.

This is not, however, implied by premiss (1) alone. Suppose that, *pace* premiss (1), everything that takes place assumes a preceding state according to which it follows according to a rule. Every event can be preceded by a temporally prior event according to a rule. The series of temporal events can regress to infinity without implying a contradiction so long as each member of every pair of such events is connected with its predecessor according to a rule. Premiss (1) requires only that there be no event that is not so related. And this is compatible with there being an infinite series of such events. None of this is true, however, if a sufficient cause demands the existence of one member of the series that does not stand as an effect to a prior cause. The combination of premisses (1) and (3) does not, however, show that we must recognize what Kant calls an absolutely first beginning in any causal series. It spawns the philosophically innocuous conclusion that premiss (3) is incompatible with premiss (1).

The argument for the antithesis of the antinomy shares this defect. Premiss (1) alone does not imply the conclusion that every event has a cause. Premisses (1) and (2) together imply at most that one of them must be false. The argument for the antithesis does not show which one of them is to be rejected; hence, it does not prove the conclusion by the assumption of its contradictory. The inference from premiss (1) to premiss (2) in the argument for the antithesis does, however, assume that all temporal relations are causal. Falsify this assumption and premiss (2) would be false. If there were some temporal occurrences that were not causally related to other temporal occurrences, then premisses (1) and (2) would be mutually compatible. The former would hold of those temporal occurrences that are not causally related to other temporal occurrences; the latter, of those which were. But premiss (1) does not *imply* the causality of all temporal relations. It merely conflicts with an interpretation of premiss (2), according to which all temporal relations are also causal.

Kant does not, then, have an antinomy. But he does have a problem. The format of the Third Antinomy disguises the real issue: Is the Second Analogy compatible with the existence of an element in a causal series that does not stand to another element in that series as an effect to a cause? The real issue of Kant's Third Antinomy does not lie in our alleged ability to infer either of two mutually incompatible propositions from the assumption of its contradictory. It concerns the compatibility of the claims that every event has a cause and that there are events that are causes but not effects.

Let me provisionally disentangle the complications that obscure the Third Antinomy. Kant presents us with an apparent fact that an event can have a prior cause and yet initiate a causal series without having a prior cause. But his proposed solution—the appeal to the distinction between things in themselves and appearances—does not show how an appearance can have both of these properties without contradiction. Nor does it show how a thing in itself is superior in this respect. This is, nonetheless, the primary strategy of resolving the Third Antinomy. And Kant makes it one of the primary reasons for distinguishing between things in themselves and appearances.

Both the strategy and the conclusion are questionable. Kant's problem must be solved, if it can be solved at all, independently of either his theory of the transcendental ideality of time or his distinction between things in themselves and appearances. Kant gives us no fewer than three resolutions of this conflict. Yet only one of them is relevant to the issue of the relation between transcendental ideality and the distinction dividing things in themselves from appearances. Examine them in turn.

2. The Resolution of the First *Kritik*

Kant's strategy here is familiar. He appeals to the transcendental ideality of our form of intuition and the distinction between appearances and things in themselves. He says this:

> I at this moment arise from my chair, in complete freedom, without being necessarily influenced thereto by the influence of natural causes. . . . For this resolution and act of mine do not form part of the succession of purely natural effects, and are not a mere continuation of them.[12]

One and the same event can stand in two relations. It can be the effect of a temporally prior event. It can also be the effect of a cause that is not in time. No contradiction is supposed to arise from any of this. Causal relations hold between one appearance and another ordered necessarily according to a rule in time. But an appearance also stands in relation to what Kant calls its ground, which is not itself an appearance.[13] The two relations do not conflict because only the relation that one appearance has to another appearance is in time. The relation of an appearance to its ground is not in time. There is no contradiction in describing an event as the effect of a prior cause without being the effect of a prior event. What *initiates* the causal series is not in time; hence, so the account goes, it cannot be the effect of a temporally prior event. The event that *begins* the series is in time and therefore must stand in a causal relation to a prior event. But it also stands in a relation to its ground. The two relational situations are logically compatible; hence, the apparent contradiction disappears and the two descriptions of one and the same event are logically compatible.

This way out assumes that there are causes of events in time that are not in time. But the dilemma it faces is as familiar as Kant's solution of the problem confronting him in the Third Antinomy: Something cannot initiate a causal series in time without itself being in time. What initiates a temporal series must precede the effects it generates and succeed the temporal causes of the event that initiates the series. But this locks the initiator of the series into the time series. What I have called Kant's problem has become a dilemma. Insofar as what initiates a causal series lacks temporal characteristics, it cannot initiate an event in time. Insofar as it can initiate such an event, it must have temporal characteristics.

The dilemma demands a closer look at Kant's doctrine of transcendental ideality. Time is transcendentally ideal because it is a form of our sensibility and therefore a condition under which objects are given to us. But this is ambiguous. Distinguish between an epistemic and an ontological version of the claim that our forms of sensibility are transcendentally ideal. According to the epistemic version, something must have, say, temporal characteristics if we are to experience it at all. This says nothing about whether it has these characteristics apart from all possible experience. That temporal or any other characteristics are either necessary or sufficient conditions for our experiencing something says nothing about whether the objects we experience have those characteristics apart from all possible experience. Both could be simultaneously true.

The epistemic version of transcendental ideality needs to be defended. Somebody might object to it in the following way. If time is transcendentally ideal, the epistemic version implies that we must *know* whether space and time are characteristics of things in themselves. For time is a condition of possible experience and to say that it might be simultaneously a characteristic of things in themselves is to imply that we can be acquainted with things in themselves since anything with these characteristics would be an object of possible experience and therefore not a thing in itself. The polemical conclusion of the objection is that the epistemic interpretation of transcendental ideality falsifies Kant's distinction between things in themselves and appearances. We can never be ignorant of whether a thing in itself really has the characteristics that are the forms of our intuition of things. But then the absurdity would seem to follow that we must be able to know whether things in themselves lack temporal characteristics. So far from being an exegetically adequate account of Kant's text, the epistemic interpretation of the distinction between things in themselves and appearances permits us to know what Kant's theory prevents us from knowing.[14]

Plausible, but faulty. The epistemic interpretation of the distinction between things in themselves and appearances requires only that time may be a characteristic of things in themselves as well as a form of our intuition of things. It does not imply that we must know that time is a characteristic of things in themselves as well as a form of our sensibility even though it may be both. Suppose time to be both a characteristic of things in themselves as well as a form of our intuition. This would not, contrary to the objection, imply that we must be able to know that things in themselves are temporal. So long as time is a form of our intuition, it is impossible to discover whether anything has temporal characteristics apart from our form of intuition. In order to discover this, we would have to be able to compare things as they are apart from our present forms of intuition with the things we perceive independently of these forms. This would be impossible even if things in themselves were temporal. We are ignorant of this, not because the temporality of things we perceive is a form of our intuition, but rather because knowing whether things in themselves are temporal for this epistemic state assumes that we can compare what we perceive under our forms of intuition with what we could perceive apart from those forms.

This generates a vicious infinite regress of forms of intuition. The issue arises because of Kant's distinction between the way things are and the forms under which they appear to us. But the ability to make the necessary comparison raises the original problem all over again. That problem arises because Kant distinguishes what a form of intuition is from what something is independently of that form. To trade one form of intuition for another merely enables us to compare what appears to us under either of our two forms of intuition with what appears to us under no forms at all. The epistemic version of Kant's distinction between things in themselves and appearances, then, is not exegetically embarrassing. To adopt it is merely to acknowledge an abiding limitation of our state of enlightenment about the characteristics of the things we perceive when they are described independently of our forms of intuition.[15]

Kant also says that what we perceive cannot have temporal characteristics apart from possible experience. Call this the ontological interpretation. This assumes a radically different account of things in themselves. If we can *know* that things lack temporal characteristics apart from possible experience, then a thing in itself is a timeless entity because it cannot be an object of possible experience. The ontological interpretation requires, then, that transcendental ideality imply the timelessness of things in themselves.[16] This interpretation and its predecessor limit Kant's ability to deal with the Third Antinomy. The epistemic interpretation requires only the existence of one particular, making the distinction between an appearance and a thing in itself into a difference between two states of enlightenment with respect to its characteristics. The ontological interpretation requires the existence of two numerically different particulars about which we know that one must and the other cannot be temporal.

Neither version of transcendental ideality can remove the contradiction that generates the Third Antinomy. The ontological version of transcendental ideality gives Kant a deceptively facile solution to the problem facing him. There are timeless particulars (things in themselves) and temporal particulars (appearances). The contradiction disappears because the thesis is true of the world of timeless particulars; the antithesis is true of the world of temporal particulars. Both the strategy and the conclusion are obvious. What Kant calls an antinomy arises because of the mistaken assumption that both thesis and antithesis are true of the same domain. The transcendental ideality of time gives us two object domains. This makes the claims simultaneously true. The illusion of contradiction exposes itself for what it is.

The epistemic interpretation of transcendental ideality ostensibly gives Kant another way of removing the contradiction. The particulars that we perceive to be temporal might not need to have temporal characteristics at all independent of our forms of intuition. The antithesis is true of the particulars that we perceive under our forms of intuition. The thesis may be true of those particulars independently of the way in which we must perceive them. The solution prevents us from *knowing* whether the thesis is true. But it removes the contradiction by restricting it to a possible world in which the particulars we now perceive may lack temporal characteristics.

Neither of these ways out of the contradiction succeeds. They merely perpetuate a common problem. Suppose, as Kant says, that the thesis ("it is necessary to assume that there is another causality, that of freedom") is true of things in themselves and that the antithesis ("Everything in the world takes place solely in accordance with the laws of nature") applies to appearances. This shift simply reproduces the antinomy at another level. Kant's problem breaks out all over again in the domain of things in themselves despite his argument for the transcendental ideality of time. Consider how this comes about.

3. The Duplication Problem Expounded

Assume that time is transcendentally ideal and, further, that the ontological interpretation is the right account of the distinction between things in themselves and appearances. This allows the problem of relating free and causally determined action to arise all over again with respect to a timeless world. The ideality of time implies for Kant that it is a condition of *our* perceiving something. But this alone implies, not that all action in a nontemporal world is free, but only that we cannot apprehend such a world in the way in which we apprehend our world. The world we cannot apprehend because of the limitations of our forms of intuition is, on the ontological interpretation, timeless. This fact does not make it independent of the law of causation but only of the way in which we apply that law to the world of our sensibility. That a world is timeless does not, therefore, make all actions free. It merely makes what is to count as a free action in that world epistemically unavailable to us.

The epistemic version of transcendental ideality is no improvement. The particulars we perceive under our forms of intuition may lack temporal characteristics if they were to exist independently of our forms of intuition. Here the antithesis of the Third Antinomy would apply to the particulars we now perceive if they were to lack temporal characteristics; the thesis of the antinomy, to the particulars as we perceive them. The shift in the interpretation of the relation between things in themselves and appearances is both forced and artificial. Kant himself does not explicitly entertain it. But it is still instructive for the strategy of my argument. Consider how the epistemic interpretation of transcendental ideality might be applied to Kant's problem in the Third Antinomy. The epistemic interpretation requires us to distinguish between things in themselves and appearances in terms of our state of enlightenment about the characteristics that things in themselves may have. They could still have the same characteristics that we observe objects to have under our forms of intuition. Suppose that our forms of intuition apply to the world described by the thesis of the antinomy while they do not apply to the world described by the antithesis. The epistemic interpretation forbids us to talk about two *worlds* and thus restricts us to our state of knowledge about one and the same world. The interpretation allows only this alteration: We could say that it enables us to describe a possible world we cannot perceive under our forms of intuition.

But the appeal to the epistemic interpretation in its present formulation is useless in resolving the Third Antinomy. The antinomy arises because we are confronted with two descriptions of the actual world, not a description of a possible world coupled with a description of the actual world. We can spin out descriptions of possible worlds in which there are agents relating to one another in nontemporal ways. But an agent in such a world is not the same agent as the one in our world. It is about the latter, not the former, agent that we must ask how he can originate a causal series without himself being the effect of a prior cause.

Nor is this all. The duplication problem persistently recurs in epistemically possible worlds. If the objects in our world might lack temporal properties when they are assumed to exist independently of our forms of intuition, the members of a possible world would be timeless. This does not, however, deprive them of causal properties. They merely lack causal properties that are temporal. The question that begins with our world—How can we relate things in themselves and appearances?—arises all over again with respect to the possible worlds the members of which lack temporal characteristics.[17] Appeals to the epistemic interpretation do not resolve the Third Antinomy. They only put it into another world in which the original problem duplicates itself.[18]

The fact is, the duplication problem mislocates the issue that confronts the Third Antinomy. Kant cannot restrict the applicability of the thesis to one domain and the antithesis to another without inviting such a problem. The ontological interpretation makes this glaringly clear. The epistemic interpretation merely obscures the presence of the problem by dropping the dangerous idiom of two worlds of things. The underlying problem is how something that may or may not have the properties of our forms of intuition relates to those forms. This generates the duplication problem. Suppose that the distinction between an appearance and a thing in itself is a function of our state of enlightenment. We can still ask the same question with respect to the object about which we have limitations of enlightenment that we have asked about that object when we might be granted considerably more enlightenment. Limitations of enlightenment do not abolish the distinction between things and their appearances. Yet this is the distinction as it has come down to us from the traditional interpretations upon which Kant supposedly makes his resolution of the Third Antinomy turn.

This, then, is the duplication problem. There is a superficially compelling reason for declaring it to be a logical fraud. It forces Kant to make the distinction between things in themselves and appearances for things in themselves just as he does for appearances. But while it is at least not self-contradictory to make that distinction for appearances, it is definitionally self-contradictory to make it for things in themselves. If they were to appear, they would not be things in themselves. The duplication problem would seem to dissolve in a semantical misunderstanding. A Kantian appearance stands in certain temporal relations to other appearances and in some other relation to a thing in itself. This alone does not imply that the thing in itself to which an appearance stands in that relation must in turn stand as an appearance to a further thing in itself and so on to infinity.

This threatens to defeat the duplication problem. If we must make the distinction between things in themselves and appearances both for things in themselves and appearances alike, we generate a vicious infinite regress. Kant must solve the problem arising from the distinction between things in themselves and appearances at the first level at which it arises or not solve it at all. Since it is logically impossible to make the distinction between things in themselves and appearances for things in themselves, there is no duplication problem at all. There is, therefore, no vicious infinite regress. And, finally, an appearance can be related to other appearances on the one hand and to things in themselves on the other. This allegedly removes the apparent inconsistency of the thesis and the antithesis of the Third Antinomy with duplicational fatality.

The objection is an instructive failure. It does not salvage the epistemic interpretation in its present form. But it suggests the basis for a new formulation. The root of the suggestion is in the proper understanding of the distinction between affection and causation. If the epistemic interpretation is to remove the duplication problem, it must be stated in terms of affection. At A19=B33 Kant says that

> intuition takes place only insofar as the object is given to us. This again is only possible, to man at least, insofar as the mind is *affected* [italics mine—M.G.] in a certain way. The capacity (receptivity) for receiving representations through the mode in which we are *affected* [italics mine—M.G.] by objects in sensibility.

The duplication problem arises only if you take the affection relation to be causal. For that problem arises once you say that affection becomes causal just because it is temporal. Affection is temporal, but it is not causal. Affection cannot be a case of necessary succession according to a rule even though it may always be accompanied by such a succession. For the succession involved in causation assumes the immediate presentation of an object to our forms of intuition as a condition of properly describing any succession of events in our experience at all. Immediate presentation of an object to our forms of intuition by affection may be always accompanied by temporal and causal relations. But it does not assume them as necessary conditions of specifying what it is to be a relation of affection.

Separating affection from causation rehabilitates the epistemic interpretation of the distinction between things in themselves and appearances. If affection is logically independent of the notion of causation, we no longer have the problem that faces our initial statement of the epistemic interpretation. We no longer need to interpret a state of enlightenment about the characteristics an object may have as a set of descriptions that may be satisfied in some possible world that is not identical with the actual world. We need only say that the satisfaction of some descriptions by the objects of our experience cannot be confirmed in this world. We can also say on the present formulation of the epistemic interpretation that things in themselves can have the characteristics that constitute our forms of intuition without contradicting ourselves. The notion of a form of intuition is defined independently of characteristics of our intuition without our being able to ascertain this fact. For the act of discovery must be subject to our forms of intuition, but space and time can exist independently of those forms.

The distinction between causation and affection removes the logical absurdity that initially threatened the epistemic interpretation of the distinction between things in themselves and appearances. Nothing Kant says in his description of the Third Antinomy commits him to such an absurdity. And the duplication problem, once it has been confronted with a more sophisticated version of the epistemic interpretation, does not burden him with that absurdity. But the new formulation of the epistemic interpretation gives his resolution a quite different problem.

The relation of affection between an event and a thing in itself removes the apparent contradiction generated by attributing two logically incompatible properties to the same event. With the affection relation Kant would have only temporal relations at his disposal if he is to remove the contradiction that begets the Third Antinomy. The relation of affection, whatever else it may be, must at least be temporal. For any thing in itself that generates an appearance by affecting our forms of intuition must accomplish this at a certain time. Without this assumption we could not distinguish, on Kant's theory, between the occurrence of an appearance at one time from the occurrence of another appearance at another. This, it might be argued, makes a thing in itself into a covert and illegitimate appearance. For it is subject to the same forms of intuition on which it is supposed to act in order to give us the appearances we perceive. Thus the temporality of the affection relation duplicates the problem it is supposed to solve. This duplication, as we have seen, must continue to infinity. And this, in turn, destroys the relation between things in themselves and appearances.

A superficially convincing strategy animates the objection. A thing in itself can affect our forms of intuition on several different occasions. The events are temporally successive. But this implies that the thing in itself that affects our forms of intuition on those successive occasions are the selves caught up in the time sequence. Even if, as we have seen, affection is not causation, we can assign places in the time series to various events involving affection. And this places things in themselves in the time order with appearances. Affection, though it may be conceptually distinguished from causation, would then seem to be subject to the Second Analogy along with the appearances that we perceive. The distinction between the two kinds of relation is powerless to separate them experientially. This would not dissolve the distinction between affection and causation. But it would make such a distinction epistemically irrelevant.

But would it? I think not. Things in themselves are an ingredient in events appearing that can be ordered as temporally successive. It does not follow, however, that things in themselves stand in temporal relations to one another. Nor does it follow that any thing in itself can be said to have a history consisting of events that are temporally related to one another. It follows only that the events in which they are parts have those relations. Temporal succession is not, then, a relation that is communicated to things in themselves merely because they are parts of events that do stand in those relations.

The appeal to a relation which Kant calls affection and which much of the tradition has wrongly assimilated to causation is only one way of engendering the duplication problem. He tells us that the thesis of the antinomy applies to a domain of things in themselves while the antithesis of the antinomy applies only to the domain of appearances. And the two domains are not related by affection. This would seem to do away with the duplication problem. If you say that things in themselves do not affect our forms of intuition at all, then what Kant calls a thing in itself does not become an appearance in a misleading semantical guise. It does not break up into an appearance that in turn requires a thing in itself affecting our forms of intuition in order to account for the presence of the appearance that is supposed to generate yet another appearance by affecting the forms of our intuition. Ontologically separate but equal status prevents all of this and avoids the duplication problem that is allegedly fatal to Kant's resolution of the Third Antinomy.

Suppose, then, that we distinguish between those entities that lack spatial or temporal properties and those that have them. Suppose, further, that there are no relations between the two kinds of objects at all. This would seem to avoid the problem of affection altogether, for the domain of things in themselves does not relate to any member of the domain of appearances. The ploy is, however, deceptive. It breaks down on the distinction between noumena and things in themselves. We have a concept, if Kant is right, of an entity (noumenon) that lacks spatial or temporal characteristics. But a thing in itself is not to be confused with a Kantian noumenon. The former, unlike the latter, is what Kant calls the ground of appearances given to us under our forms of intuition.[19] The latter is, however, superficially but deceptively similar to the former because it has characteristics that are not available to our sensibility.

But the deception soon ends, for the similarity between the two notions trades on an ambiguity in the notion of what it is to be unavailable to sensibility. What makes something into a thing in itself is that it can be schematized in different ways for different forms of intuition. The concept of a noumenon cannot be schematized at all. A thing in itself has characteristics that we cannot know that it has even though we may be presented with them under some schema or other. This is not so for a noumenon. It cannot, therefore, be a thing in itself except in the trivial sense in which it lacks spatial or temporal properties. A thing in itself may lack these properties. But it does not lack alternative schematisms. We could be acquainted with noumena if we lacked any forms of intuition at all. But we could never be acquainted with things in themselves if we lacked any forms of intuition. Otherwise a thing in itself could not, as Kant says, be the ground of the appearances given to us. The duplication problem remains. An appeal to a domain of noumena will dispense with the relation of affection. But it will also dispense with the distinction between things in themselves and appearances. It cannot, therefore, be used to reconstruct that distinction.

The distinction between a thing in itself and a noumenon alone is not enough to remove the duplication problem. Another objection must be answered if that problem is to be taken seriously. It runs like this. The duplication problem and the vicious infinite regress that attends it can start only on the assumption of the ontological interpretation of the relation between things in themselves and appearances. The epistemic version of that distinction in its received form does not prevent what Kant calls a thing in itself from being only a semantically disguised appearance. But all that remains is to substitute a noumenon for what Kant calls a thing in itself. This would require us to claim that the relation of affection holds between phenomenal substances and their appearances. But there is no necessity to insinuate that relation into the distinction between a noumenon and an appearance. The solution of the duplication problem, then, would require that we confine the relation of affection to spatial and temporal objects and the way in which they appear to us. And this would dispense with the difficulties of both the ontological and the epistemic version in its received form of the distinction between things in themselves and appearances. Both of those theories assume, falsely, that the relation of affection must hold between noumena and appearances. The revised version of the epistemic interpretation is, then, at best obsolete and at worst false: Obsolete, because it is addressed to a problem that does not exist; false, because it assumes that affection is a relation that can hold only between things in themselves and appearances.

The objection breaks down, however, on a stubborn fact. A substance that is spatially and temporally ordered according to the forms of our intuition may not stand in any relation to things in themselves once they are assimilated to noumena. It may also be true that the affection relation stands only between substances thus ordered and their appearances. But the concept of substance can be schematized in ways other than the schemata we employ to apply it to our experience. The fact of alternative possibilities of schematism introduces problems that the appeal to phenomenal substances appearing to us under our forms of intuition was supposed to remove. We may know that a perceptual object may affect us in various ways in a world governed by our forms of intuition, but we do not know whether that substance has the properties that our schematism requires it to have apart from that schema.

This does not involve an appeal to other possible forms of intuition. It does not involve an illicit claim about the existence of entities in our world that lack the properties that we employ as forms of intuition. Nor does it involve an implicit but equally illicit appeal to the characteristics of things in other epistemically possible worlds. Alternative schematisms do, admittedly, determine for Kant alternative epistemic worlds. But this is not all they do. Schemata also determine the extent to which we can know about the characteristics of objects in our world apart from the schemata in terms of which we apply the categories we have in that world. Grant for the sake of argument that affection holds, not between things in themselves and appearances, but rather between phenomenal substances and their appearances. We still do not know whether these substances, even though they are temporal and spatial, have those characteristics apart from our schematism. This is the problem that demands the restoration of all the original distinctions even though we might try to remove the problem by changing our description of them.

The objection to the revised version of the epistemic interpretation must, then, be rejected. But it is useful dialectical confirmation of the truth of that interpretation. And it also helps to explain why the problems to which that interpretation is intended as a solution do not disappear with a shift in terminology. Saying that the relation of affection can hold between objects that are spatial or temporal and their appearances while assimilating the notion of a thing in itself to the concept of a noumenon merely shows once again that the issue here has nothing relevant to do with whether the objects that affect the forms of intuition stand in a spatial or temporal relation to them. Affection and causation are, as we have already seen, two and not one. The relation of immediate awareness is not, therefore, either temporal or spatial, although it is accompanied by whatever relations the forms of our intuition demand. Whether what affects us is a spatial or temporal entity or, rather, something that lacks these properties is irrelevant to the viability of the affection relation and to the explication of the relation between a thing in itself and an appearance. The issues can be raised with respect to either noumena or phenomena.

The failure of the objection tells us even more. It is an instructive reminder of the importance of Kant's distinction between a category and a schema as the key to his distinction between things in themselves and appearances. A thing in itself is an object that can be schematized in indefinitely many ways. This is only another way of saying that a Kantian schema is different from a pure concept or, what for Kant comes to the same, the concept of an object of experience in general. The ground-consequent relation, for example, is the pure concept or category of which one schema is the necessary connection of events in time. Schemata can change from one possible world to another. This does not, however, imply a similar change in the pure concept. Nor does such a distinction imply that the objects we do perceive under our forms of intuition have or lack the characteristics we perceive them to have independent of those forms of intuition. It implies merely that what we call a thing in itself is an object in our world that can be schematized differently in other possible worlds. Thus the concept of an object that affects us is independent of the concept of the forms of intuition under which it affects us. And this merely confirms the revised version of the epistemic interpretation of the distinction between things in themselves and appearances.

An unsympathetic critic might object to this gloss. We might be told that we cannot schematize concepts, but that it makes no sense to say that we can schematize objects at all, let alone objects answering to the description Kant gives of things in themselves. A schema is a way in which we apply a concept to an object. To claim that we schematize *objects* is at best a semantical slip and at worst a contradiction in terms. We schematize concepts. We do not schematize objects.

The unsympathetic critic is helpfully wrong: helpful, because he locates the fundamental ambiguity in Kant's notion of schematism; wrong, because he clings to one and only one sense of that notion. A Kantian schema is a mark in the object in virtue of which we can tell that such an object corresponds to an element that we think in the concept of that kind of object. If we insist that only a concept can be a Kantian schema, we invite the hopeless problem of specifying just how the concept that we call a schema is to be applied to objects. And this merely gives us our original problem of applying concepts to objects all over again. If we are to avoid attributing this consequence to Kant's theory, we must recognize that a schema must ultimately be a characteristic of things that has its counterpart in our concepts of those things. The narrow view of schematism invites a problem it cannot solve. A recognition of the ambiguity of Kant's use of that notion remedies it.

My reconstruction of the distinction between a thing in itself and an appearance faces two consequences that superficially threaten its adequacy. The first is this. The duplication problem may arise all over again just because there is a distinction of some kind demanded by the fact that the forms of our intuition dictate the only way in which we can perceive the objects that are given to us. To say that a thing in itself is an object that can be schematized in indefinitely many ways in as many possible worlds perpetuates the problem it is supposed to solve. The problem arises from the necessity to perceive any object under some schema or other. To transfer the issue from the schematism required for our world to the schematism appropriate to other epistemically possible worlds only reproduces the problem from one world to another.

The objection trades on a confusion. We cannot explicate the relation between a thing in itself and an appearance by appealing to the difference between the schema of a pure concept in our world and the schema of that same concept in another possible world. But we can give the required explication by appealing to the distinction between a pure concept and a schema of that concept in this world. The objects falling under that concept in this world may have characteristics different from those given to us in the schema of that concept. That the object given to us may have even the characteristics that are those of the schema cannot be confirmed or disconfirmed in this or any other world just because a schema prevents us in each world from discovering what the object that falls under the pure concept is like. The possibility is not, then, shifted to other schemata in other possible worlds. It remains in this world. But the distinction between a thing in itself and an appearance is preserved by separating the concept of an object apart from a schema and the object as given to us through a schema. And this merely serves to support the revised version of the epistemic interpretation of the distinction between things in themselves and appearances.

But the epistemic version faces another objection. We might be told that it undermines Kant's resolution of the Third Antinomy. Suppose that the concept of a thing in itself is really the concept of an object that can be schematized in different ways in different possible perceptual worlds. This conception of a thing in itself avoids the duplication problem by appealing to the notion of schematisms in possible worlds as distinct from the schematism that dominates our perceptual world. But the problem that generates Kant's Third Antinomy is how something in *this* world can, as Kant says, absolutely initiate a causal series without itself being the effect of a prior cause in the series of events that constitute our perceptual world. The antinomy arises because of the seeming unavoidability of assigning mutually exclusive predicates to one and the same event.

How, then, can we avoid simultaneously ascribing to a subject in this world both the predicates "absolutely initiates a causal series" and "is the effect of a prior cause"? An appeal to a thing in itself as an object in a possible world would seem merely to return us to the traditional version of the epistemic interpretation. This would remove the contradiction. But it would not explain how the initiating occurrence can take place in this world. We are presumably faced with the philosophically disastrous results of the duplication problem. We are to shift the issue of things in themselves to worlds that are possible but not actual.

First, a preliminary caution: *The Kantian distinction between the transcendental reality and ideality of time is irrelevant to the solution of the problem of the Third Antinomy.* The same antinomy can be generated if we assume that time is transcendentally real. And the transcendental ideality of time is powerless to resolve the antinomy. The antinomy can be constructed by assuming either alternative. The transcendental ideality of time only gives birth to the duplication problem with the attendant vicious infinite regress of appearances affecting appearances. At each stage of this regress the problem facing the Third Antinomy can be raised again.

This occurs whether you assume the ontological or the traditional version of the epistemic interpretation of transcendental ideality. The former confuses a noumenon with a thing in itself. And once the assimilation of the one to the other has been accomplished, we have seen that even a noumenon can affect forms of intuition in some way or other. The ontological interpretation makes what is supposed to be an entity that lacks the characteristic of our forms of intuition into something that must have them because they affect those forms. The received version of the epistemic interpretation fares no better. For it, too, must either assume the relation of affection or generate an infinite regress through possible epistemic worlds in order to avoid solving a problem that it cannot solve at the first stage of that regress without destroying the relation between things in themselves and appearances.

But what about the assumption that the forms of our or any other kind of intuition are transcendentally real? The alternative fails. The problem that hounds the assumption of transcendental ideality also undermines transcendental reality. Let us suppose, then, that the objects we call appearances have the characteristics we perceive them to have independently of our forms of intuition. What we observe to have spatial or temporal characteristics has those very characteristics (Forget for now how we are supposed to *know* this!) no matter what the forms of our intuition are. This contra-Kantian assumption neither removes the duplication problem nor abolishes the distinction between things in themselves and appearances. Both of these claims are startling. Both of them are true. But they both require defense.

The transcendental reality of time and space does not relieve us of the distinction between things in themselves and appearances. The assumption merely stipulates that what we perceive under our forms of intuition has the same characteristics as the forms under which we perceive them. The transcendental reality of time and space does not alter the fact that we perceive things under forms of intuition. It requires only that the characteristics of the things we perceive be the same as the modes of intuition under which we perceive them. The transcendental reality of space and time does not abolish the distinction between things as they are in themselves and things as we perceive them. It merely perpetuates that distinction.

Kant's doctrine of forms of intuition is still with us, even if we are somehow allowed to know that the things we perceive have the characteristics we perceive them to have under our modes of intuition. The relation of affection still holds between those things and the modes of our intuition. And this is enough to preserve Kant's distinction between appearances and things in themselves. But the problem of the Third Antinomy can be raised for things in themselves that are temporal just as it can be raised for appearances that are temporal. Transcendental realism does not escape the duplication problem.

The same point can be put in a different way. Continue to assume that what we perceive has the characteristics it is perceived to have even though those characteristics are also what Kant calls the forms of our intuition of things. Whether the characteristics of what we perceive really belong to the things given to our modes of intuition or not, Kantian affection must still be the relation between what we perceive and the forms under which we must perceive them. The objects that generate the appearances that we are given to perceive under our forms of intuition may themselves be appearances. But the explanation of the mechanism by which I come into perceptual contact with an appearance offered to me is that another appearance affects my forms of intuition. The appearance that, on the assumption of transcendental realism, affects my forms of intuition is logically no better off than the appearance I get from its affection. The epistemic problem has merely been duplicated. And all of this—the duplication problem as well as the distinction between things in themselves and appearances—remains even if we assume transcendental realism.

The issue that confronts Kant's Third Antinomy has nothing to do with the issue about the transcendental ideality or reality of time. Nor has it anything to do with the issue about the distinction between things in themselves and appearances. You can adopt a realist or idealist view of time and still leave Kant's problem untouched. This leaves the problem unresolved. Both of the solutions camouflage the genuine issue raised by the Third Antinomy. My intermediate conclusion, then, is twofold. Kant's resolution of the Third Antinomy is not an independent argument for the distinction between things in themselves and appearances. The issue raised by the Third Antinomy is logically independent of the issue about whether time or, for that matter, any alleged form of intuition is transcendentally ideal or real.

Consideration of an alternative interpretation should help to place this conclusion in sharper focus. Somebody might try to apply Bertrand Russell's treatment of the Paradox of Self-Reference in set theory to Kant's problem in the Third Antinomy. It goes like this. To suppose that the class of all nonself-membered classes is self-membered is to imply a contradiction. Russell works his way out of this by running a theory of types and denying that there is any self-membered class. If we apply this to the Third Antinomy, what Kant is concerned with is whether the world as a whole is a self-membered class. By assuming that "everything" is a something, we get the antinomy that Kant seeks to resolve.

This resolution supposedly parallels Russell's solution of the paradoxes of self-reference. For Kant's distinction between appearances and things in themselves is allegedly a precursor of Russell's theory of types. If there were no distinction between appearances and things in themselves, then all totalities are legitimate. But if space and time are transcendentally ideal, we can justify talking about something that is not a part of the totality of appearances in a metaphysically harmless way. For we can then describe appearances transcendentally (thus moving to a higher type level) without generating a contradiction with respect to a totality of things of a lower type level. This, we are told, removes the duplication problem, for it establishes that nothing answers to the definite description "the world." The absence of a distinction between the world of appearances and the world of things in themselves would generate self-referential paradoxes. Conceiving the world transcendentally avoids them. Thus the Third Antinomy does assume the transcendental ideality of space and time. And this implies the distinction between things in themselves and appearances.

Ingenious, but wrong. To think of appearances transcendentally may avoid self-referential paradoxes with respect to the world of appearances. But it carries no such guarantee with respect to the world of things in themselves. Referential talk about the world of appearances may be carried on from what, on this interpretation, might be called the type level of transcendental idealism. But we still have the problem of how we are to talk about the world of things in themselves. Talk about one world takes place on a different logical level from talk about the other. But the present view has much to explain, for it must still explain how we are to avoid the duplication problem in the world of things in themselves. Appealing to another type level does not do. It applies to things in themselves and appearances alike. And this shows that the issues involved in the self-referential paradoxes are independent of Kantian distinction between things in themselves and appearances.

But it shows even more. The appeal to the type distinction fails instructively, for it gives us additional proof that the distinction between transcendental ideality and reality is independent of the distinction between things in themselves and appearances. This shows, further, that the argument of the Third Antinomy is independent of both the ontological and the traditional epistemic interpretation of the distinction between things in themselves and appearances.

4. *Holzwege*: The *Groundwork* and the Second *Kritik* Resolutions

The *Groundwork* and the second *Kritik* face the problem that Kant described in the third Antinomy of the first *Kritik*. Both offer arguments that differ from the strategy of the first *Kritik*. But the solutions they offer still suffer from the defects of one or the other of the received interpretations of what a thing in itself is.

Consider the *Groundwork* resolution of the apparent contradiction involved in describing one and the same act as free and caused. Here Kant introduces the notion of an alien cause:

> Will is a kind of causality belonging to living beings so far as they are rational. *Freedom* would then be the property this causality has of being able to work independently of *determination* by alien causes; just as *natural necessity* is a property of characterizing the causality of all non-rational beings—the property of being determined to activity by the influence of alien causes.[20]

But is there a distinction between causes that are alien and those that are not? Kant answers:

> He [a rational being] has therefore two points of view from which he can regard himself. . . . He can consider himself *first*— so far as he belongs to the sensible world—to be under laws of nature (heteronomy); and *secondly*—so far as he belongs to the intelligible world—to be under laws which, being independent of nature, are not empirical but have their ground in reason alone.[21]

Kant begins by asking how a temporal occurrence can have two apparently incompatible causes. He ends with a reference to different ways in which an agent can conceive of himself. But the problem can be raised all over again about the agent who is able to conceive of himself in different ways. The act of conceiving is itself temporal; hence, we can ask whether this act is the result of what Kant calls an alien cause. The problem concerns the relation between the object of what the agent conceives. Removing the issue to a claim about conceptual ability not only provides another example of the first *Kritik* problem, but it also substitutes another description of the original statement of the problem. The antinomy that Kant faces in the first *Kritik* does not tax our conceptual abilities. It questions our ability to demonstrate what we can conceive. The *Groundwork* solution of the antinomy ignores this.

Let us assume that an act is heteronomous just in case it is an event that follows necessarily upon another event according to a rule.[22] The alien cause would be whatever antecedent events were sufficient conditions for the occurrence of the heteronomous act. This may be true. But this tells us only how to distinguish heteronomous from autonomous acts. It merely baptizes Kant's first *Kritik* problem with a new name. Heteronomous acts may be the effects of antecedent events. But the first *Kritik* problem arises within the context of what Kant calls autonomous acts. We want to know how an autonomous act can be at one and the same time a member of a temporal causal series and still be the absolute initiator of a causal series. The distinction between two kinds of act in time does not solve a problem that is raised solely in the context of only one kind of temporal act.

But worse is to come. The heteronomy-autonomy distinction is logically independent of the distinction between free and causally determined action. Kant defines the distinction between autonomous and heteronomous action in terms of the kind of reason we give to explain the motivation of our acts. Autonomous acts are done from what he calls rational grounds; heteronomous acts are done from grounds that are given to us by our sensuous nature. As far as this characterization goes, even autonomous action can be causally determined. To say that an action is autonomous is merely to say that we act in accordance with a motive of which we are aware. But the fact of our awareness of such a motive can be the effect of causal antecedents.

But this revision of the problem is irrelevant to the Third Antinomy. The distinction between things in themselves and appearances cannot, then, imply the autonomy-heteronomy distinction any more than the distinction between autonomy and heteronomous action implies the distinction between things in themselves and appearances. The problem facing Kant in the Third Antinomy is, therefore, fundamentally different from the problem facing him in the defense of the heteronomy-autonomy distinction. We can accept the distinction between things in themselves and appearances and reject autonomous action without contradiction. The heteronomy-autonomy distinction applies to different *kinds* of temporal occurrences. The distinction between things in themselves and appearances applies to *every* temporal occurrence.

The second *Kritik* gives us a different resolution of the Third Antinomy. Here Kant tries to resolve the antinomy by appealing to what allegedly follows from the assumption that there are necessary connections between appearances.

(1) If we assume that the objects we experience are things in themselves, "it is impossible to see how, if *A* is granted, it would be contradictory not to grant B, which is altogether different from *A*."[23]

(2) What is impossible for things in themselves is possible for appearances because "*A* and B as appearances in one experience must necessarily be connected in a certain manner . . . and that they cannot be separated without contradicting that connection by means of which experience is possible."[24]

(3) The unity of experience implies the distinction between things in themselves and appearances.

(4) Therefore, the concept of causation applies to noumena although we cannot experience the objects to which it applies.[25]

(5) Therefore, "[t]hrough it [the concept of a *causa noumenon*] I do not strive to know theoretically the characteristic of a being insofar as it has a pure will; it is enough for me to denote it as such by means of this concept and thus to couple the concept of causality with that of freedom."[26]

The argument confirms my contention: Necessary connections in our experience of objects are irrelevant to the distinction between things in themselves and appearances.

Suppose that appearances can exist independently of our forms of intuition. This alone does not show that premiss (1) of the second *Kritik* argument is true. There might be necessary connections between events even if we could not observe them. Saying that time is transcendentally ideal no more guarantees the existence of necessary connections among events than the denial of such a connection implies the transcendental reality of time.

Kant himself supplies the evidence for this conclusion. The issue about the transcendental ideality of time can be raised independently of the connection that any occurrence in time has to another. That is a lesson of the Aesthetic of the first *Kritik*.[27] There Kant infers the transcendental ideality of time from arguments about the relation of appearances in general to inner sense. His argument here depends on the characteristics of individual appearances and not on their relations to one another or to whatever affects our sensibility.

Even if we forget that lesson, the Transcendental Analytic of the first *Kritik* gives us another. The apprehension of the manifold of perceptions is always successive.[28] But some manifolds are irreversible. Others are not. This implies that the distinction between necessary and accidental connections between temporal occurrences is drawn independently of the issue of the status of time itself. The existence of necessary temporal connections cannot, therefore, decide whether time is transcendentally ideal or whether there are things in themselves. Those connections assume a prior account of temporal succession in general; hence, any local peculiarity of temporal relations cannot help us decide whether time is transcendentally real or ideal.

The complexity of this issue does not end here. Kant does admittedly say that we cannot *know* necessary connections between events a priori if time is transcendentally real.[29] If we cannot know the characteristics of time independently of inductive evidence, then we can never know whether the connection we perceive among the events in our experience must invariably hold between events of a like kind. Concede all of this for the sake of argument. None of it shows, however, that the transcendental ideality of time follows from the assumption that we can know that there are necessary connections among temporal occurrences independently of experience. Transcendental ideality may be a necessary condition of our *knowing* such facts. But it cannot be a necessary condition of there *being* such facts. Transcendental ideality guarantees our ability to know a priori that there are necessary connections in our experience. It does not show that there are such connections. Nor does the argument permit any inference to a conclusion about whether these connections obtain independently of our ability to experience them.

The second *Kritik* solution of the antinomy may tell us something about our ability to know that there are necessary connections between temporal occurrences independent of experience. And this may, in turn, assume the transcendental ideality of time. But it is silent about whether time can also be transcendentally real. *The transcendental ideality of time is logically compatible with the transcendental reality of time.* This undermines the second *Kritik* argument for the distinction between things in themselves and appearances; but it is also a prima facie contradiction. Consider how this comes about.

The second *Kritik* resolution requires our ability to know some things about the pervasive features of our experience. We are told that we can know these features just in case we can assume that, say, time is a necessary condition of our being able to experience anything. That for Kant makes time transcendentally ideal. But none of this prevents time from being a characteristic of things independent of our ability to experience them. Our ability to know certain things about the character of time independent of experience requires that we restrict these *epistemic* claims to time insofar as we perceive it. Nothing follows about the relation of time to things insofar as we cannot perceive them.

A superficially plausible objection may temporarily obscure this point. Assume that time is a condition of the possibility of our experiencing objects. Somebody might argue that such an assumption prevents time from being a characteristic of things in themselves. To invest such things with temporal properties immediately implies that they are objects of possible experience for us just because temporality partially specifies what is to count as an object of possible experience; hence, time cannot be transcendentally real. If it is, then what we claim to exist independently of possible experience both is and is not an object of possible experience.

The objection breaks down on a confusion of an ontological with an epistemic claim. To say that time is transcendentally ideal is to say that it is a necessary condition of our perceiving anything. This claim is epistemic. It tells us something about the conditions under which perceptual awareness is possible. It does not tell us whether those conditions are characteristics of things apart from possible experience. It is thus compatible with the ontological claim that what is to count as a necessary condition of our ability to perceive anything is also a characteristic of the thing independently of possible experience. The epistemic claim, however, is incompatible with the claim that we are able to verify the truth of the ontological claim. Temporality may be a necessary condition of the possibility of perception. But it may still be a characteristic of objects existing independently of possible experience. This is just a result of the fact that the faculty of intuition for Kant is logically independent of any form of intuition that we may have. And it shows that the second *Kritik* resolution of the antinomy sustains the epistemic, not the ontological, interpretation of transcendental ideality.

The difficulties continue. Premiss (4) of the argument says that we can apply the category of causation to noumena even though the transcendental ideality of our forms of intuition prevent us from experiencing such objects. Kant's argument provides only two alternatives for the interpretation of premiss (4). We can say that what we apply to noumena when we extend the category of causation to them is the unschematized category of causation. We can, however, say that we apply that category schematized in a different way to what Kant calls noumena. This exhausts the options, neither of which makes premiss (4) any more viable than the other. Eliminate them in turn.

The unschematized category of causation goes first. A category in this state is compatible with any world that is consistently describable.[30] But to say that a category can be applied in any such world is one thing. That it has objects falling under it in every such world is quite another. Kant's argument needs the latter. Premiss (4) yields only the former. The argument must show that we can consistently think of objects that are not spatial or temporal. What it shows on this interpretation is that we can consistently think of an object in general without respect to any form of schematism at all. But the thought of an object in general is not the same as the thought of a particular kind of object that does not conform to our forms of intuition.

The second alternative aggravates the issue. Suppose that our conception of a noumenon is really the thought of an object conforming to the category of causation when that category is schematized differently from the way in which we are forced to schematize it. This may be true of noumena, but it only duplicates the issue already facing Kant's argument.[31] Kant tries to resolve the Third Antinomy by distinguishing between appearances and the things in themselves. That distinction allegedly succeeds because the transcendental status of the forms of intuition that, in turn, are the schemata of the categories. The introduction of a different set of schemata merely reproduces the distinction between appearances and things in themselves for another possible world. It does not solve the problems facing the distinction in this world.

5. The Third Antinomy: The Aftermath

What, then, remains of Kant's treatment of the Third Antinomy? It lacks the formal structure of an antinomy. Kant does not give us mutually incompatible propositions each of which generates the other without further assumptions. He supplies only what purport to be equally cogent arguments for the logically incompatible propositions. His problem cannot be solved by assuming the transcendental ideality of our forms of intuition whether we adopt either the ontological or the traditional epistemic version of that doctrine. The problem of the Third Antinomy arises independently of Kant's distinction between the transcendental reality or ideality of those forms. And it cannot be solved by assuming any of the standard, received accounts of the distinction between things as they are in themselves and appearances.

None of this undercuts Kant's argument. It merely exposes the defects of the traditional interpretations of that argument and the basis on which they were erected. The tradition confuses two very different issues that are to be found in Kant's discussion of the Third Antinomy. One of them is essential to the success of the resolution. The other is not. There is, first of all, the problem about the possibility of a cause that can initiate a series of events but that itself does not stand as an effect to any prior cause. There is, secondly, the issue of whether there can be a temporal event that can initiate a temporal series without standing in the relation of effect to cause to any prior temporal event.

The issues are logically independent. Whether there can be a temporal occurrence that is not the effect of a prior cause can be resolved without implying any conclusion about whether there is an absolutely first occurrence in time. Kant's exposition of the problem in the Third Antinomy obscures the difference between the two issues. But it does not obliterate that difference. The tradition does. The traditional views of the relation between a thing in itself and an appearance are responsible for the assimilation of these two issues. This assimilation is responsible for the duplication problem and the collapse of the distinction between causation and affection. The removal of the confusion does not give Kant an independent proof for the transcendental ideality of our forms of intuition. But it nevertheless assumes the transcendental ideality of those forms as a condition of the resolution of the Third Antinomy.

Suppose that every temporal occurrence must be preceded by an occurrence that is temporally prior to it. The arguments that such a procession is possible are legion in the history of philosophy.[32] The assumption of such a series is either possible or actual and is compatible with the claim that no causal series properly so called is infinite. The assumption that an infinite temporal series is either possible or actual is compatible with the fact that there are events that are occurrences that are causes of other occurrences that are not themselves effects of prior causes. The contradiction arises when we assume that the same occurrence in time is both the result of a prior event and that it can cause another event to occur without itself being caused by a prior event.

But the assumption is false. The occupation of a place in the temporal order does not imply being caused. But being caused implies that what is caused occupies a place in the time order. This is the key to Kant's resolution of the Third Antinomy. His exposition shows that the question facing the antinomy can be answered by formulating it differently. The question cannot be how one and the same *event* both is the effect of a prior cause and lacks that relation. This makes the solution of the problem impossible by making the conditions of its solution impossible of fulfillment. Suppose that there is an infinite regress of temporal occurrences. There need not be anything answering to what Kant describes as an occurrence that is the first member of the series. But the problem about the regress of events (not occurrences) cannot be dismissed in this way. For one thing, it does not arise with respect to the world as a whole but concerns every member of the temporal series of occurrences. To say that there is an infinite or finite regress of temporal occurrences does not remove the problem facing the Third Antinomy, for that problem can be raised with respect to every occurrence in that series. For another thing, the distinction between an event and an occurrence removes the problem from a merely temporal sequence and places it squarely in the context of causal sequences.

The distinction between an occurrence and an event is crucial to Kant's resolution of the Third Antinomy. It enables something that is not an effect of a prior cause to initiate a series of events. But this does not imply that the initiating event lacks temporal antecedents that are occurrences and that may also be events. Both causal and noncausal occurrences are locked in the time order. For one occurrence can be described both as a member of that series and as an event. The former does not imply a causal relationship with anything else. The latter does. The description of an occurrence in time is neutral with respect to either causal or noncausal descriptions. What takes place in time can be an effect of a prior cause. It can also be an occurrence that initiates a series of temporal occurrences without itself being the effect of a prior cause.

The neutrality of location in the time order removes the contradiction that otherwise makes it impossible to resolve the Third Antinomy. The dilemma arises only on the assumption that Kant must reconcile the existence of events that are both caused and not the effects of prior causes. It arises because the only way out of the dilemma, once you have accepted the notion of event and not that of occurrence as the subject to which these mutually exclusive descriptions are given, is to introduce the existence of atemporal causes.

But this is merely another case of the false assumption that dominates most traditional descriptions of what Kant is doing in his exposition and resolution of the Third Antinomy. Kant must prove only that it is possible for something to initiate a temporal series without being the effect of a prior cause. This does not, however, imply that it cannot be the successor of another temporal occurrence. Nor does it imply that it is impossible by the occurrence by which a series of events is initiated to be the effect of a proper cause. For there is no contradiction between the two descriptions applied to the same temporal occurrence.

Suppose that an occurrence can be both the effect of a prior cause and an instance of what Kant calls the initiation of a temporal series without being the effect of a prior cause. Does this not merely return the contradiction that Kant undertakes to remove? Not at all. The two descriptions involved in such a case can be conjointly fulfilled without a contradiction, for those descriptions apply to occurrences and not to events. The contradiction arises only if those descriptions were restricted in their applicability to events. The notion of occurrence, however, is neutral with respect to any causal relations that one occurrence may have to others. An occurrence can have both relations to two different things. An event cannot have those relations without generating a contradiction. An occurrence does not become an event by being the effect of a temporally prior cause. The event is the relation in which an occurrence stands to another occurrence. The occurrence does not, therefore, cease to be an occurrence when it stands in that relation. This is what permits it consistently to relate to other occurrences in the time series as effect to cause and to relate to something else as a cause that is not the effect of a prior cause.

At this point the issue of the transcendental ideality of space and time enters Kant's argument in the Third Antinomy. Neither of the two traditional interpretations of the distinction between things in themselves and appearances can resolve the antinomy. Both import the duplication problem. The *TWT* enables us to postulate two subjects of predication. The member of a causal series in time is an appearance. It is related to a thing in itself that is not a member of that series. But insofar as a thing in itself initiates a series of events in time, it is itself caught up in the time series and thus becomes a member of the causal series it allegedly escapes. And mere absence from a temporal series does not exclude a thing in itself from causal relations with other things in themselves. It merely signals our ability to schematize the category of causation independently of temporal relations in a world populated by things in themselves. And this duplicates the problem that the *TWT* is supposed to solve.

The same problem vitiates Kant's resolution of the Third Antinomy if we read the *TDT* into Kant's argument. It may be possible for us to give two different descriptions of one and the same item of our experience. We might describe it in terms of its temporal relations with other items. We might also leave it open whether it might satisfy different descriptions in other possible worlds not epistemically accessible to us because of the limitations of our forms of intuition. This enables us to say that the item in question is causally related to all other items in our experience but need not stand in that relation to other times in another possible but epistemically unavailable world.

But this way of reading Kant's attempt to resolve the antinomy had to go the way of its predecessor. There is, to be sure, some evidence for it in Kant's discussion of the problem he faces in the *Groundwork* and in the second *Kritik*. That evidence is neither exegetically conclusive nor philosophically helpful. It is not exegetically conclusive because the argument in both the *Groundwork* and the second *Kritik* appeals to two ways in which the agent can conceive of his acts. He can view them as part of the causally ordered series of events in time or, alternatively, as part of the actions of a member of what Kant calls the Kingdom of Ends. But this is at most a description of how the agent can conceive of what he does. It does not provide a foundation for the legitimacy of that distinction. Nor is it philosophically helpful to Kant, for the alternative ways of conceiving of one's actions are themselves events in the time order. This leaves open whether there is any foundation for action in reality other than our own conception.

The revised view of the epistemic interpretation of the distinction between things in themselves and appearances does not share this fate. The distinction between two descriptions of an occurrence in time escapes the duplication problem. It solves the original problem with respect to our world and does not postulate a world of entities that are neither temporal nor spatial. It does not remove the problem facing the relation between things in themselves and appearances to another possible world. The revised version of *TDT* enables us to construe the relation between things in themselves and appearances as a case of affection, not causation. And the relation of affection, as we know, can hold between any object and how we perceive it to appear to us. This, as we also know, is compatible with the temporality and spatiality of the object that is a thing in itself. The distinction between a thing in itself and an appearance, then, is not reconstructed as the difference between how something appears to us under our forms of intuition and how that thing may appear to us under other forms of intuition. It is the distinction between how something appears to us under those forms and what it may or may not be independently of those forms.

We now have independent confirmation of the revised version of the epistemic interpretation. For, as we have seen, the interpretation is compatible with the possibility that things can have the same characteristics apart from our forms of intuition that they appear to have under those forms. The distinction, essential to Kant's resolution of the Third Antinomy, between occurrences and events assumes that things in themselves might have the same characteristics as appearances. This enables Kant to resolve the Third Antinomy without having to rely on either the *TWT* or the traditional version of the *TDT*. Only the revised version of the *TDT* can avoid the duplication problem so fatal to its alternatives.

7. Concluding
Aporetical Postscript

THE MAJOR parts of the case for the revised version of the epistemic interpretation of the distinction between things in themselves and appearances are now before us. We have Kant's own statement of the conditions for distinguishing between things in themselves and appearances. We have seen how the traditional attempts to explicate Kant's meaning rely upon distinctions other than those that Kant makes between things in themselves and appearances in his epistemology and thus violate Kant's conditions of a proper explication of that distinction or, in fact, contradict other parts of Kant's epistemology. And we have also seen how the revised version of the epistemic interpretation must be assumed if Kant is to be credited with a viable resolution of the First and Third Antinomies.

1. Causation, Affection, and Temporality

The problems that the traditional explication faces are basically these. What we have inherited assimilates affection to causation and ultimately fails to account for the place of either in Kant's theory of perceptual objects. Both the *TWT* and the *TDT* first assume that temporal succession is causation and then fail to account for the place that either has in Kant's theory of knowledge. Affection is an epistemic relation that is assumed by Kant's account of causation. If we hold with Kant that causation is a necessary connection of events according to a rule, we must at least be able to stand in an epistemic relation to the events in a causal series in order for us to be able to identify the members that constitute such a series. Any attempt to transform the cognitive relation called affection into a causal relation between members of a temporal series and our acts of perceiving would be circular. We must be able to stand in a noncausal epistemic relation to any member of that series as a necessary condition of our ability successfully to claim that what we experience is a member of a Kantian causal series.

Suppose we appeal to the causal relation between a member of such a series and an act of perceptual awareness in order to explain how we can be perceptually aware of the member as a part of any temporal series at all. This would seem to avoid the circularity inherent in the claim that affection is a kind of causation by exploiting an ambiguity in the description of what is to be explained. If we describe the member of the series the parts of which we must be able to identify as a member of a causal series, then the appeal to a causal explanation of our ability to make such an identification would be circular. But we can describe the perceptual situation in terms of an acquaintance with something merely as a member of a temporal but not necessarily a causal series. But this escapes one circle only to generate another. The act of perception that occurs simultaneously with whatever state of affairs we claim ourselves to perceive still assumes an immediate, noncausal epistemic state called affection that is logically distinct from whatever causal relations that obtain between them. The problem of explicating the relation between things in themselves and appearances has been generated historically mainly by the implicit and philosophically dangerous assumption that affection is a variety of causation and that the relation between things in themselves and appearances must be understood as causal in character. But the assumption distorts the character, not only of affection, but also of the nature of Kant's theory of causation. And, finally, both of these blunders conspire to generate what I have called the duplication problem. The *TWT* falls back on causation because it cannot explain the fact of affection. And this merely reproduces the original problem of explaining how we can be in epistemic contact with something that cannot be given to us. The traditional *TDT* reproduces the problem it is introduced to solve by transferring the description of that problem from our world to a possible world.

The basic theme pervading all of these assimilations and misappropriations is the continuous distortion of the affection relation. Affection, we are correctly told, is the immediate presence of an object to our forms of intuition. But much of the tradition *defines* that relation in terms of the simultaneity of an object to an act of perceptual awareness. This maneuver is behind the confusions about the relation between affection and causation, temporal and causal connections, and ultimately the nature of transcendental ideality itself. The definitional assimilation of affection to causation generates a dilemma that vitiates most of what has been said about the character of Kant's transcendental idealism. It is this.

If things in themselves affect us, then they have temporal characteristics. Events of affection are at least simultaneous with our acts of perceptual awareness. This destroys the distinction between things in themselves and appearances. It makes what affects our forms of intuition into part of what is presented to us under those forms. And this requires us to distinguish what affects us and the act that is affected all over again from what is given to us under the forms of our intuition. We must then recognize the existence both of an object with spatial or temporal characteristics and of yet another object lacking them in order to account for affection. This is a process of fission and it goes on to infinity.

The second horn of the dilemma is no less objectionable. If we definitionally transform affection into a relation between two temporal entities in order to avoid a vicious infinite regress, we will have joined a significant part of the tradition in implicitly denying any distinction between a thing in itself and an appearance. The relation of affection now holds between temporal and therefore phenomenal entities. Neither horn of this dilemma is acceptable. The former makes a thing in itself into an entity that cannot stand in any relation to our forms of affection. And the latter makes it into something that can stand in a relation to our forms of intuition that is not affection. In one case, we prevent the relation of affection from doing what it is supposed to do in Kant's theory. In the other, we prevent it from doing what it is supposed to do by calling it a name that it cannot bear. And both horns of the dilemma can, as we have seen, be traced back to the definitional assimilation of affection to causation.[1]

2. Affection and Intuition

All of this disappears once we realize, as the tradition does not, that Kant's theory contains two mutually compatible claims that are ostensibly incompatible. Things can have spatial or temporal characteristics and still affect our forms of intuition without themselves becoming appearances among appearances. Much of the tradition has either denied or ignored this. And here it has gone wrong. What has come to us as the *TWT* and the *TDT* are superficially incompatible alternatives. The former tells us that things in themselves are objects that lack the characteristics of our forms of intuition; the latter tells us that a thing in itself is an object that satisfies descriptions that it cannot satisfy in our world. But both of these theories assume that to say that something has spatial or temporal characteristics implies that it cannot be a thing in itself.

The *TWT* assumes that what affects our forms of intuition cannot have the characteristics of the forms of intuition that they affect. But it assumes that to have or lack the characteristics of our forms of intuition is the principle of division for things in themselves and appearances. The *TDT* in its traditional form diverges from its alternative only to make the same mistake in a different way. To say that a thing in itself satisfies a description in another possible world that it does not satisfy in this world rests on a mistake. For it falsely assumes that things in themselves cannot have the characteristics of the forms under which they are intuited. This is the structural motive for making the distinction between a thing in itself and an appearance into the distinction between the characteristics something has in this world and the characteristics it has in some other possible world.

Both the *TDT* and the *TWT* in its received version attempt to avoid saying that things in themselves can have the same characteristics as our forms of intuition. The *TWT* appeals to things in this world that lack the characteristics of our forms of intuition. The *TDT* merely transfers the problem to another possible world to which we do not have access. But the differences between the two theories are dialectically indistinguishable. The ostensible difference resides merely in the location of the *incognisabilia*. Both alternatives are dialectical deceits. And we know now the illicit inference that generates those deceits.[2]

The epistemic interpretation of the distinction between things in themselves and appearances, revised in its present form, removes this difficulty. The revision of that theory requires us to distinguish between the fact that affection is necessarily accompanied by causation and the very different fact that affection is the same relation as that which always occurs with it. We can now explain how affection can obtain without implying the illegitimate application of the category of causation to things in themselves. We must also distinguish between the claim that things in themselves have or lack the characteristics of our forms of intuition from the very different claim that we cannot know this. This enables us to expose the objectionable assumption dominating the standard interpretations of the relation between things in themselves and appearances. That distinction is epistemic and not ontological.

In the first place, given the distinction between affection and causation as it is epistemically interpreted, we do not illegitimately apply the Kantian category of causation when we claim that things in themselves conform to it. To say that the particulars affecting us also have causal characteristics permits us to say that the relation of causation obtains between the properties those particulars have and not between the particulars themselves. This conclusion is reinforced by a basic fact about Kant's theory of schematism. When we refer to things in themselves, we can apply only the unschematized category of causation to the particulars thus identified. And this aids in the explanation of affection as distinct from causation because we can understand how something can affect us in terms of the unschematized category while we cannot do so if we are restricted to the schematized category of causation. The epistemic interpretation of the distinction between things in themselves and appearances also enables us to avoid the objectionable consequence sometime imputed to Kant's that we surreptitiously claim to know what a thing in itself is independent of possible experience. There is, on this interpretation, a limit to our cognitive capacity but not to the ontological possibilities that are epistemically impossible.

The difference can be generalized. We are also obliged to distinguish between standing in the relation of immediate awareness to an object and standing in a relation of immediate awareness to spatial or temporal characteristics. This, again, requires the distinction between immediacy and what uniformly accompanies that state without being a definitional component of it. This further exposes the mistake of the traditional assumption about the nature of the things in themselves and how they are available to us. Certain characteristics may always be present in case of direct awareness. But their presence does not define direct awareness.[3]

3. Affection and Reflexivity

The revised version of the *TDT*, then, fits what Kant says about the distinction between things in themselves and appearances. It also shows that the theory is philosophically defensible. But the theory still faces objections that might threaten to obscure both the structure of the argument from which it is derived as well as the conclusion that follows from it. The first is this. Self-knowledge would seem to constitute a damaging counterexample to the theory. If the relation of affection holds between things in themselves and appearances in general, it must also hold between the self as it is in itself and the self as it appears to itself. But the relation of a self to what is given to it in cases of self-awareness would not, it seems, be the relation of affection.

The whole mechanism by which the relation between a self and objects other than itself has been explicated ultimately breaks down on the Paradox of Self-Knowledge.[4] The relation of affection requires numerical diversity of relata. The self cannot be aware of itself without perpetually supplying as the object of such an awareness something that is not identical with the intended object of awareness. If self-knowledge is possible, then the affection relation cannot obtain between the self and what presents to itself in cases of self-awareness. If perceptual awareness is a case of affection, then Kant's theory makes self-knowledge impossible.

The dilemma is specious. The problem of reconciling the fact of self-knowledge with Kant's theory of affection arises because of the Paradox of Self-Knowledge. And the fact of self-knowledge is an exception to the affection relation. But an exception need not be a counterexample. The putative exception does not disqualify the affection relation as an explanation of how things in themselves are connected with appearances. Nor is it a legitimate counterexample to Kant's theory of affection.

It does not undermine the affection relation because the difficulty raised by the Paradox of Self-Knowledge arises independently of any theory of self-knowledge. The relation of affection does not solve the problem that the epistemic idiosyncrasies of self-knowledge generate. But neither does it generate that problem. And the relation of affection that holds between things in themselves and appearances does not perpetuate the problem. What makes self-knowledge an exception, then, is that it can be stated without any reference to the problem that faces an account of the distinction between things in themselves and appearances.

But the Paradox of Self-Knowledge does not, after all, supply even so much as a counterexample to the use of affection in cases of self-knowledge. A paradox arises because the self of which each of us can claim immediate awareness is not the same as the self that is the subject of awareness. This assumption undermines any theory of self-knowledge. There is, however, a hidden assumption in the paradox. The paradox is ambiguous about whether the object of self-awareness must exist simultaneously with the act of awareness. Nothing in the case for the affection relation demands that the object affecting us be simultaneous with the subject affected. The self that affects us need not, on this revision of the assumptions governing the argument, be simultaneous with the self it affects. The paradox becomes acute only on the assumption that both selves be simultaneous with each other. This is a threat to the Kantian account of affection only on the assumption that all affection relations must obtain between relata that exist simultaneously with each other. The theory is formulated only for simultaneously existent entities. But it is completely neutral about whether we can apply it to entities that do not exist simultaneously. It does not, to be sure, explain how this is to be done. But it does not forbid the possibility. The theory of affection is not a genuine counterexample of Kant's theory. It remains as it was before: It is an exception that is neither accommodated nor contradicted by the fact of self-knowledge.

This, however, is only a fact about the relevance of Kant's account of self-knowledge in the Transcendental Analytic to his general theory of affection in cases of self-knowledge. The argument of the Transcendental Aesthetic makes other demands on the notion of affection. There, as we have learned, we are told that the self does affect itself. And there, once again, the distinction between causation and affection enables us to avoid the philosophically and exegetically serious consequences of having to say that self-affection is either a contradiction in terms or that it is an abiding mystery of Kant's theory of affection. All instances of causation, on the Kantian account, involve two numerically different terms. Such a condition does not apply to all relations of affection because it, like the relation of identity, need not have two terms. Thus just as the use of the notion of self-knowledge in the Transcendental Analytic is an exception to the use of the notion in the Transcendental Aesthetic, Kant's employment of that notion in the Transcendental Aesthetic is not a counterexample to his use of it elsewhere.

4. Epistemic and Ontological Overlap

Two distinctions have figured prominently in the revised version of the *TDT*. There is the distinction between the *TWT* and the *TDT*. They are both theories about the nature of the distinction between things in themselves and appearances. The issue dividing the two theories is whether the forms of our or any other intuition characterize things in themselves or only appearances. But this distinction can be interpreted either ontologically or epistemically. If we interpret the relation between the *TWT* and the *TDT* ontologically, then we claim that we can know whether the forms of intuition characterize things in themselves or not. This is knowledge that the epistemic interpretation of that distinction denies to us.

The interpretations overlap. And this generates the aporetic embarrassment. If you suppose that the difference between the two theories is ontological, then you claim that you do know whether things in themselves have or lack the characteristics of whatever forms of intuition we have. This claim immediately threatens to undermine *TDT* in both its traditional and its revised form. Both versions claim that the distinction between things in themselves and appearances is a matter of our state of enlightenment about the characteristics of things in themselves. But if we can know what those characteristics are and what they are not, the knowledge would destroy the distinction between things in themselves and appearance. A thing in itself that can perceptually disclose the characteristics it has and lacks only succeeds in ceasing to be what it is supposed to be. The distinction collapses. The *TWT* follows close behind. If we can know what we are supposed to be able to know on the ontological interpretation of the distinction between the *TDT* and the *TWT*, the distinction we are to explicate collapses. We are once again placed in an epistemic position that makes it impossible for us to distinguish between acquaintance with a thing in itself and an appearance.

The epistemic interpretation of the distinction gets no further. If we cannot know whether the characteristics that we ascribe to perceptual objects are the characteristics they really have, then we cannot know whether either the *TWT* or the *TDT* is true. The same doubt that is involved in the case of the *TDT* arises again with respect to the truth of that theory with respect to its alternative. If the conclusion of the *TDT* is true, then we cannot know whether the theory that implies that conclusion is true. For the claim that we cannot know which of the two alternative theories is true is in fact an admission that the truth of the *TDT* is undecidable.

There is a way out. The ontological interpretation of the distinction between the two theories is false, and it illustrates the hopelessness of clinging to the *TWT*. Here the objection is right. It fails, however, when it is used against the revised version of the *TDT*. To say that we cannot know whether things in themselves have or lack the character- istics of the forms of intuition does not imply that we cannot know whether the *TDT* is true or false. The demonstrability of ignorance is a confession of an incapacity to decide the limits of one's knowledge.

The objection rests on a failure to understand the fatal consequence of its application to the *TWT*. The ontological interpretation of the distinction between the two theories fails because it allows us to know what we cannot know. This claim destroys the interpretation of the distinction, but it does not do away with the distinction itself. It merely supplies the evidence we need in order to justify the claim that we can know that the revised version of the *TDT* is decidable. This follows directly from the falsity of the ontological interpretation of the distinction between the two theories. If we can know that the inter- pretation is false, it follows that then we can know whether its alter- native is true. The epistemic interpretation is removed from the objec- tion once we understand that it applies, if it applies at all, equally to the ontological and to the epistemic interpretations of the distinction. We have seen that it does not apply to the former. And this enables us to see through the pretensions of the alternative. To demonstrate igno- rance of the properties that things may have independent of possible human experience does not show that we are in principle unable to decide which theory of the relation between things in themselves and appearances is true. It shows, on the contrary, that we can demonstrate the truth of one rather than the other theory just because the demonstration of something about a fact of our ignorance implies nothing about our ignorance of the truth or falsity of a theory about what such a fact involves.

5. Schematism and Things in Themselves

Things in themselves differ from appearances as an unschematized differs from a schematized category. The reason for this is that a thing in itself cannot differ from an appearance as one kind of *object* differs from another. The distinction must hold if it is to be at all defensible between two states of enlightenment about one and the same object. We can say that a thing in itself is a substance if a substance is what Kant calls whatever is a subject but never a predicate.[5] This does not involve the application of the pure category of substance to things in themselves.[6] The trouble arises only if you apply the schematized category of substance to things in themselves. This relates that object to the objects that we perceive under our forms of intuition. The unschematized category does not shift an object that we cannot intuit under our forms of intuition into membership in a group all members of which are open to our intuition. The unschematized category only relates a concept to something indeterminate with respect to any forms of intuition at all.

This solution does not, however, escape objection. The aporetical complaint is this. The distinction between unschematized and schematized categories is arguably irrelevant to the relation it is supposed to explicate. The distinction between a thing in itself and an appearance is supposed to hold between an object and the forms of intuition. It is not, therefore, a distinction between two kinds of concept. Rather, the problem of relating a thing in itself to an appearance arises about the relation between what falls under a schematized category and something that does not fall under such a category.

The objection fails. True, things in themselves are distinguished from appearances within the context of objects that fall under the schematized categories. True, also, that distinction is made with respect to objects and not concepts. But all of this misses the point. The schematized category is a complex concept. You can divide it into what Kant calls a pure category and whatever must be added to that category in order to restrict its application to our forms of intuition.

This conceptual complexity is what enables us to apply the pure category to things in themselves and the schematized category to appearances without smuggling the latter into our thought about the former.

It is no objection to this to say that the concept of existence is being illegitimately extended to things in themselves. The unschematized category of existence does apply to them, for it is compatible with any schema. We can thus claim truthfully that there are things in themselves. But this claim, understood properly, does not imply that we either do or can know their characteristics, for we are limited to the use of the schematized categories in making good on such claims. So much for this aporetical puzzlement.

6. Schematism and Appearances

The affection relation is still not out of trouble. It may be true that the relation between things in themselves and appearances can be partially explicated in terms of the relation between a schematized and an unschematized category. But this gives us another problem. The relation between a thing in itself and an appearance holds, not between things and appearances, but rather between a thing in itself and our perception of an appearance. If we assume the revised epistemic version of the *TDT*, the relation of affection does not hold between two kinds of objects. It obtains between things in themselves and our acts of perception. The shift here is from a relation between two kinds of objects to a relation between an object and an act. The difference is crucial. For it is both necessitated by the requirements imposed on the relation of affection and at the same time a serious threat to the adequacy of the epistemic interpretation of the *TDT*. The necessitation arises out of the fact that only a thing in itself can satisfy the Affection Condition as well as the Cognitivity Condition. Only a thing in itself can stand in the affection relation to any form of intuition because that relational complex is what Kant's theory requires in order for it to provide a successful explanation of what it is for something to appear to us. It satisfies the Cognitivity Condition because what appears to us cannot itself be given to us independently of forms of intuition. This account leaves us with the problem of translating the vocabulary provided by Kant's distinction between schematized and unschematized categories. Here the relation between two kinds of concept—one schematized and the other not—does not work. We have already seen that the affection relation is logically prior to the relation of causation or to the relation of entities presented in any of the modes of time. It would seem that the relation of affection cannot be understood in terms of the distinction between a schematized and an unschematized category. The distinction between things in themselves and appearances holds between an object and an act of perceptual awareness. But the logical priority of this relation to any relation a thing in itself might have to a category, schematized or unschematized, would seem to prevent our understanding of the relation of affection in terms of a relation that is logically posterior to it.

Suppose there are two objects one of which is a thing in itself and the other an appearance. The relation of affection cannot hold between them. That relation can obtain only between an object of immediate awareness and a mental act. The affection relation is defined in terms of immediate awareness. And the distinction between things in themselves and appearances is defined in terms of affection. This connection prevents the affection relation from obtaining between two objects. If a thing in itself is not a possible object of such awareness, then it cannot affect our forms of intuition. The requirement, as we have seen, is that it do so directly.

The consequence of all of this is the ostensible collapse of the distinction between things in themselves and appearances. Once you reject the claim that the distinction between things in themselves and appearances holds between two objects, the affection relation threatens to undermine the very distinction it is supposed to explicate. If the affection relation holds between an object and a mental act, the object can be what it appears to be. It may be the case that one of the conditions of affection is that what stands in such a relation to us also has the characteristics of our forms of intuition. But this does not imply that what affects us is unknowable. It implies only that what does affect us is accompanied by characteristics that function as our forms of intuition.

The objection is instructively wrong. So far from heralding the collapse of the distinction between things in themselves and appearances, making the affection relation hold between acts and objects preserves the distinction that the alternative to it only erases. That distinction is cancelled if we try to transform it into a relation between two kinds of objects. Once we do this, we prevent the affection relation from holding between a thing in itself and an appearance. The object that affects us is accompanied by our forms of intuition. What we perceive is a thing in itself. But we do not perceive it independent of forms of intuition.

There remains, finally, the claim that we cannot use the distinction between schematized and unschematized categories as an explication of the relation of affection because that relation holds between an object and an act while the relation between a schematized and an unschematized category holds between two concepts the applicability of which assumes our understanding of the affection relation. The problem is not genuine because it overlooks the task that the relation between a schematized and an unschematized category performs in the total context of our understanding of how a thing in itself relates to an act of perceptual awareness. The distinction between a schematized and an unschematized category cannot account for what it is to stand in the relation of affection to anything. But that distinction nevertheless supports the existence of the affection relation because it explains how we can be conceptually aware of a thing in itself without assimilating affection to causation. An unschematized category is merely the concept of an object in general. It does not give us any information about the characteristics of what an object must have if it is to constitute an appearance that conforms to our or any other forms of intuition.

This confirms the revised version of the epistemic interpretation. The distinction between things in themselves and appearances on that interpretation is neither a duality of object nor a single object that can satisfy various descriptions in different possible worlds. The difference resides in the diversity of two states of enlightenment about the descriptions that a single object can satisfy in the world that is epistemically accessible to us. We can be appeared to by an object about which we do not know whether it satisfies certain descriptions. We can be aware of the object that satisfies descriptions that we cannot know it to satisfy.

7. The Antinomies Again

Kant uses the First and Third Antinomies to support the claim that our forms of intuition are transcendentally ideal. But both antinomies arise even if we assume that our forms of intuition are transcendentally real. Kant's resolution of both antinomies would, then, seem to be independent of the ideality-reality issue of space and time. It would seem to follow that neither argument proves the transcendental reality or ideality of space or time, nor is it capable of providing corroboratory evidence for the truth of the epistemic revision of the distinction between things in themselves and appearances.

The fact remains, however, that both antinomies provide the corroboratory evidence for the truth of such a revision even though they would both arise independently of the ideality or reality of space and time. Neither the conclusion of the thesis nor antithesis of the argument in either antinomy demonstrates the transcendental ideality of our forms of intuition. But this does not show that the arguments are irrelevant to the issue of the transcendental ideality of our forms of intuition. For Kant's strategy in both of the antinomies is to show that neither the conclusion of the thesis nor the antithesis of both antinomies can be demonstrated. Both arguments are compatible with the transcendental reality of space and time. But neither is compatible with the claim that we *know* whether space or time is transcendentally real or ideal. This conclusion does not support either the *TDT* or the *TWT*. But this is not a weakness in the appeal to the argument of either antinomy to support the revised version of the *TDT*. It is, however, fatal to the claims of either theory as it has been traditionally expounded.

We cannot, for all the argument of the First Antinomy shows, know whether there is a first occurrence in time or whether there is a region of space that encloses all other regions of space. This does not show that space or time is transcendentally ideal or real on either of the received theories. But it does show, as it should, that the revised version of the *TDT* is true and that the assumption of any other version makes the argument of the antinomy irrelevant to the ideality-reality issue or, even worse, that the argument begs the question about whether space or time is transcendentally ideal.

The resolution of the Third Antimony falls into place when it is seen in this context. The problem of compatibly ascribing two mutually exclusive descriptions to one and the same temporal occurrence arises, as we have seen, irrespective of whether temporal characteristics exist independently of our forms of intuition. But, here again, the conclusion that the argument commits us to accept reinforces the revised version of the epistemic interpretation of the *TDT*. There is, to be sure, a twist in the argument of the Third Antinomy not present in the resolution of the First Antinomy. Here the distinction between an event and a temporal occurrence is crucial to the resolution of the antinomy. But what is equally crucial is that an occurrence can also be an event and, further, that the distinction between an event and an occurrence assumes the truth of the revised version of the *TDT*. Take these in turn.

First, to be an event for Kant is to follow necessarily according to a rule upon a temporally prior event. But the version of causation presented in the Second Analogy applies to events, not to occurrences. There are no events that are not occurrences. But there can be occurrences that are not events. This removes what would otherwise be insoluble in Kant's argument about whether one and the same subject of predication can simultaneously satisfy an event- and an occurrence-description. Thus something can be initiated without a causal antecedent but not without a temporal antecedent. There is, in other words, a difference between saying that one and the same event can simultaneously instantiate the properties, "is the result of a prior cause," and "is the initiator of a causal series without being the effect of a prior cause," on the one hand, and saying that occurrences can take place that instantiate the former property without instantiating the latter. The neutrality of the notion of an occurrence allows the first but forbids the second.

Neither the *TWT* nor the traditional version of the *TDT* can explain the possibility of Kant's resolution of the Third Antinomy. Both of them break down on the duplication problem. But once we recognize that the distinction between things in themselves and appearances holds between two states of enlightenment about the objects of our perceptual experience, the duplication problem cannot arise. This also puts Kant's resolution of the antinomy in proper perspective. Kant shows the possibility of initiating causal series without being a member of another causal series. He does not purport to show that such initiation actually takes place but only how it is possible. For something can have spatial and temporal characteristics and still instantiate such a series. For all we know, the initiator of such a series can be an element in an event as well as an element in an occurrence. This is a matter of our state of enlightenment about the occurrence we describe. And this, in turn, assumes the revised version of the *TDT* if it is to be intelligible, let alone true.

APPENDIX: SUMMARY OF
CONTROVERSIES

1. "Antinomy" Controversy

Norbert Hinske's "Kants Begriff der Antinomie und die Etappen seiner Ausarbeitung," pp. 448ff., distinguishes three senses of Kant's use of "antinomy": (1) There is a conflict (*Widerstreit*) of opposed assertions; (2) there is a conflict of accepted principles; (3) an antinomy is a phenomenon of pure reason. All of this may be philologically accurate, but it is philosophically useless. The first claim gives us, at best, just another description of a plain contradiction. This may be true of antinomous argumentation, but it does not distinguish an antinomy from a plain contradiction. The same holds for Hinske's second characterization. The contradiction that obtains in antinomies may always and everywhere hold between what we might want to call received or accepted principles, but this no more exclusively characterizes an argument than saying that it is constructed solely out of empirical propositions. *Modus ponens*, for example, does not alter its character whenever we substitute solely analytic for synthetic propositions contained in the syllogism. And what Hinske singles out as the third concept of a Kantian antinomy gets us no further. Suppose we call an antinomous argument a phenomenon of pure reason. This, too, may be true of all such arguments. But it is also true of arguments containing propositions the concepts of which contain no marks of anything that can be intuited in sensory experience. And these arguments can be called antinomies only at the cost of depriving that notion of all of its meaning.

W. Windelband also attempts to distinguish different senses of thing in itself that Kant allegedly invokes at different periods of his development. In the *Vierteljahresschrift für wissenschaftliche Philosophie und Soziologie*, Windelband gives us four stages: (1) The period of *Inaugural Dissertation*, during which Kant calls anything a thing in itself that is an object of thought as distinct from an object of the senses; (2) The period in which anything counts as a thing in itself that is generated (created, produced) by our intellect rather than being received by our senses; (3) The period in which the thing in itself is a postulated or limiting concept (*Grenzbegriff*) that is the last stage in an infinite series of appearances; and (4) The period in which the thing in itself is a postulate the existence of which we must assume to explain the fact of free action.

The principles of division overlap misleadingly. (1) This confuses a noumenon, which is an entity that lacks spatial-temporal characteristics, with the quite different notion of a thing in itself, which is an entity about which Kant repeatedly asks what its relation to the forms of our sensibility is. The *Inaugural Dissertation* discusses the former, not the latter. (2) A thing in itself may be created by our intellect, but this does not distinguish a thing in itself from things like perceptual particulars that could be generated by our intellect if it were—what it is not—an *intellectus archetypus*. (3) Kant did hold this view of the thing in itself, but it is irrelevant to the problem of the Third Antinomy. All the notion of a limiting concept gives us is the *thought* of the end of an infinite series of appearances. It does not show us that there is or must be anything answering to that thought as a necessary or sufficient condition of our ability to experience what we do experience. (4) This treats the thing in itself as a postulate of moral action. But a postulate is not a proof. It is a proof and not a postulate that he needs to get the argument of the Third Antinomy off the ground. Swetomir Ristititsch, "Die indirekten Beweise des transzendentalen Idealismus," laboriously continues the tradition by distinguishing three senses of a thing in itself. (1) There are things that lack the subjective characteristics of space and time. (2) There are concepts of things in general that can be given no objects in intuition because the concepts in question are not schematized. And (3) there are Ideas of Reason (*Vernunftideen*) for which no objects can be given in possible experience (e.g., God, freedom, and immorality). All of these count for Ristititsch as things in themselves.

None of these classifications can possibly count as a Kantian thing in itself. (1) goes at once. It is a confusion of a noumenon, which does not affect our sensibility, with things in themselves, which do affect that sensibility. (2) follows closely its predecessor. The concept of a thing in general is not a thing in itself in the first place, for what should be the transparent reason that it is a concept from which all reference to any sensibility has been abstracted and for the slightly less transparent but still evident reason that the concept of a thing in itself is a notion that is compatible with any sensibility whatsoever—which is very far from being a concept of something that cannot be given to any sensibility at all. And (3) merely lists concepts that cannot be given to our sensibility. But this is very different from claiming, as the doctrine of things in themselves does claim, that there are entities that cannot be given to our sensibility but that nonetheless exist and affect our sensibility.

This massive confusion is not, however, isolated. Kuno Fischer, *A Commentary on Kant's Critick of the Pure Reason*, pp. 135ff., simply gives us a more ancient anticipation of Ristititsch's mistakes. As if that were not enough, Fischer continues (p. 218) the tradition of confusing the argument of the Third with that of the Fourth Antinomy. See chapter 2 for an attempt to prepare the way for getting all of this straight. See also chapter 3 for the application of this conceptual thicket to the problem of self-knowledge according to Kant.

James Ward, *A Study of Kant*, was the first philosopher known to me to address the issue of how the noumenal self is related to appearances on the one hand and the quite different problem of how things in themselves are related to our sensibility on the other. I raise this problem only to drop it because my present interest is solely in separating the philosophical issue of the status of noumenal objects from the very different philosophical issue of the relation of things in themselves to the forms of our sensibility. Ward recognizes (p. 183) what frequently escapes Kant that noumenal selves are causes of the appearances that we are given in our sensibility. This distinction is important for the viability of Kant's theory. For one thing, the relation of affection does not hold between noumenal and phenomenal selves. For another, once we make the distinction that Kant frequently obscures between the relation that a thing in itself has to what appears to us and the relation between a noumenal and a phenomenal self, we can ascribe moral responsibility to moral agents without having to assimilate the relation of the moral self and the empirical self to the very different relation between a thing in itself and an appearance. And, finally, whatever the difficulties associated with the relation between things in themselves and the way in which they affect the forms of our sensibility, they are not inherited by the relation between the phenomenal and noumenal selves. The general result is this: *This noumenal self does not affect the phenomenal self.* This puts the problem in its proper perspective. The issue is not how an agent in time can generate a causal series and still act freely. It is, rather, how the noumenal self can act at all without falling prey to the philosophical difficulties of the duplication problem. Ward (pp. 185ff.) saw all of this quite clearly. My chapter 3 is an attempt to work out in some detail what Ward correctly saw but imperfectly elaborated.

Paton, *Kant's Metaphysic of Experience*, 2:387ff., is largely responsible for contributing to an already muddled issue. Paton reports (p. 387) that "by inner sense we know ourselves." Paton continues to report (pp. 388–89) that "when Kant speaks of the self as 'affecting inner sense,' he is not using the word 'affects' in the same way as when he speaks of physical objects, or things in themselves as affecting outer sense. . . . The difference between outer and inner sense appears to lie in this—that outer sense might receive impressions . . . apart from the transcendental synthesis of imagination and the unity of apperception; but apart from the transcendental synthesis of imagination and the unity of apperception nothing could be received by inner sense at all." Both parts of Paton's report are faulty. Suppose, in the first place, that we grant the distinction between a noumenal and a phenomenal self. The noumenal self cannot affect the phenomenal self at all. The problem of self-affection arises only on the assumption, which Paton uncritically accepts from sources he fails to cite, that the *noumenal* self is a *thing in itself*. But Kant nowhere says that the noumenal self is a thing in itself; hence, he nowhere has to raise the issue of how the noumenal self can affect itself; hence, whatever the Paradox of Self-Knowledge may be, it cannot be what Paton says it is. The problem is his, not Kant's.

Once you grant the distinction between noumenal selves and things

in themselves, whatever paradox of self-knowledge there is to be resolved at all must be resolved independently of the distinction between
the noumenal and phenomenal self. There is, I grant, a paradox of self-
knowledge. But that paradox can be stated independently of the distinction between appearances and things in themselves, the accompanying problems of applying the Kantian doctrine of affection to
such a situation, and the maddeningly dismaying problem of explaining how a noumenal self can affect the sensibility of a phenomenal self
cannot be duplicated to infinity whenever a noumenal self affects itself.

The second part of Paton's report betrays signs of awareness of all
of this. But Paton's description of the muddle into which he has ma-
nipulated Kant's text is by this time beyond repair. Listen to Paton
again. Having just said that we can know ourselves in inner sense as
we appear to ourselves but not as we are in ourselves, Paton continues
to say that Kant is working with two distinct senses of "affection."
When things in themselves affect what Kant calls outer sense, we receive these impressions without being aware of any synthetic activity
of the ego or, for that matter, without having to be aware of the ego
that is being affected. Not so with what we get from inner sense. Here
we are automatically aware of the ego and the act of synthesis. And
this, for Paton, marks out a different sense of "affection."

The distinction is banally relevant. True, should we be aware of
ourselves as we appear to ourselves, this could only occur in inner
sense. But this is merely to say that Kant's doctrine of affection is restricted to time in cases of self-knowledge. It is not to say, as Paton
claims, that the *sense* of "affection" changes but only that the *medium*
of affection differs when we are affected by our noumenal egos. We
can, I believe, agree on all hands that we can think about ourselves.
But the issue here is whether such a thought is a case of affection. Paton distinguishes two senses of "affection" without asking whether the
very notion of affection can be applied to self-knowledge without
contradiction.

Paton dramatizes an already perilous hermeneutical situation when,
in his *The Categorical Imperative* (p. 235), he tries to show the peculiarity of self-affection by asking us to imagine a historian describing a
battle: "It looks—from one point of view—as if he stood above the
battle as a timeless observer assigning to each historical event its place
in a causal series that he understands. Yet when we turn to consider
what he has done in composing his history, this too appears as an historical event in the same causal series, and in no way different from

any other historical event. . . . Every man is, as it were, the historian of his own life, and it looks as if Kant were right in saying that we must regard ourselves from two different points of view." The example is irrelevant to the problem. Yes, there is a history of the historian's composition of historical events. Both are series of events in history. But the former series does not stand in the relation of affection to the latter series. That there can be more than one series of historical events is one thing. That the member of one of those series relates to a counterpart member in the other by what Kant calls affection is quite another. The existence of the former is compatible with the absence of the latter; hence, in cases of two series of historical events members of one of which can also view themselves as members of the other series are not valid illustrations of the epistemic relation of affection nor, consequently, of the relation between a thing in itself and an appearance.

Beck, *A Commentary on Kant's Critique of Practical Reason*, says what has to be said here to avoid the muddle that Paton generates for Kant's notion of self-knowledge (pp. 186ff.): "We cannot apply the category of causation to things in themselves so as to have knowledge of them; but we can apply the category by analogy to the relation of *noumena* to *phenomena* and think of the former as a free cause of the latter without infringing on the principle of mechanical causation so far as our possible knowledge is concerned." Here Kant says only that freedom (noumenal causation) does not affect the forms of our sensibility at different places and times but only, as Beck aptly points out, that noumenal causality is compatible with mechanical causality. This avoids the serious philosophical difficulty imported by Paton into Kant's argument according to which noumenal selves as well as things in themselves affect our sensibility. Beck's version of the argument requires only that we be able to apply the *unschematized* category of causation to things that lack the characteristics of our sensibility. This is not a different kind of affection. It is not a kind of affection at all; hence, Paton's puzzle dissolves. This is not to deny that there is a problem of self-knowledge in Kant's theory. Here I have tried to show only that the paradox in Kant's theory of the distinction between the transcendental ideality and reality of time cannot remove the paradox that Paton claims to find in Kant's text.

But Paton is not the worst offender. Paton does—mistakenly, I believe—conflate the relation of a noumenon and an appearance with the very different relation of a thing in itself to an appearance. And this conflation costs him dearly when it comes to explaining how the doctrine of affection can apply to the relation between noumena and appearances. Weldon's *Kant's Critique of Pure Reason* worsens matters by saying that "the noumenon is the concept of the thing in itself, and the thing in itself is the alleged object of which the noumenon is a concept" (p. 193). Weldon goes on to identify both of these notions with that of the transcendental object. A noumenon, whatever else it may be, cannot be the concept of which a thing in itself is the alleged object. A thing in itself assumes a relation to some form of sensibility. Otherwise there could be no affection. A noumenon rests on no such assumption; hence, a thing in itself cannot be even a putative object of a concept of a noumenon. To say that a transcendental object is a Kantian thing in itself is textually unfounded. The concept of a transcendental object is the concept of an object in general (A92=B125). But the concept of such an object is in part the concept of an object falling under the categories. And this is precisely what a thing in itself does not do. (Cf. esp. A251: "[T]he categories represent *no special object* [italics mine], given to the understanding alone, but only serve to determine the transcendental object, which is the concept of something in general, though that which is given in sensibility, in order thereby to know appearances empirically under concepts of objects.")

Consult also Gerold Prauss, *Kant und das Problem der Dinge an sich*, where he distinguishes between things in themselves and what he calls transcendental-philosophical and transcendent-metaphysical interpretations (p. 9). This distinction approximates to the distinction I defend here and elsewhere between an epistemic and an ontological interpretation of transcendental ideality. On the other hand, Peter Heintel, "Die Dialektik bei Kant," tells us that Kantian dialectic is a case of reasoning in which the categories are used "nicht als Bestimmungen von Erscheinungen, sondern als tatsächliche Bestimmungen der Dinge an sich . . . [in thus behaving, the philosopher] sich insofern nicht als transzendentaler Idealist, sondern Realist ausgibt" (p. 451). But, as I show in chapter 6, the issue of the Third Antinomy can be raised irrespective of the issue of transcendental ideality or reality. Heintel merely provides us with yet another example of the history of egregious misunderstandings of just what the antinomy is and what, if anything, Kant takes to resolve it.

Heinz Heimsoeth, "Zum kosmologischen Ursprung der Kantischen Freiheitsantinomie," argues that what he calls the psychological concept of freedom is founded on the cosmological idea of freedom; "Die

Freiheitsantinomie muss in Wahrheit ganz in einem ursprünglichen Seinszusammenhang und gleichsam in Kooperation mit der Vierten Antinomie gesehen werden" (p. 208). The alleged dependence, however, just muddles the issue. No matter how we resolve the Fourth Antinomy, whether the world has or lacks a beginning in time, we still have the problem of deciding whether each event in the world's history, though it has a beginning in time, must stand as a result of a temporally prior cause in time. Moreover, the issue of the Third Antinomy is not whether an act has temporal antecedents but whether an act that does have *temporal* antecedents also has *causal* antecedents.

The irrelevancy of the two antinomies can be set forth even more drastically. Concede that there must be a first cause of all causal chains that is a paradigmatic case of free action just because it cannot stand as an effect to a prior cause. This may be true, but it says nothing about any event of human agency within the cosmic series thus caused. The issue besetting the Third Antinomy is not whether there is a paradigm as the Fourth Antinomy defines it but rather whether every case of human agency has all of the relevant characteristics of the paradigm. The question is, then, whether there are cases of human agency that can have both temporal and causal antecedents but that are nonetheless free in the sense in which the first cause of the Fourth Antinomy is. Here the properties of the absolutely first cause of the Fourth Antinomy cannot be transferred to the elements that allegedly generate the Third Antinomy. The mistake is not isolated. Compare Joong Fang's argument in *Das Antinomienproblem im Entstehungsgang der Transzendentalphilosophie* (pp. 78–79).

In addition, Martin Kalin, "Inference and Illusion in Dialectic," faithfully perpetuates the hermeneutical mistakes in our understanding of what goes on in Kant's Third Antinomy. I restrict my comments here to what Kalin says about the kind of conflict that allegedly takes place in the Third Antinomy. What is wrong, Kalin tells us, is that both thesis and antithesis of the antinomy rest on the assumption that "if the conditioned is given, then the entire sum of conditions, and consequently the unconditioned, also is given" (p. 259). This is, of course, taken from Kant himself, for the literal quotation occurs at A409=B436. Kalin sets up the structure that presumably fits the argument of the Third Antinomy and focuses on what he identifies as a residing assumption of that argument, the assumption, namely, that "[i]f the conditioned is given, then so must all its conditions including the ultimate one(s)" (p. 260). Here Kalin joins the issue. He says that the antinomy arises because the second premiss is ambiguous. If it is analytic, then it is what Kalin calls a "harmless clarification for the concepts of the conditioned and unconditioned" (p. 260). Or if we choose to take the premiss as synthetic, it "can be dismissed as a false—or, again, an empirically unsupportable—claim about the unconditioned as an object of possible sensory experience" (p. 260). So, there is no antinomy. The second premiss is either otiose or false. In either case the conclusion of Kant's argument does not follow. Kalin's dissolution makes the whole issue seem philosophically unimportant.

There is, as I have already argued, no genuine antinomy here. But Kalin cannot explain its absence. That everything that is conditioned requires a condition may be analytic, but it is hardly harmless. What makes the claim philosophically explosive is whether there is something that is unconditioned once we allow the truth of the claim that everything having a condition requires a causally prior conditioned. And the claim that there is or that there is no such thing as an absolutely unconditioned, so far from being a harmless analytic proposition, is not even analytic. It is paradigmatically synthetic. One premiss in Kant's argument for the thesis of the Third Antinomy is, I grant, that every conditioned has a condition. This, as Kalin points out, is merely a semantical unpacking of the notion of conditioned. What is not such a harmless exercise, however, is the claim, essential to the argument for the thesis of Kant's Third Antinomy, that the admission of the series of conditions must end in something that is unconditioned. This is synthetic because it is a thinly disguised existence claim and not an exfoliation of the relation between one condition and another.

To say that the crucial proposition is synthetic makes the issue facing Kant's Third Antinomy no less grave just because we can admit for the sake of the argument that the unconditioned is not an object of possible sensory experience. Kant never makes that a requirement for there being an entity with such a property; and, even if he did, his problem could be easily reformulated without such a property that would just raise the issue of the Third Antinomy all over again.

Finally, suppose there were one solution of the Fourth Antinomy—an absolutely first cause. This would show only that what we *call* an absolutely first cause logically cannot stand as an effect to a prior cause. But it does not show that the absolutely first cause logically might not have occurred. To claim that the Third Antinomy is merely a specialized instance of the Fourth Antinomy confuses two very different senses of what it is to be an absolutely first cause. Something can have this characteristic simply if it is not the effect of a prior cause. But something can have this characteristic only if it is logically impossible for it not to have occurred. This latter characteristic is essential to an absolutely first cause. Without it, the demand for a causal explanation can continue perpetually. But with it, the notion of an absolutely first cause is incompatible with a *free* cause. Thus so far from exemplifying what Kant calls the spontaneous initiation of a causal series, the initial member of such a series is logically incompatible with such an initial member.

Sadik J. Al-Azm, on the other hand, in *The Origins of Kant's Arguments in the Antinomies*, offers an assimilation of the proof of a first cause to the proof of free agency (pp. 87ff). And Jonathan Bennett, *Kant's Dialectic*, gives the most admirable philosophical antidote known to me of the distortions perpetuated by Al-Azm (pp. 186ff.). Stephan Körner sees all of this in "Kant's Conception of Freedom" when he argues (pp. 196ff.) that the argument about a first cause as the sum total of phenomena is logically very different from the argument whether any member of that series can spontaneously initiate a further series. The former assumes an infinitely populous series; the latter does not. H. W. Cassirer, *Kant's First Critique*, is one of the few commentators who join him in this (cf. esp. pp. 306ff.). This point, however, is marred by Körner's claim that the alternative ways in which the pure category of causation can be schematized shows that causation is not applicable to all objective phenomena; hence, causation and freedom are allegedly applicable to one and the same categorial framework. But this move confuses the restricted applicability of a Kantian category to a sensuous manifold with the applicability of one and the same category to different forms of intuition. Kant's argument shows the latter, not the former. The Third Antinomy is not, as Körner claims (p. 110), to be resolved by restricting the applicability of causation within one of its potentially indefinite many schematisms. For the freedom-determinism issue can be raised all over again with respect to each of these schematisms.

W. T. Harris, "Kant's Third Antinomy and His Fallacy Regarding the First Cause," dimly perceives the distinction that Körner so clearly makes between the two logically very different problems facing the Third and the Fourth Antinomies. Harris correctly distinguishes (pp. 5ff.) between the relation between the relation of an event to its initiator on the one hand and the relation between one event and another on the other. But he then wrongly continues to argue that the

Fourth Antinomy is really a case in which there is an initiator of an event and not a case of the existence of a first event.

2. "Trendelenburg-Fischer" Controversy

I distinguish between the ontological and the epistemic interpretations of transcendental ideality. The distinction can be simply stated and is essential to my further claim that there are no things in themselves as they have been traditionally described. We might say that time is transcendentally ideal and mean that it is a necessary condition of our ability to perceive any object whatever without implying that it is only a characteristic of a state of our perceptual consciousness or committing ourselves to saying that the things we perceive would lack this characteristic if there were no states of perceptual consciousness at all. But it does commit us to say that the perceptual objects of our world do have, say, the transcendentally ideal characteristic of time. It is not merely the case that, for example, time is a necessary condition of our ability to perceive things in our world. It is also the case that the things in this world really have the characteristic, albeit contingently, of being temporal. I will not repeat my arguments for this view here because I have already presented them elsewhere. But the Trendelenburg-Fischer controversy, augmented by Vaihinger's attempt at mediation, threatens to undermine my distinction between ontological and epistemic interpretations of transcendental ideality and ultimately to leave the dispute about the relation between a thing in itself and an appearance in the same epistemologically disreputable state in which I found it. But this is simply not so.

Concede for the sake of this hoary dispute that, as Trendelenburg assures us, there are three possibilities for the status of space and time, declared by Kant to be transcendentally ideal. In the first place, we might say that space and time are objective either in the sense that they are absolute (i.e., that what we call space and time are really places and moments, respectively) or that they are characteristics of things that exist independently of acts of consciousness. In the second place, we might say that space, for example, is a subjective characteristic of our minds. (Trendelenburg: "er haftet nur an der subjektiven Beschaffenheit unseres Gemüts.") But there is a third possibility, we are told, that Kant does not consider, that is internally consistent, and the existence of which even as a logical possibility vitiates Kant's argument for the transcendental ideality of space and time: Both the first and second alternatives might be simultaneously true without internal inconsistency. Thus Trendelenburg.

In this controversy, Fischer flatly rejects the third possibility as logically inconsistent. Space and time are merely subjective (Fischer: "sind nur subjektiv und nicht real . . . "). And this precludes them from being objective as well because the claim that space and time are merely subjective (transcendentally ideal) implies that their alleged objectivity is internally inconsistent. To say that something is objective is to imply that it is real; hence, Trendelenburg's third possibility, so far from being a conceptual possibility, is merely a flat contradiction.

Here Vaihinger intervenes (p. 137). He distinguishes what he calls the question of validity (*Geltungsfrage*) from the question of origin (*Ursprungsfrage*). Once we apply this distinction to the notion of transcendental ideality, the whole issue dividing Trendelenburg and Fischer dissolves because each participant in the dispute is interpreting the notion of transcendental ideality in a different way. Time and space can belong to things in themselves if we mean that we acquire our notions of such characteristics from an examination of the things we perceive. But if we mean that space and time are necessary conditions of our perceiving anything and go on to say that they might still be characteristics of things in themselves, then we do contradict ourselves. For we are saying both that we can learn what a necessary condition of our perceiving anything is by experience while at the same time assuming the validity of that condition in order to establish that it is necessary for us to be able to perceive what we claim to perceive.

I recount this ancient quarrel only to show that, whatever its outcome, it does not endanger my distinction between an epistemic and an ontological interpretation of transcendental ideality. Trendelenburg's third possibility and Fischer's attempt to rebut it are as foreign to my distinction as Vaihinger's effort at conceptual illumination is to the issue facing any of the issues involved here. Begin by supposing that things in themselves have the very properties that are the necessary epistemic conditions of our perceiving them. This is the Trendelenburg claim and its very logical possibility should be able to shatter my distinction between an epistemic and an ontological sense of the notion of transcendental ideality.

If Trendelenburg is right, then the third possibility he allows (called the *Trendelenburgische Lücke*) assumes what I have called the ontological interpretation of transcendental ideality and tacitly denies the possibility of the epistemic interpretation of that notion. To say, as Trendelenburg does, that the third alternative constitutes the claim that forms of intuition are both objective characteristics of things as well as subjective characteristics of our perceptual apparatus is just to assimilate the epistemic to the ontological interpretation of transcendental ideality. To adopt Trendelenburg's third alternative is, accordingly, not to say merely that we cannot know whether things have or lack the characteristics under which we perceive them but rather that we can know the properties they have both within and without the bounds of possible experience.

But this is not so. The principles of division are different. Trendelenburg claims that the characteristics that are necessary conditions of our perceiving objects are also properties of the objects we observe. For in order to find this out we should have to be able to compare the necessary conditions of the objects that we now observe with those same objects lacking those conditions in order to find out whether what we now perceive has the same characteristics when they exist outside the possibility of our perceiving them. In order to know this we would *per impossibile* have to compare one and the same object under the conditions necessary for us to perceive it and those under which we could not be able to perceive it. And this is so even if the latter conditions are ontologically no different from the former. Nothing follows about the epistemic identity of those conditions. The Trendelenburg claim is, therefore, in its own perverse way true: We could be put in a situation in which the conditions that are necessary for us to perceive an object are really characteristics of the object even though we could not be put in a position to know that such a claim is true. There is a distinction between epistemic and ontological senses of transcendental ideality. If what is to count as transcendentally ideal is understood epistemically, then we are claiming only that we cannot know whether the objects governed by our forms of intuition are spatially or temporally independent of those forms. But if we impose the ontological interpretation on Kant's notion of a form of intuition, then we make an implicit claim that we do know something about the characteristics of things independent of our forms of intuition. For we claim to know that they lack spatial or temporal properties.

All of this leaves Fischer in an equally perverse situation. True, it is logically impossible to say that the epistemic conditions under which we perceive objects can also be ontological characteristics of those objects—but not for the reasons that Fischer gives. He assumes, falsely, that we can *know* that the epistemic conditions are or are not also on-tological characteristics of what we perceive. But in order to know this, we would have to have a way of putting ourselves in the same impossible position toward which Trendelenburg wants to push us. And this gives us the conclusion that both parties to the dispute actu-ally agree, that Vaihinger's intercession is superfluous, and my distinc-tion between epistemic and ontological sense of transcendental ideality is still intact.

Furthermore, Ristitisch, *Die indirekten Beweise des transzenden-talen Idealismus*, argues that Trendelenburg fails to show that space and time have exclusive subjectivity (pp. 22ff.). They might also be properties of things in themselves (*die Trendelenburgische Lücke*). But there is no such *Lücke*. Trendelenburg's claim concerns only our abil-ity to *know* whether things independently of possible human experi-ence are spatial or temporal. This is right. But Ristitisch does not rec-oncile this with the claim according to which Trendelenburg calls the forms of our intuition subjective and thus does not explain how there can be a *Lücke* in the first place. Nor does Trendelenburg's claim re-quire this; hence, no collapse of the epistemic interpretation of the dis-tinction between things in themselves and appearances.

3. "Epistemic Interpretation of Transcendental Ideality" Controversy

The older literature burgeons with claims that what I have called the epistemic interpretation of transcendental ideality is indispensable to the resolution of the Third Antinomy. Simon Brysz, for example, in *Das Ding an sich und die empirische Anschauung in Kants Philoso-phie*, tells us that the antinomy can be resolved only if we take time to be transcendentally ideal (pp.4–5). Brysz says that Kant's inability to prove this theoretically enables us to decide it practically (p. 19). Hermann Lotze's *Metaphysic* follows this line in saying that the anti-nomy can arise in the first place only if you assume, incorrectly, that space and time are real characteristics of objects and that it can be re-solved only on the assumption that they are not (1 : 201ff.).

All of this slides by the real issue that the Third Antinomy raises. The problem here arises independently of whether we take time to be transcendentally real or ideal. Whether there are events that can be initiated without being caused by preceding events is a question we can ask even if we assume that all temporal relations are somehow mental or subjective. This shows that the freedom-determinism issue is logically independent of the real-ideal issue with respect to the forms of our sensibility. And—what is even more philosophically bizarre —the distinction between things in themselves and appearances applies to a world that is purely temporal just as much as it applies to a world in which we distinguish between temporal and physical items. Thus the introduction of the transcendental ideality of time merely gives us the same problem we had before in another rather thin disguise. In a world in which every item is temporal, you still have the problem of what is caused. The issue of universal causation, then, is logically independent of whether time is transcendentally ideal or real; hence, the assumption of the transcendental ideality of time no more resolves the Third Antinomy than it provides us with an independent proof of the transcendental ideality of time. It is not the answer to this difficulty to say that there are objects that appear to us to have temporal characteristics but that really lack them apart from our sensibility. The antinomy arises with respect to the situation in which objects appear to have temporal characteristics with respect to our sensibility. It also arises for a domain that lacks time and space as forms of intuition.

What I have been calling the duplication problem and linking with the problem of affection was completely ignored by the older literature. One paradigm here can stand for many. John Watson, *The Philosophy of Kant Explained*, says, for example, that the Third Antinomy cannot be resolved if phenomena are regarded as things in themselves (pp. 272ff.). For then, according to Watson, a spontaneous cause would merely be a member of the same series as its effects; hence, there could be no absolutely first initiator of a causal series. Watson's argument is intellectually transparent. If there were only appearances, each member of the causal series would have to stand as an effect of a causally prior appearance. Concede the transparency for the sake of the argument. Watson's reconstruction of the Third Antinomy fatally collapses at two places. To claim that there are entities called things in themselves that, among other characteristics, do not stand as effects to prior causes, so far from giving us an indirect argument for the distinction between things in themselves and appearances, merely perpetuates the very problem it is alleged to solve. If a thing in itself is supposed to be an uninitiated initiator of a temporal causal series, then it must stand in a temporal relation to the other members of the set of effects it initiates. And this merely reproduces the problem that a thing in itself is supposed to solve. Even if we suppose that things in themselves are timelessly related to one another, the same problem about initiating a causal series without itself being an effect of a prior cause can be defined, according to Kant's theory of schematism, independently of any reference to temporal relations at all. So whatever the problem, it has nothing to do with the temporal relations of the entities that are caused, but rather with the possibility of there being a cause that is not the effect of a prior cause—all of which can be raised, as Kant himself acknowledges, without any reference to the accidents of our schematism of the category of causation. Watson continues this confusion in his *Kant and His English Critics*, chapter 10.

4. "Affection" Controversy

Kant asks us to suppose that the relation of a thing in itself to an appearance is the affection of the former on the forms of our intuition. He says at A20=B34 that "[t]he effect of an object upon the faculty of representation, so far as we are *affected* by it, is *sensation*" (first italics mine). Compare A19=B33: "But intuition takes place only insofar as the object is given to us." Consider further also A44=B61 and A494=B522. Two points are crucial to my argument here. (1) Affection is not causation. It is not a connection between one event and another necessarily according to rule. Nor can it be a relation between something and an object that is produced by the action of that thing on our sensibility. The presence of an object to our modes of sensibility may be a necessary condition of our ability to *perceive* it, but it cannot *mean* the same thing as our perceiving the object. If it did, then the explication of what it is to perceive something would be circular since it assumes that we are affected by the object we perceive as a necessary condition of our perceiving it. (2) Affection designates the fact that something is present in our sensory field. It is, therefore, compatible with any theory of what it is to perceive what is present in such a field.

Otto Riedel, *Die Bedeutung des Dinges an sich in der Kantischen Ethik*, was the first to distinguish between the use of affection as an answer to a psychological question of how we acquire the sensations we have and the transcendental question of how the objects, irrespec-

tive of how we learn about them, are given to us. Thus Riedel concludes that "das Gegebensein und das Afficiertwerden durchaus kor-
respondierende Begriffe sind" (p. 19). The issue for Riedel is not the
relation of a cause to its sensations but rather the transcendental
meaning of the concept of what it is to be given to intuition irrespective of the apparatus by which this fact is explained. In *Die monadologischen Bestimmungen in Kants Lehre vom Ding an sich*, Riedel
anticipated the later view on affection. Affection cannot be causation,
then, because the latter is a relation that holds between one appearance and another and not between an appearance and its ground. But
since this is so, then what we are asked to call affection is no more
than the designation of the fact that we stand in a relation of perceptual awareness to an object—in which case what Kant calls a noumenon cannot be a thing in itself because we would be perceptually aware
of what by definition we cannot be perceptually aware. Compare here
what Goethe says: "Wer ein Phänomen vor Augen hat, denkt schon oft
drüber hinaus; wer nur davon erzählen hört, denkt gar nichts" (*Werke*,
12:434).

This can be put in another way. The Third Antinomy allows us two
ways in which we can relate affection to causation. We can say, on the
one hand, that our sensibility is affected just in case something of one
event-kind always precedes something else of another event-kind necessarily according to a rule. This is just a truncated statement of Kant's
Second Analogy. But, on the other hand, the notion of Kantian affection allows us just as easily to say that our sensibility is affected whenever something acts directly upon our sensibility. This counts, not as
the simultaneous occurrence of two different events nor as a successive
occurrence of two numerically different events, but rather as the occurrence of one and the same event.

Kantian affection must be a case of the third and not of the first or
second situations, and for the following reasons. (1) This is why affection is not a theory about the mechanism of perception at all. It gives
us only a semantical means of designating a commonsensical state of
affairs that any adequate theory must account for. (2) The notion of
affection does not imply the existence of the distinction between
things in themselves and appearances. (3) Nor does it commit one to
the adoption of what I have called the epistemic or the ontological theories of transcendentality. (4) The notion of affection shows the logical
irrelevance of the distinction between the transcendental reality and

ideality of time to the solution of the problem facing Kant's Third Antinomy. Even if you say that time is transcendentally real, all you are saying is that the temporal characteristics of the things we perceive belong to them whether they are objects of possible experience or not. And this tells you nothing about whether what is present to your perceptual consciousness might not also be an event-kind that does, after all, follow upon an antecedent event of another kind necessarily according to a rule.

The general issue of affection is complicated enough. In chapter 1 I trace that doctrine to its sources in other theories that Kant holds. But the whole issue of affection shifts with what Kant calls the Paradox of Self-Knowledge. Here, again, I raise an issue only to ignore it because it is irrelevant to my present purpose. That issue is, however, peripherally relevant to the distinction between noumenal and phenomenal selfhood in Kant. Kant repeatedly tells us that we can conceive of ourselves in at least two ways. We can think of ourselves as being members of a kingdom of ends (noumenal selves) or as belonging to the phenomenal world (phenomenal selves). The issue of affection does not apply here. In conceiving of myself, for example, as a member of one or the other of the two worlds, I am not providing a case in which the self affects itself or of what Kant considers to be a case of the Paradox of Self-Knowledge. Here there are two deceptively similar but actually quite different issues. (1) Does our ability to *conceive* of ourselves in a certain way imply the existence of a relation of affection between the object we conceive ourselves to be and the subject that conceives himself to be that way? (2) Does Kant's distinction between phenomena and noumena (I do not say "things in themselves"!) imply the existence of two different selves?

If we say "Yes" to the second question, then we commit ourselves to the doctrine of affection and the Paradox of Self-Knowledge in our answer to the first question. And this is just wrong. Nothing in what Kant says about our ability to conceive of ourselves in different ways shows that there are, in fact, two selves or that there exists the problem of reconciling this with the fact that the subject of thought can be aware of itself. There is, of course, the Paradox of Self-Knowledge. But it is not generated by the distinction between phenomena and noumena. Nor can the introduction of such a distinction solve the paradox.

See Martin, *Immanuel Kant,* for an instance of a confusion of these two questions (pp. 203ff.). Here the semantically seductive play is on the word "spontaneity." And this is where the confusion of the two questions that I have sketchily distinguished above touches on the issue of Kant's Third Antinomy. Speaking for Kant, Martin says that "wir auch im Selbstbewusstsein der objektiven Realität der Freiheit gewiss sein können, dass wir aber trotzdem nicht erkennen können, wie Freiheit im eigentlichen realen Sinne möglich ist" (p. 205). Martin goes further. He claims that there is no freedom without consciousness of freedom—that what is called the intelligible existence of the spontaneous subject just doesn't exist if we don't think it does (p. 207). And, finally, Martin tells us that spontaneity cannot grasp itself as spontaneity because, if such were the case, we would be both the observer and what is observed (pp. 210–11). And this would allegedly exclude the very possibility of observing pure spontaneity as such. But, Martin concludes for Kant, we cannot know (*erkennen*) the intelligible subject that is the noumenal ego, but we can nevertheless think (*denken*) it.

None of this resolves the problem that Kant sets himself in the Third Antinomy. We can concede that we can conceive of ourselves in two different ways. But nothing follows from this about the existence of a noumenal and a phenomenal self; hence, it does not show how it is possible to initiate a causal series without standing as the effect to a prior cause. Yet this is precisely what Kant purports to do in his attempt to resolve the Third Antinomy. Every member of the causal series in time might be able to conceive of himself in two different ways without curtailing the infinite regress of causes.

So, too, with the distinction between thinking and knowing: It suffers fatally from two wounds. It cannot solve the Paradox of Self-Knowledge. And, what is equally damning, it cannot establish the distinction between a phenomenal and a noumenal self that might be used, successfully or not, to stop the infinite regress of causes. Concede, momentarily, the fact that I know myself in that I am presented with an object in intuition that I correctly describe on some criterion or other as *my* self. This admittedly generates the Paradox of Self-Knowledge. Martin sees this and I concede it. But suppose now that we change our jargon, as Martin proposes, and say, rather, that in such a case I am only *thinking* and not really *knowing* my *self*. There is, however, still an object of thought before me when I think of myself. This is enough to generate the Paradox of Self-Knowledge even if what I think is something that I cannot intuit. From here it is only one quick step to the irrelevance of the distinction between thinking and knowing as to the Third Antinomy. Even if I could think of my self without knowing (intuiting) it, the problem of the infinite causal series of phenomena does not go away. For there remains the problem of a possibly infinite series of selves who, try as they might, succeed only in thinking of themselves but not ever really knowing themselves. In either case, the problem of the Third Antinomy remains.

NOTES

Chapter 1. Double Affection

1. *Critique of Pure Reason*, A20=B34. (All unspecified references in the sequel are to the foregoing work.) The major statement of double affection is in Erich Adickes, *Kants Lehre von der doppelten Affektion unseres Ich*, pp. 27–59, pp. 32ff. (hereafter cited as *KL*). Cf. Herbert Herring, *Das Problem der Affektion bei Kant*, for a review of the history of the problem. Cf. also Hans Vaihinger, *Commentar zu Kant's 'Kritik der reinen Vernunft'* (hereafter cited as *CZ*), for a review of the sources out of which the theory of double affection grew. See T. D. Weldon, *Kant's "Critique of Pure Reason,"* pp. 252–56, and Norman Kemp Smith, *A Commentary to Kant's "Critique of Pure Reason,"* Appendix C, for brief English summaries of the Adickes view. I consciously restrict my discussion of *DA* to the first *Kritik*. I do this despite the claim of Norman Kemp Smith, *Commentary*, p. 614, that the *Opus postumum* is the place at which *DA* emerges in its most explicit form. What distinguishes Kant's view in the first *Kritik* from his view in the *Opus postumum* is primarily a thesis in the latter concerning the productivity of the ego. Thus in the *Opus postumum* Kant claims that the thing in itself is "the mere representation of the self's activity" (cited by Erich Adickes, *Kant's "Opus postumum," dargestellt und beurteilt*, p. 654). This marks a distinction between the two works, but it does not mark an advanced form of *DA* for the simple reason that *DA* assumes a relation of affection and such a relation cannot obtain if one of the ostensible terms of that relation is a product of the other term. The theory to be found in the *Opus postumum* is not, I conclude, relevant to the assessment of the quite different theory that

217

adherents of *DA* allege is to be found in the first *Kritik*. Significantly, where the two theories do agree, Adickes cites the argument from the first *Kritik*. If the basis for *DA* in the first *Kritik* can be disqualified, the corresponding passages in the *Opus postumum* will also be disqualified. Cf. Norman Kemp Smith, *Commentary*, pp. 625 ff., for a comprehensive list of references to the peculiarity of the *Opus postumum* theory.

2. Kant says that things in themselves are the primary sources of sensible experience at A538=B566, A540=B568, A557=B585, A564=B594, A565–66=B493–94, and A613=B641–42.

3. Cf. Smith, *Commentary*, pp. 217–18, 275 ff., for an enumeration and discussion of the relevant passages.

4. A19=B33.

5. A19=B33; cf. A493=B522. For a critical assessment of this alternative, see Henry E. Allison, *The Kant-Eberhard Controversy*, pp. 29 ff.

6. I follow here the statement of *DA* given by Adickes in *KL*; Hans Vaihinger in *CZ*, 2:35–55, gives a similar formulation. For a good summary of Vaihinger, see Anton Thomson, "Bemerkungen zur Kritik des Kantischen Begriffes des Dinges an sich," p. 254 ff.

7. Cf. Adickes, *KL*, p. 14. The textual basis for the coinage "appearance in itself" is A28–29=B44–45. The defense of such a notion is in Adickes, *KL*, pp. 22 ff., especially p. 22: "Die räumliche Aussenwelt ist also zwar Erscheinung, aber nicht eine solche des empirischen Ich; ihm ist sie vielmehr gleichgestellt, steht ihm selbständig und unabhängig gegenüber, wird nicht von ihm produziert, sondern (als eine vom Ich an sich geschaffene) vorgefunden besitzt also im Verhältnis zu ihm eine Art von An-sich Charakter."

8. The terms "empirical affection" and "transcendent affection" are Vaihinger's but are also used by Adickes, *KL*, p. 4. Adickes, *KL*, pp. 22 ff., puts it as follows: (1) the empirical ego generates empirical representations because it is affected by spatial objects; (2) but these objects are also appearances; and (3) they are produced (*geschaffen*) by the ego in itself; (4) appearances exist in themselves (*an sich*) for the empirical ego but are mere appearances (*blosse Erscheinungen*) for the ego in itself; and (5) the result of empirical affection is sensation (*Empfindung*).

Robert Pippin, *Kant's Theory of Form*, especially pp. 199–200, follows a similar line. We can consider appearances empirically or transcendentally. In the former case, we have objects that are caused by outer objects; in the latter, we consider all objects as conditioned by the form of sensibility we have. The former is a case of causation, the latter, of affection. Cf. p. 204, where he appeals to the phenomenal object considered independently of its relation to our forms of experience as distinct from the same object considered as given to us under those forms. But the problem about affection versus causation arises within the context of the empirical relation in which we stand to objects. We may be able to consider them transcendentally, but the description of what we are considering in this way does not remove the problem concerning the relation between affection and causation when an object acts on our sensibility.

The notion of an object considered independently of the forms of experience has been exploited to the same end by different means. Cf. H. Herring, *Das Problem der Affektion*, pp. 80–96, where he introduces Kant's notion of a transcendental object in order to account for what it is to be a thing in itself. Our notion of the transcendental object is a thought of something indeterminate and represents a thing in general. But the solution is defective. What affects us is a determinate object, not an object in general. And a determinate object cannot be understood by an appeal to an indeterminate object. Cf.

George Schrader's insightful "The Thing in Itself in Kantian Philosophy," for the antidote to this kind of theory.

Cf. also Richard Aquila, "Things in Themselves and Appearances: Intentionality and
Reality in Kant," p. 297, for a correct understanding of the revised version of the *TDT*.
But he incorrectly concludes that theory like the *TDT* as revised involves two different
senses of "existence." Thus p. 298: "Existing as thing in itself would be existing in a
sense which requires no appeal to the possibility of experience." The argument here
feeds on a confusion of what Aquila calls two senses of "existence" with two different
states of affairs in which one and the same particular can be a part. See also Richard
Aquila, "Is Sensation the Matter of Appearances?" Here he correctly reinforces the
claim that Kantian appearances are not a kind of particular numerically diverse from
Kantian things in themselves by distinguishing between sensation (*Empfindung*) and appearance (*Erscheinung*). To say that sensation is not the matter of appearance is to remove the temptation to make the particular in a phenomenal state of affairs into something other than the particular in a thing in itself. Sensation may itself be one kind of
appearance. But what is important here is to see that the form-matter distinction must
be made independently of the distinction between a sensation and an appearance. Each
has a form and a matter. A sensation cannot be the matter of an appearance with which
it is associated. Aquila confirms this approach in his "Intentional Objects and Kantian
Appearances," where he argues that Kantian appearances are not particulars in their
own right but rather so many ways in which the particulars present in things in themselves appear to us.

Aquila explores the consequences of this position in "Two Lines of Argument in
Kant's Transcendental Aesthetic." He argues that the Kantian notion of a sensation
designates not an object of intuition but rather the means by which we come to be acquainted with such objects. Sensations are the effects of an object on our sensory apparatus. They need not, therefore, be what we are aware of by means of this causal activity.
Kantian objects of immediate awareness need not be causal objects. This provides further evidence for the integrity of the affection relation and the revised version of the
TDT. In his "*A priori* Form and *a priori* Knowledge in the Transcendental Aesthetic,"
Aquila makes the same point by appealing to the distinction between *de re* and *de dicto*
perception.

Aquila's suggestion is that we must distinguish between something through which
something else is presented to us and something that is presented by means of it. The
validity of this suggestion must, however, be protected from an ostensibly strong objection to it. The fact is that we can introspect our sensations even though we cannot accomplish such an act while we perceive something else through it. Our ability to introspect sensations would seem to violate the distinction between affection and causation.
Such an ability would seem to allow sensations to function as objects of perceptual
awareness and stand only in a causal relation to the objects we claim to perceive. Cf.
Peter Krausser, "Kant's Theory of the Structure of Empirical Scientific Inquiry and Two
Implied Postulates Regarding Things in Themselves." The antidote to such an objection
is the understanding that the distinction between being something through which we
are aware of something else and the object of which we are aware does not *define* a
sensation as distinct from an object of a sensation. A sensation, considered merely as a
matter of general fact, performs the task of being that through which we gain perceptual
access to objects. But this is a fact about and not a definition of the notion of sensation.
The validity of the more basic distinction between affection and causation thus remains
intact.

9. Cf. Adickes, *KL*, p. 22, and Vaihinger, *CZ*, 1 : 35.

10. What follows is a summary of Adickes, *KL*, p. 35. The theory has not died out. More recently Wilfrid Sellars in *Science and Metaphysics* has endorsed it. Cf. especially p. 52: "The doctrine of 'double affection' is an essential feature of Kant's thought. Correctly understood, it simply tells us that the transcendentally conceived non-spatial, non-temporal action of the non-ego on human receptivity, generating the manifold of sense (which action is required to explain how the *esse* of the experienced world can be *concipi* and yet non-arbitrary and inter-subjective) has as its counterpart in the represent*ed* world the action of material things on our sense organs and, through them, on the sensory faculties of the empirical self."

11. For this distinction see especially the *Opus postumum*, AA 22, 339, 363–65.

12. A28=B45.

13. B307.

14. I am aware that Kant has more than one way of distinguishing between sensuous and nonsensuous faculties of intuition. One such way apparently diverges from the claim I make about the implications of the inevitability of some kind of account of the distinction between our acquaintance with particulars and our acquaintance with concepts. Thus as early as *De mundi sensibilis atque intelligibilis forma et principiis*, §10, he claims that the distinction between these two kinds of apprehension would not apply to a being with nonsensuous intuition. The same claim runs through Kant's entire development. It emerges again in a letter to Marcus Herz dated 21 February 1772 (*AA* 8, 689). Passages like these do not disconfirm my claim that we must be able to make the distinction between sensibility and intellect even with respect to beings that have nonsenuous forms of intuition. All that it requires is the distinction between beings that lack any faculty of intuition at all and those that have a faculty of intuition with characteristics unlike ours.

15. Cf. *Prolegomena*, §13, n.II; A28=B44; A358ff. Other passages containing what purports to be discussion of empirical affection are *De mundi sensibilis atque intelligibilis forma et principiis*, §3, §4, and §15A; cf. also *Reflexion* 4972. Adickes, *KL*, p. 13n.1, gives an extensive list of similar passages in the *Opus postumum*. but if my argument is correct, none of them establishes the existence of two kinds of affection.

16. A45=B63–A46=B64; cf. A232=B285, A257=B313, A393. Adickes, *KL*, p. 35, cites this as a case of implied empirical affection without distinguishing it from the rose example.

17. Cf. my "Causation and Direct Realism."

18. P. F. Strawson, *The Bounds of Sense*, pp. 41ff., exemplifies the confusion of causation and affection. He claims, for example (p. 41), that for Kant a thing in itself is what science tells us is the constitution of nature, whereas phenomenal objects are the result of the causal action of entities so constituted on our sensory apparatus. Strawson rightly objects that such a doctrine is intelligible only so long as we think of the thing that affects us as being spatio-temporal. Without this provision, the notion of affection is, I agree, meaningless. What goes wrong with the Strawsonian criticism, however, is that it falsely assumes affection to be a kind of causation. It thereby fails to lay bare the real relation between things in themselves and the forms of intuition in affection. A similar mistake is to be found in Jonathan Bennett, *Kant's Analytic*, pp. 19ff. For a more extended discussion of this issue set in a different context, see my "Causation and Direct Realism."

19. A28=B44; *Prolegomena*, §13.

20. Adickes, *KL*, pp. 67–74.

21. A28=B44 and A36=B52.

22. A26=B42ff; A33=B49ff. Cf. A36=B53 and A44=B62ff.

23. Cf. Adickes, *KL*, p. 69, where he claims that for Kant "die Subjektivität der sekundären Sinnesqualitäten einen ganz anderen Ursprung hat als die Idealität von Raum und Zeit: hier kommt die geistige Organisation des Ich an sich, dort die des empirischen Ich als Quelle in Betracht."

24. Cf. Adickes, *KL*, p. 69.

25. The major passages here are A29=B44ff., A29, and *Prolegomena*, §13. Cf. also Hans Vaihinger, *CZ*, 2:353ff. For the classical statements of the primary-secondary distinction, see John Locke, *Essay Concerning Human Understanding*, bk. 2, chap. 8, and George Berkeley, *The Principles of Human Knowledge*, secs. 9–20. The most thorough recent discussion of the distinction is given by Reginald Jackson, "Locke's Distinction between Primary and Secondary Qualities."

26. Cf. Adickes, *KL*, pp. 74ff; Vaihinger, *CZ*, 2:180.

27. A431=B459. Cf. *Metaphysische Anfangsgründe der Naturwissenschaft* (*AA* 4, 510), translated into English by James Ellington (Indianapolis: Bobbs-Merrill Company, 1970), pp. 58–59.

28. Cf. *De mundi sensibilis atque intelligibilis forma et principiis*, §4, §16, §22, and §27. See also Erich Adickes, *Kant und das Ding an Sich*, pp. 7, 12, 28.

29. Cf. Adickes, *KL*, pp. 78–79.

30. CF. A251, A538=B566, A566=B594; *Prolegomena*, §32, §57. Cf. Also Adickes, *Kant und das Ding an Sich*, pp. 4ff.

31. Cf. Adickes, *KL*, pp. 81ff.

32. A127ff, B165.

33. For Kant's definition of "affinity," see A113. Cf. A122 and A600=B628.

34. B164, A125, A127, and B134ff.

35. Cf. Adickes, *KL*, pp. 84ff.

36. Ibid., pp. 91ff.

37. Ibid., p. 91.

38. For a discussion of this issue in a wider context, see my *Kant, Ontology, and the A Priori*, chap. 5 esp. For further discussion of the distinction between general and particular rules of synthesis, see my "Must Transcendental Arguments Be Spurious?" pp. 304ff. For a more microscopic study of the development of this whole issue, consult my "Do Transcendental Arguments Have a Future?" pp. 23ff.

39. The suggestion I consider here was first made by Trendelenburg and led to the famous Trendelenburg-Fischer controversy. For a good description of the course of that controversy, see Vaihinger, *CZ*, 2:134ff.

40. A19=B34. Cf. also A320=B376 and *Prolegomena*, §8. In his "Kant's Philosophy of Arithmetic," Charles Parsons has stated this and the following criterion in some detail. Manley Thompson, "Singular Terms and Intuitions in Kant's Epistemology," p. 332, adds what he calls a uniqueness condition to the application of terms denoting the contents of intuition. I consciously ignore this. Even if the criteria for application of "intuition" were to be supplemented in this way, nothing follows about the necessary spatio-temporality of what is uniquely designated.

41. Cf. A25=B39.

42. Cf. A25=B39.

43. Cf. A32=B47ff.

44. For a discussion of this issue in a broader context, cf. chap. 2.

45. A41=B52.

46. A38=B54.

47. A26=B42.

48. Cf. Edwin B. Allaire, "Existence, Independence, and Universals," for a discussion of this kind of dependence.

49. Ibid.

50. Much of what I argue here is seriously blurred by a hermeneutical tradition most recently represented by J. N. Findlay, *Kant and the Transcendental Object*. He begins (p. 1) by saying that a thing in itself and an appearance are not different objects but rather the same object "conceived in respect of certain intrinsically unapparent features." He goes on to say (p. 2) that "we must also conceive of what is thus non-apparent as so *affecting* [italics in text] us that it can appear before us, or be variously given in experience." Each of these claims has adverse consequences. Are these nonapparent features possessed by objects in our world or in some other, possible, world? If the claim is about our world, then we have just another version of the *TWT* with a new twist. Here what constitutes the duality of worlds is not the *particulars* that have the properties some of which are apparent and others not but rather *states of affairs*. This illustrates the inherent instability of Findlay's description. If "object" means "particular," then there is no difference between a thing in itself and an appearance. If "object" means "state of affairs," then we have a disguised version of the *TWT*. This is instructive because it correctly mirrors the inherent instability of the tradition. Findlay's description requires that what is inherently nonapparent affect what is apparent. But the consequence of his first claim prevents this. It fulfills the Cognitivity Condition but not the Affection Condition.

Cf. Lauchlan Chipman, "Things in Themselves," in which he represents a tradition of writers who ignore the distinction between particulars and states of affairs as it applies to the distinction between things in themselves and appearances. He argues that such an identification would imply the applicability of Kant's categories to things in themselves. (Cf. ibid., pp. 499–500.) Chipman suggests an amendment to Kant's list of categories. We must remove the categories of existence (reality) and identity (unity). He tries to avoid such an amendment by introducing what he calls qua-predication. We can talk about an object as though it possessed a property without committing ourselves to the subsumption of that object under a category. Qua-predicates enable us to talk about things in themselves without applying categories to them. The issue facing the epistemic availability of Kantian things in themselves cannot, however, be resolved by talking about them as though they fell under categories. This merely postpones the problem we have with things in themselves in our world to a possible world and thereby inherits the problems of the traditional version of the *TDT*. Chipman's way out ignores the more convenient expedient of saying that things in themselves fall under the unschematized but not the schematized categories. It is in this sense that they are unknowable. Cf. Josef Simon, "Phenomena and Noumena: On the Use and Meaning of the Categories."

Chapter 2. Things in Themselves (I)

1. *Critique of Pure Reason*, A191=B236; A249–50. All unspecified references in the sequel are to the foregoing work.

2. A46=B63. Cf. B69. The vagueness about the relation between appearances and phenomenal substances on the one hand and the relation of appearances and things in themselves on the other gives superficial support to skeptical interpretations of Kant's notion of substance. See my "The Skeptical Attack on Substance: Kantian Answers" for an attempt to remove the temptation of this skeptical tendency.

3. Characteristic statements of this position occur at A39=B56; A276=B332; A492=B520–A493=B522; A525=B563.

4. B69.

5. Cf. A36=B52.

6. Hermann Cohen, *Kants Theorie der Erfahrung*, p. 252; Hans Vaihinger, *The Philosophy of 'As-If'*, chap. 17 esp. Cf. Kuno Fischer, *Geschichte der neueren Philosophie*, 3:219–21. All of them hold that a thing in itself is the end of an infinite series of appearances. Cf. Eva Schaper, "The Kantian Thing in Itself as a Philosophical Fiction," for a discussion of Vaihinger's interpretation of Kant.

7. A249; cf. A252–53; B310; A287=B344; *Prolegomena*, para 32; *Nachlass*, 4522. Cf. W. Westphal, "In Defense of the Thing in Itself," for a discussion of these passages in relation to Kant's notion of intellectual intuition. The claim is that we should understand the relation between a thing in itself and an appearance in terms of two kinds of awareness. The same object can appear to us under forms of intuition (a Kantian echtypal intellect) or it is logically possible for an intellect (a Kantian archetypal intellect) to be aware of that object without any forms of intuition at all. In the former case, we are aware of an appearance; in the latter, we would be aware of the same object without any forms of intuition at all.

The evidence does support the conclusion that it is logically possible for an intellect to be aware of objects apart from any forms of intuition at all. But it fails to explain the relation of things in themselves to appearances when we are presented by objects under forms of intuition. The theory confirms my view that things in themselves are particulars that are logically independent of the forms of intuition under which we happen to be perceptually aware of them. It does not, however, show that the hypothetical case of an archetypal intellect is an awareness of a thing in itself apart from all forms of intuition rather than an awareness of a Kantian noumenon. The importance of Westphal's argument is that we can specify the individuation of a perceptual object apart from any given form of intuition under which it is given to us.

Cf. my "Intellectual Intuition: The Continuity Thesis," where I distinguish three different kinds of intellectual intuition (*intellektuelle Anschauung*) that occur in Kant's thought. First, Kant counts as a case of intellectual intuition any intellect that can be aware of objects independently of all forms of intuition whatever. He also counts as intuitive any intellect that is perceptually aware of the sum total (*der Inbegriff*) of all appearances. And, finally, an intellect is intuitive for Kant if it creates the objects of which it is aware by the very act of conceiving them. Despite the differences in specification, all of these uses of the notion of intellectual intuition share the common feature that they are used to specify objects that are not given to us in intuition but not things in themselves as such. Thus the first sense of the notion requires that an intuitive intellect be able to know objects independently of sensibility. This, however, is silent about whether those objects are things in themselves properly so called. The second use of the notion stipulates only that intellectual intuition enables its possessor to be aware of a set of things that is not itself an appearance. This capacity is independent of the issue of the relation between an appearance and a thing in itself. Even though such a set is not an appearance, it still does not follow that it is a thing in itself. And, finally, an intuitive intellect may be one that creates its objects by the very act of conceiving of them. But this does not distinguish noumenal entities and, for that matter, entities like the round square and the golden mountain, from bona fide things in themselves that affect our sensibility. Cf. Walter Bröcker, "Kants Lehre von der äusseren Affektion," pp. 152–53, and Martin Heidegger, *Kant und das Problem der Metaphysik*, pp. 36–37, argue for the rejection of the *TWT*.

Cf. Eric Stenius, "On Kant's Distinction between Phenomena and Noumena" (p. 233), who distinguishes between a noumenon as a limiting concept and an independent entity in its own right. He then reports Kant's distinction between a positive and a negative noumenon, saying that the former is the object of nonsensible intuition and the latter "what remains when we abstract from a phenomenon all that is attributed to it by our sensible intuition" (p. 239). He concludes that a thing in itself and a noumenon are identifiable if we regard a noumenon in the negative sense (p. 241). But a negative noumenon is really a bare particular—a thing devoid of properties. Such an entity is not thinkable; therefore, Stenius concludes, there is no genuine distinction between a noumenon and a phenomenon.

This representative of the critical tradition runs afoul of several distinctions that it deploys in order to arrive at its conclusion. There are, first of all, two senses of "limit" when it is used in the employment of a concept. We can speak of the sum of an infinite number of representations that we cannot synthesize because we cannot complete the enumeration of an infinite series. We can also speak of a limit when we talk about something that is not an object of awareness independent of some forms of intuition or other. The former is a noumenon. The latter is a thing in itself. A negative noumenon is a bare particular. But this conclusion does not generate the further conclusion that no such particulars exist at all. Stenius's argument is faulty because it moves from the fact that we can never think of particulars that lack properties to the conclusion that we cannot distinguish a particular from its properties. The bareness of a particular required by Kant's theory is merely that we must distinguish between a particular and its properties, not that we must be able to be aware of that particular divested of any property whatever.

8. Arnulf Zweig also argues for the distinction between a noumenon and a thing in itself in his introduction to *Kant: Philosophical Correspondence*, p. 16. Cf. Norman Kemp Smith, *A Commentary to Kant's "Critique of Pure Reason,"* pp. 410 ff. Ralph Walker, *Kant*, p. 107, pursues a similar line of argument when he first suggests that the transcendental object can be assimilated to a noumenon and then uses the concept of a noumenon to elucidate the concept of a thing in itself. But, as we have seen, the concept of the transcendental object concerns any object conforming to some modes of intuition or other and not any specific object that so conforms. The concept of a noumenon, however, is the notion of an object which does not conform to any modes of sensuous intuition.

Cf. Nicholas Rescher, "Noumenal Causality," for an attempt to come to terms with passages like A190=B235, A288=B344, and A494=B422, where Kant ostensibly claims that things in themselves are causes of the appearances we have. Rescher distinguishes (p. 176) between authentic causation and generic grounding. The former is, for Rescher, a Kantian constitutive principle formulated in the Second Analogy. The latter is to be understood by Kant as a regulative use of the Principle of Sufficient Reason, according to which we infer from our acquaintance with appearances to something that lies outside of those appearances (p. 178). Rescher concludes that the relation between things in themselves and appearances is not causal. The conclusion is defensible. His explanation for it is not. A Kantian regulative principle governs our cognitive relation to appearances and things in themselves. The explanation confuses our putative relation to a series of appearances that we are incapable of completely synthesizing with the very different relation between each member of any such series and a thing in itself that is its ground.

The allegedly troublesome passages remain. At A190=B235 Kant says that representations (*Vorstellungen*) are the way in which things in themselves affect us. Once we are forced to assimilate affection to causation, the claim becomes philosophically troublesome. The difference between the two notions forbids the conclusion that the category of causation applies to things in themselves. The argument at A288=B344 and A492=B422 is initially more troublesome. In both passages a thing in itself is allegedly first a transcendental object and then the cause of appearances. The philosophical mischief disappears once we see that Kant claims a transcendental object is like a thing in itself in that both of them are nonsensible objects with the qualification that a transcendental object is the thought of a cause of appearances not available to us an appearance. None of this shows that a thing in itself is either a transcendental object or a noumenon. We are told only that the thought of a nonsensible cause is the thought of something not given to sensibility. The connection between such a thought and a thing in itself is left totally open. I consciously ignore for the present discussion passages like A249 in which Kant identifies a noumenon with a thing in itself. Such passages are relevant to a problem very different from mine. I am asking about the relation between a thing in itself and the intuition we *do* have and not, as Kant does, in passages like A249, the relation of possible objects to a mode of intuition we *might* have. I also ignore the relevance of noumenal causation to the tenability of the *TWT*. As Kant raises that issue in A444=B472 ff., the possibility of noumenal causation concerns whether any agent can cause a series of events to begin without have an antecedent event causing it. Whether this is possible *assumes* a resolution of the distinction between things in themselves and appearances; hence, it cannot help to decide for one solution or other. Cf. Gottfried Martin, *Kant's Metaphysics and Theory of Science*, p. 149, for a different reason for separating the two issues.

9. D. P. Dryer, *Kant's Solution for Verification in Metaphysics*, p. 513. For similar statements see Adickes, *Kant und das Ding an Sich*, pp. 20 ff.; H. J. Paton, *Kant's Metaphysic of Experience*, 2:75; George Schrader, "The Thing in Itself in Kantian Philosophy," p. 173. Cf. also Bröcker, pp. 152–53, and Heidegger, pp. 36–37. Westphal, pp. 118 ff., reviews most of the recent literature on the *TDT*. Typical statements of the theory in Kant are Bxxvi–Bxxvii; A38=B55; B69; A538=B566; *Prolegomena*, sec. 49.

10. Bxxvii; cf. A38=B55.

11. A19=B33.

12. A19=B33.

13. A24=B39.

14. A23=B39.

15. A24=B39.

16. A26=B42; cf. A22–B37, where he calls space "a property of the mind"; A42=B59, where he says that space and time "cannot exist in themselves, but only in us"; A43=B60, where he says that space and time are "conditions which are originally inherent in the mind." Here I ignore two other arguments by which Kant tries to arrive at the same conclusion. (1) The first moves to the subjectivity of space from the assumed synthetic a priori character of the propositions of geometry. (Cf. B41: "Our explanation . . . makes intelligible the possibility of geometry." Cf. also A39=B56; A47=B64–A48=B65.) Even if we grant that geometrical propositions are what Kant says they are, this does not imply Kant's conclusion. That space is subjective is, rather, assumed in order to explain how we can have such knowledge; hence, Kant's argument for geometry is not an independent demonstration of the subjectivity of space. The argument is irrelevant to my present purpose for yet another reason. Even if we grant that such an argument proves the subjectivity of space, it could not be used to establish the distinction between things in themselves and appearances. We could, for example, do geometry in a world without things in themselves; hence, that synthetic a priori propositions in

geometry require the subjectivity of space does not imply the distinction between things in themselves and appearances. (2) Kant claims indirect confirmation for the subjectivity of space and time at A506=B534, where he purports to resolve the First Antinomy. Here the issue is whether the world is a finite or infinite collection of appearances. Kant argues that neither assumption is true, drawing the inference that no such collection exists. This does not, however, give indirect support to the claim that space and time are subjective. Even if we grant that the collection of all the appearances there are is neither finitely nor infinitely large, nothing will have been shown about the subjectivity of space and time with respect to each individual appearance. The issue about subjectivity can be raised all over again at the level of each appearance. Consult "Kant's First Antinomy," in chap. 5, for the basis of this claim.

    17. A28=B44.

    18. A32=B49.

    19. Cf. A22=B37, where he says that outer sense is "a property of our mind." Cf. also A38=B55, where Kant says of the form of intuition that it "is not to be looked for in the object in itself, but in the subject to which the object appears." The sentence that follows illustrates the conflation of epistemic and ontological senses of "transcendental ideality": "[N]evertheless, it [the form of intuition] belongs really and necessarily to the appearance of this object." H. J. Paton nicely transcribes this confusion when he reports that "[t]hings as they are in themselves are the very same things that appear to us, although they appear to us . . . as different from what they are in themselves" (*Kant's Metaphysics of Experience*, 1:61). A more trenchant evaluation is in H. A. Prichard, *Kant's Theory of Knowledge*, chap. 4.

    20. A19=B33.

    21. A19=B33. Cf. Charles Parsons's instructive discussion of immediacy, in "Kant's Philosophy of Mathematics," pp. 569 ff. He attacks affection indirectly by exposing an alleged ambiguity in the very notion of transcendental ideality. He claims (pp. 74–76) that Kant illegitimately assimilates the assertion that things appear to us in certain ways to the very different assertion that things produce appearances in us. The slide is from an attempt to explain how something appears to us to the illegitimate conclusion that what does appear is an entity different from the one with which Kant begins his argument. Thus Kant allegedly cannot appeal to affection as a relation between a thing in itself and our sensibility. Causation is the relation Kant must employ in order to account for our cognitive relation to appearances. The slide exists only if we assume, mistakenly, that particulars in the phenomenal objects we perceive cannot be identical with the particulars in things in themselves. Cf. Stephen Barker, "Appearing and Appearances." See also my "The Sense of a Kantian Intuition," for a defense of the claim that the problem can be avoided if we specify what it is to be a particular independently of what it is to have the characteristics of forms of intuition.

    22. The present discussion applies to the distinction I make in chap. 5, "Kant's First Antinomy" (note 16), between an epistemic or criteriological and an ontological sense of "thing in itself" to the notion of transcendent ideality. There I hold that a thing in itself is ontological just in case it is a kind of object that remains when we abstract from the conditions under which we intuit it. And I hold, further, that a thing in itself is epistemic in relation to the verifiability of claims made about its nature. More recently, however, R. Meerbote, "The Unknowability of Things in Themselves," pp. 413 ff., has offered a different account of the distinction. The ontological use of "thing in itself," according to Meerbote, involves a distinction between two kinds of things; an epistemological use, the occurrence of the term in a discussion of the conditions of empirical knowledge. The difficulty with this way of stating the distinction is simply that the two

uses overlap. Thus a duality of objects might still occur in an epistemological discussion of the conditions of empirical knowledge. That a term occurs in two different contexts is still compatible with there being two different *referents* of the term. For all that the present distinction between ontological and epistemic uses of the term "thing in itself" shows, the ontological use can be embedded implicitly in the epistemic use of the term. In like manner, the epistemic use of the term might be explicable by means of the ontological use of that term just because what is seen as two uses of the same term really amount to a diversity of access to one and the same referent.

Cf. Gerold Prauss, *Erscheinung bei Kant*, pp. 15–38, for a discussion of the epistemic and ontological uses of the distinction between things in themselves and appearances. Prauss distinguishes between what he calls a transcendental and an empirical use of "thing in itself." This allows him to speak of empirical things in themselves. The move enables us to talk about objects of experience that can appear to us in different ways but cannot be presented to us without any form of intuition at all. Regarded empirically, objects of experience are independent in that they are logically distinguishable from the forms of intuition under which we perceive them. Regarded transcendentally, they can exist independently of possible human experience.

Chapter 3. Things in Themselves (II)

1. The argument for this claim is presented more fully in chap. 2. All lettered references otherwise unspecified are to the *Critique of Pure Reason*.

2. This reviews the argument of sec. 3 of the first part of this chapter (note 1).

3. A19=B34.

4. A20=B34.

5. A19=B34.

6. A42=B59–A43=B60.

7. Cf. B153 and A33=B49ff., for the source of the paradox. Other passages pertaining to the paradox are A399=B400; A443=B471; A371; A379. Cf. also *Reflexion* 6316 in *Gesammelte Schriften* (edited by the Prussian Academy of Sciences), 22:613. There are passages, however, in which he seeks to deal with the paradox by offering no theory at all and merely citing the existence of self-awareness as a fact as in B155ff. For a historical review of the treatment of affection, see Herring, *Das Problem der Affektion bei Kant*.

8. B153. Cf. B156; B158; A226=B273ff.

9. B156 (Kant's italics). Cf. B158.

10. A typical supporting text is B158, in which Kant distinguishes between the kind of awareness of the self that he counts as knowledge and the kind that is peculiar to the awareness we have of the self. When this characterization is compared with A146=B145, A719=B747, A19=B33, A50=B74ff., B146ff., A702=B730, what emerges is that we are, according to Kant, allowed to call something a case of knowledge only when what we purport to know relates to intuition. And this implies that whatever is aware of a content of consciousness cannot be a self as it appears to us. Cf. esp. B277.

11. Cf. B55. and chap. 2, sec. 1.

12. Cf. A19=B33 and A49=B67.

13. A19=B33.

14. A19=B33.

15. Cf. B156.

16. B153.

17. B155 (italics mine).

18. A20=B34 (italics mine).

19. Cf. A20=B34.

20. A10=B34 and A49=B66ff.

21. Cf. A49=B60.

22. The major source for the shift in the meaning of "affection" is B155: "The understanding does not, therefore, find in inner sense such a combination of the manifold, but *produces* it, in that it *affects* that sense" (Kant's italics).

23. B157. Cf. also A350, B278, B408, A546=B574.

24. I find the textual support for this conclusion from two sources: (1) that Kant frequently refers to the acquaintance we have with self as an awareness of a thought and not an intuition (see note 22 above); and (2) the passages in which Kant refers to the way in which I am conscious of myself as an ability to determine my own existence in time. Cf. B275ff. and my article, "Transcendental Arguments," for further discussion of the passage.

25. B131; cf. the discussion beginning at A362.

26. B133 (Kant's italics). Cf. A113, A116, A123–24, A265=B320, B135, B412.

27. Cf. B275.

28. B134.

29. Cf. B133 and esp. the definition of "object" given in the Analytic at B137: "an *object* is that in the concept of which the manifold of a given intuition is *unified*" (Kant's italics).

30. A401.

31. Ibid.

32. A402 (Kant's italics).

33. Ibid.

34. Ibid. He quaintly calls this the subreption of hypostatized consciousness.

35. Cf. A157=B196, A722=B750. I have consciously ignored two problems that superficially bear on my account of Kant's theory of the self. There are, first, the problem of noumenal causation and, secondly, whether we are allowed to infer that the ego is discontinuous through time from the argument that Kant gives in the Paralogisms. Take these in turn. The possibility of a causation that is not in time is raised in the Third Antinomy (A444=B472). Kant argues as follows: Since we can distinguish between a noumenal and a phenomenal self, we can also conceive of a kind of causation that acts in such a way that it is not subject to natural law (cf. A549=B575 and esp. A559=B487). The possibility of free action is, according to Kant's argument in the first *Kritik*, made to depend on the possibility of a kind of ego that stands outside a temporal series but nonetheless acts causally on those subjects that apprehend that series. But this makes the entire argument of the Third Antinomy depend upon the very assumption that, as I argue in chapter 6, vitiates the distinction between a noumenal and a phenomenal self; hence, I ignore it here. For a review of the whole issue, see Lewis White Beck, *A Commentary on Kant's Critique of Practical Reason*, pp. 176ff., and, for a discussion of narrower parts of this issue, see my "Kant's Arguments against Material Principles." The second issue that I raise only to drop is whether Kant's argument in the Paralogisms proves that there is one continuous self through them (cf. A349ff). What he shows there is merely that you cannot infer the continuity of the ego from concepts alone without providing some relation of that concept to intuition. He does not show that there is no way of establishing the continuity of the self at all. Heinz Heimsoeth gives the most recent discussion known to me in his *Transzendentale Dialektik*, pp. 79. Cf. Heim-

soeth's earlier discussion of the issue in his *Studien zur Philosophie Immanuel Kants*, chap. 5.

36. Cf. A106: "But a concept is always as regards its form something universal which serves as a rule." Others have suggested a different way around the Paradox of Self-Knowledge. Karl Ameriks, *Kant's Theory of Mind*, pp. 252–55, distinguishes between apperceptive and reflective affection. We are said to be reflectively affected whenever we bring our representings to explicit consciousness. Apperceptive affection occurs whenever we synthesize individual intuitions by bringing them under a concept. He offers this distinction as a solution of the Paradox of Self-Knowledge. We are actively affected when we synthesize what is given to us in acts of apperceptive affection; passive, when we are reflectively affected. The distinction is valid; but it does not resolve the paradox. The problem generating that paradox arises entirely in the context what Ameriks calls reflective affection. The relation of the perceptual content to the mental act when they are, *ex hypothesi*, numerically the same cannot be explained by introducing the fact that we can be aware of ourselves as synthesizing one perceptual content with another. The distinction between passivity and activity arises with reflective affection. We cannot solve the problem it faces by transporting that problem into a context that assumes the existence of reflective affection.

Chapter 4. Things in Themselves: The Historical Lessons

1. Friedrich Heinrich Jacobi, *Werke*, 2:304. Others argued a claim that is only superficially similar to and philosophically less respectable than Jacobi's. Cf. K. L. Reinhold, *Versuch einer neuen Theorie des menschlichen Vorstellungsvermögens*, p. 243, and *Beiträge zur Berichtigung bisheriger Missverständnisse der Philosophen*, 1:185–86, where he tells us that things in themselves are in principle not imaginable with what is thinkable (*denkbar*). I can consistently conceive of an object that the limitations of my imagination prevent me from representing pictorially. Those limitations do not, however, prevent me from consistently *thinking* of an object that I cannot picture. Solomon Maimon, *Versuch über die Transzendentalphilosophie, Gesammelte Werke*, 2:226ff., claims that what Kant calls a thing in itself is really only the concept of a complete series of appearances that the limitations of our perceptual capacities prevent us from completing. Cf. Maimon, *Philosophisches Wörterbuch, Gesammelte Werke*, 3:176: "Nach mir . . . ist die Erkenntnis der Dinge an sich nichts anders als die *vollständige Erkenntnis der Erscheinung*" (Maimon's italics). But no sooner has he said this than he reverses himself (*Versuch über die Transzendentalphilosophie, Gesammelte Werke*, 2:226ff.), saying that the concept of a thing in itself is that of an imaginary and irrational entity like the concept of $\sqrt{-a}$ in mathematical analysis. The conditions of its cognition cannot be given to us. We employ the notion only in order that we may demonstrate the impossibility of an object that corresponds to it. But asymptotic approximations and their conceptual relatives will not do. For one thing, the issue about the status of a thing in itself arises at the level of every member of such series. For another, the kind of series that Maimon mentions may be impossible for us to complete. This does not show that the concept of the last term in such a series, available perhaps only to an angelic intellect, is logically incoherent. I have argued all of this more exhaustively in chaps. 2, 3, and 5.

Gottlob Ernst Schulze in *Aenesidemus* (1792) tells us that the notion of a thing in itself is polymorphous. It can be the faculty of representation (*Vorstellungsvermögen*), simply a concept of reason, a designation of a noumenon, or a merely negative or limiting concept. For Schulze the basic issue is whether a thing in itself is a concept or a thing. If it is a thing, the problem for him is how Kant can account for the form-matter distinction with respect to appearances without assuming the logically prior distinction between things in themselves and appearances. This generates a dilemma. Either the form-matter distinction can be made for concepts and intuitions alike or intuitions supply the matter while concepts supply the form of experience. If the former, then the distinction between things in themselves and appearances cannot be explicated: A distinction that applies both to intuitions and concepts cannot account for the peculiarity of the matter of an appearance. If the latter, the relationship between the ground of an appearance and the appearance of which it is the ground arises all over again with respect to the matter of experience. Hence, there are no things in themselves.

Emphatically not. The dilemma is misleading. True, intuitions supply what Kant calls the matter of an appearance. But the dilemma Schulze associates with this is harmless. The form-matter distinction is not used to account for the peculiarity of intuitions. And Kant does distinguish between the ground of an appearance and the appearance that it grounds. But this is just another way of formulating the distinction between things in themselves and appearances. Cf. Richard Aquila, "Is Sensation the Matter of Appearance?" See also my "What Kant Really Did to Idealism."

2. Jacobi, *Werke*, 2:304.

3. Ibid.

4. Ibid., p. 305; cf. p. 307: "Kurz unsere ganze Erkenntnis enthält nichts, platterdings nichts, was irgend eine wahrhaft objektive Bedeutung hätte."

5. *Critique of Pure Reason*, B137, B138, B139, A106. (Unspecified references to this work are hereafter cited only by the pagination of the A or B editions.) Cf. Immanuel Kant, *Prolegomena to any Future Metaphysics*, sec. 22. (Unspecified references to this work are hereafter cited as *Prol.* and the relevant section number.)

6. Jacobi, *Werke*, 2:502ff.

7. Ibid., p. 305. Cf. the 1787 edition of Jacobi's book, where he argues (pp. 118–23) for the immediacy of our awareness of objects independently of us and for the superfluity of the notion of a thing in itself. The argument confuses the distinction between things in themselves and phenomena with the very different distinction between things outside us—which may be phenomena—and appearances. Cf. also pp. 220–25 of the same edition, where he claims that Kant applies the principle of causation to sensory impression and then goes on to substitute what he calls transcendental uncertainty (*transzendentale Ungewissenheit*). Here he confounds things outside us with the transcendental object and then interlards both of these notions with that of a thing in itself.

8. Ibid. Schelling repeats this argument in his *System des transzendentalen Idealismus, Werke* 2:95ff and again in his *Darstellung des philosophischen Empirismus, Werke*, 3:527, where he confronts Kant's theory of things in themselves with a dilemma: A Kantian thing in itself is either a thing (*ein Existierendes*) or it is by definition unknowable. If it is the former, then it is necessarily an object of possible experience—in which case it is not something in itself. If it is the latter, then it is not a thing—in which case the very notion of a *thing* in itself is a contradiction in terms.

9. J. G. Fichte, *Erste Einleitung in die Wissenschaftslehre*, vol. 1, sec. 6. Cf. Fichte's review of *Aenesidemus*, ibid., 1:15ff. and esp. p. 17 for the parallel argument that "der Gedanke von einem Dinge *an sich*, und unabhängig von irgendeinem Vorstellungsvermögen, Existenz und gewisse Beschaffenheit haben soll, eine Grille, ein Traum, ein Nicht-Gedanke ist." (Unless otherwise indicated, all italics are Fichte's.) Both Fichte and

Schelling claim that there are no things in themselves and that the distinction between things in themselves and appearances cannot be made for cases of self-awareness.

These are, however, two logically independent problems. In cases of self-awareness the subject and object are the same. This admittedly raises the issue of how a self can be its own object and yet remain identical with itself. This, however, is irrelevant to the distinction between things in themselves and appearances. Both Fichte and Schelling conflate these issues. In his argument of 1800, Fichte repeatedly concludes from his argument against the existence of things in themselves and appearances that all we can really perceive is a state of our own self. Cf. *The Vocation of Man*, p. 38; cf. esp. p. 51: "[Y]ou have no consciousness of things, but only *a consciousness . . . of a consciousness of things.*" Cf. also p. 57, where he concludes that "all knowledge is merely knowledge of yourself," repeating this on p. 61. Schelling echoes all of this in his *System des transzendentalen Idealismus* (1800), in *Werke*, 1:180ff.; 2:24–25, 39, 41, and 625ff.

But the two issues are logically independent. We cannot conclude anything about the collapse of the distinction between things in themselves and appearances when it is applied to cases of self-awareness. The latter issue concerns the relation between two things that are identical with each other. The former involves the relation of an appearance to what appears. We already know that the relation of identity applies to the self and its object when it is aware of itself. In the case of the problem about relating a thing in itself to an appearance we want to know the nature of the relation of an object admittedly different from the apprehending subject and the appearance it apprehends to that appearance. This question does not arise in cases of self-awareness.

10. Fichte, *Erste Einleitung*, 1:435: "Ich denke mir dieses or jenes Objekt . . . : ich bringe gewisse Bestimmungen in mir hervor, wenn das Objekt eine blosse Erdichtung ist; oder sie [objects] sind ohne mein Zuthun vorhanden, wenn es etwas Wirkliches seyn soll; *und ich sehe jenem Hervorbringen, diesem Seyn zu.*"

11. Ibid. Cf. pp. 428–31.

12. Ibid., p. 436.

13. Fichte, *The Vocation of Man*, p. 7.

14. Ibid., p. 36.

15. Ibid.

16. Ibid., p. 37.

17. Ibid., p. 11; cf. pp. 56, 64, and esp. p. 19, where he applies the substratum-attribute distinction to the self as well as to material objects.

18. Ibid., p. 37.

19. Ibid., p. 38.

20. Ibid., p. 37.

21. Ibid., p. 40; cf. p. 74, where he finally concludes that "a thing *in itself* is itself a thought; namely, this, that there is a great thought which yet no man has ever thought out."

22. Ibid., p. 46: "*I.* I maintain that were I to divide a corporeal mass to infinity, I could never come to any part which is *in itself* imperceptible . . . *Spirit.* Thus there is nothing remaining of the object but *what is perceptible*, what is a property or attribute . . . and the true bearer of the attributes of things . . . is, therefore, only the space which is thus filled?" The interlocutor concedes.

23. Ibid., p. 47; cf. pp. 52, 56, 64. Schelling echoes this argument. Cf. note 8, supra. To say that there are things in themselves is to confuse a noumenon with a thing in itself. Kant allows the application of the *unschematized* categories to noumena. In such a case, however, the categories are merely empty designations for any world that has a logically

self-consistent description. Schelling then concludes that there are either no things in themselves or that we wrongly take noumena to be things in themselves. We are left without sensations. And they are not things in themselves at all but rather things that are always perceptually available to us.

24. Cf. Arthur Schopenhauer, *Die Welt als Wille und Vorstellung*, 2:240ff. Whatever else may be wrong with Schopenhauer's argument against the existence of things in themselves, he carefully distinguishes this distinction from the quite different distinction between primary and secondary qualities, calling the latter a juvenile preamble (*jugendliches Vorspiel*) to the former because the primary-secondary property distinction arises within the context of appearances and therefore cannot be used to explicate the distinction between an appearance and a thing in itself. Cf. Paul Carus, *The Surd of Metaphysics*, pp. 3ff., for an example of this confusion, which can be traced to Alois Riehl, *Der philosophische Kritizismus*, 1:405ff.

25. Schopenhauer, ibid., 1:599ff., and 2:chap. 4, where he tries to show that matter is the condition of all causal sequences and that everything else is conditioned by (*beruht auf*) causation. He continues this in his "Über den Satz vom Grunde," 3:sec. 21. I ignore this argument because its conclusion is compatible with the fact that a thing in itself is not material in Schopenhauer's sense or, even if it were, that material objects can never be objects of possible experience although they must conform to the unschematized category of ground and consequent.

26. Ibid., 1:598, says that what we call a thing in itself is added to (*hinzugedacht*) objects of experience (*Vorstellungen*) by the intellect. Elsewhere, however, he says that things in themselves do exist and can be known (2:sec. 18). He presents this as a report of a datum of experience (p. 254). His evidence: Our acts of volition are given to us immediately and not by means of representations. His explication: In cases of volition we cannot distinguish what Schopenhauer calls a representation from what generates that representation in our consciousness. I am aware, for example, not of a representation of the source of an act of willing, but rather of the source itself. I ignore this issue here because it is irrelevant to the existence of things in themselves. The problem of the distinction between a thing in itself and an appearance arises whenever you distinguish between an object and the representation of an object. That problem cannot arise whenever it is impossible to distinguish between, say, the self and its object when that object happens to be the self; hence, Schopenhauer can consistently hold both positions. Cf. Schelling, *Werke*, 2:95ff., for the same position. See my "Intellectual Intuition: The Continuity Thesis" for a short critical history of the claim that cases of self-awareness demand the acknowledgment of a special kind of awareness. Cf. Goethe: "Von dem Ding weiss ich nichts und auch nichts von der Seele, Beide erscheinen mir nur, aber sie sind doch kein Schein."

This misunderstanding has shaped the course of the reception of the distinction between a thing in itself and an appearance by German literature in the nineteenth century and beyond. The famous *Kantkrise* which is said to have gripped Heinrich von Kleist is our most celebrated example of this influence. Kleist dramatizes that crisis in his letters to his girlfriend and to his sister. Cf. the letters to Wilhelmine von Zeuge of 18 September 1800 and 22 March 1801 as well as to Ulrike von Kleist of August 1800 and especially 23 March 1801. Kleist seems to have thought that Kant's distinction prevented us from knowing anything, leaving us with only a precarious grasp of the phenomena that Kant says we can know. Robert Musil's *Die Verwirrungen des Zöglings Törless* and *Der Mann ohne Eigenschaften* continue that tradition with a notable twist. The distinction is said to demand the recognition of two kinds of knowledge. The one is appropriate to appearances since it involves the use of concepts; the other, appropriate to something that is not the appearance of something we cannot grasp but rather available to us only in feeling and cannot be communicated rationally. An adequate history of the fortunes of Kant's distinction in literature has yet to be written.

27. All citations from Hegel are from the Glockner edition. The translations are mine, although in the case of *Die Phänomenologie des Geistes*, I cite in parentheses the corresponding passages in the English translation by J. B. Baillie.

28. Hegel, 4:603.

29. Ibid., 4:605. Cf. Hegel, *Enzyklopädie*, secs. 77–83, for a parallel argument.

30. Ibid., 2:108–38 (Baillie, pp. 180–213).

31. Ibid., 2:81–92 (Baillie, pp. 149–60).

32. Ibid., 2:81–91, for his attack on the "Here" and the "Now" (Baillie, pp. 149–66), as examples of universal terms in the disguise of designators of particulars.

33. Ibid., 2:92–107 (Baillie, pp. 162–78).

34. The account I give here is neutral with respect to any theory about the structure of Hegel's dialectic. My present purpose is solely to record the sequence of objections he makes to theories of perceptual knowledge, not to speculate about the relations among those theories. I have discussed this elsewhere in another context in my "Gadamer on Hegel's Dialectic: A Review Article."

35. Hegel, 2:108ff. (Baillie, pp. 180ff.).

36. Ibid., 2:110ff. (Baillie, pp. 186ff.).

37. Ibid., 2:121ff. (Baillie, pp. 188ff.).

38. Ibid.

39. Ibid., 2:121 (Baillie, p. 188).

40. Ibid., 2:126 (Baillie, p. 126). The parallel argument is in Hegel's *Enzyklopädie*, secs. 75–108. There Kant is said to divide objects of perceptual awareness into things (*Dinge*) that have properties (*Eigenschaften*) distinguishable from one another standing in a relation to the thing (Hegel calls it the relation of *Haben*). But the thing is indistinguishable from the properties it has because of the inherent incoherence of the notion of *Haben*. A thing ceases to exist without its properties. Hegel concludes that the relation of *Haben* does not exist: There is no relation between a thing and its properties; hence, there is no such thing in itself. Hegel puts it this way: "[T]he properties of the thing are equally independent and freed from their dependence on the thing" (sec. 77). Hegel further concludes in sec. 99 that "substance is thus the totality of the accidents in which it reveals itself as *absolute power* and as the *richness of all content*."

Arguments like this die hard. They were perpetuated in the tradition by Otto Liebmann, *Kant und die Epigonen*, pp. 114ff., and Carus, pp. 3ff., in an even more egregious form. Both of them begin by claiming that substances are really bundles of properties, continue by inferring that there is no substance-accident distinction, and fallaciously conclude that Kant's distinction between things in themselves and appearances is spurious.

41. Cf. Hegel's *Wissenschaft der Logik*, in *Sämtliche Werke*, 4:603ff., where he argues that the notion of a thing in itself is essentially unstable because it can exist only because it is "das Existierende als das durch die aufgehobene Vermittelung vorhandene, *wesentliche Unmittelbare*." At the same time, however, it is mediated by its properties: "Aber das Ding-an-sich und sein vermitteltes Sein sind beide in der Existenz enthalten, und beide selbst Existenzen; das Ding-an-sich existiert, und ist die wesentliche, das vermittelte Sein aber die unwesentliche Existenz des Dinges." Here Kant's distinction is equated with the distinction between essential and accidental properties. The issue

worsens when Hegel begins on p. 608 of the *Logik* to argue that things in themselves are causes of phenomenal effects. Having reduced a thing in itself to a kind of property, Hegel then makes these properties into so many causes of other properties.

42. Hegel tacitly realizes this in the section of the *Phänomenologie*, pp. 129ff. (Baillie, pp. 203ff.), entitled the Inverted World (*die verkehrte Welt*), and again in the *Logik*, *Sämtliche Werke*, 4:636. In both he attacks the notion of a thing in itself because it duplicates the problem it is supposed to solve even though the members of the inverted world supposedly have properties that are the opposite of the properties that the members of the world of appearances have.

43. Cf. A109, A250, and A251.

44. Friedrich Nietzsche, *Jenseits von Gut und Böse, Werke in Drei Bänden*, sec. 16, dramatically illustrates the chameleon-like character of a description of a Kantian thing in itself widespread in the tradition. Nietzsche's description runs as follows: To know a thing in itself implies that we have what he calls absolute knowledge of a phenomenal thing. But this in turn implies that I can be perceptually aware simultaneously of that object from all the perspectives from which it can be perceived. And this conflicts with the fact that every case of perceptual awareness is perspectival. To say that I can be simultaneously aware of an object from all possible perspectives at once contradicts the claim that all perception is perspectival; hence, things in themselves cannot be known.

The description shows, however, only that we cannot have a certain kind of awareness of phenomenal objects, remaining silent about the relation between a thing in itself and an appearance. What is even more instructive for the hermeneutical tangle in which that distinction has been involved is that Nietzsche's description can be used to show either that the notion of a thing in itself is logically incoherent or that such a notion is logically coherent but that it is impossible to be perceptually acquainted with any object falling under that concept. The concept of a thing in itself is logically incoherent when you choose to conclude from the premises that anybody can perceive an object from all perspectives at once while tacitly assuming that all cases of perceptual awareness are necessarily perspectival. The same set of premises will support the conclusion that the concept is logically coherent but that it is impossible for anybody to *perceive* an object falling under it apart from a perspective. This ambiguity has undermined most of the traditional discussion of the subject. Cf. G. Dawes Hicks, *Die Begriffe Phänomen und Noumenon*, for a palmary case of such a confusion.

Horst Seidl, "Bemerkungen zu Ding an sich und transzendentalem Gegenstand in Kants Kritik der reinen Vernunft," pp. 604ff., is joined by Henry Allison, "Things in Themselves, Noumena, and the Transcendental Object," pp. 42ff., and "Kant's Concept of the Transcendental Object," pp. 165ff., in showing the ambiguity of Kant's use of that notion. Both agree that Kant uses the notion in two senses but disagree about what these senses are. Allison tells us that Kant sometimes equates the transcendental object with a noumenon and at other times with whatever object to which we refer the appearances in the sensuous manifold. Seidel, however, tells us that Kant sometimes equates the transcendental object with a thing in itself and at others with a noumenon. What I am saying here should help to resolve this issue. To say that what Kant calls the transcendental object is a variable is to explain how we can say that the transcendental object is indeterminate: The notion is a place-marker for a range of specific empirical objects and is, therefore, not itself given as one more empirical object among others. To say that the transcendental object is a determinate object to which we assign the various components of the sensuous manifold is to say that the variable in question can be satisfied by any number of empirical objects since it can be multiply instantiated. There is no inconsistency in claiming, as Kant does, that the transcendental object is both determinate and indeterminate. Allison and Seidl are right for the wrong reason. They both correctly discern an ambiguity in Kant's usage of the term but each in his own way mislocates the source of that ambiguity.

45. A90=B122. Cf. A112, A203=B248, and esp. A542=B570.

46. A19=B34.

47. Cf. esp. A44=B61, where affection does not imply causation. A494=B522 confirms this as does Kant's *Anthropologie*, 7:sec. 7, *Anmerkung*. The structure of Kant's text supports this on independent grounds. To assume that affection and causation are two terms designating the same thing is to do irreparable harm to Kant's text. The assumption would force us to conclude that there is no distinction between the transcendental ego and the empirical ego because what Kant calls the transcendental unity of apperception would be subject to the Second Analogy—which would make Kant's distinction into a distinction without a difference.

The assumption cuts even deeper. It brings about the collapse of the distinction between a schematized and unschematized category. If "affection" were just another word for "causation," Kant's categories would apply only to our world because their application would be restricted to our way of schematizing the category of causation. If affection were simply a case of causation, consider just what kind of causation we would be given. In the first place, we have already seen that the applicability of Kant's category of causation to any sensuous manifold assumes as a logically prior condition that the relation of affection holds between individual acts of perceptual awareness and the various elements comprising a sensuous manifold. If this were not possible, then Kant could not claim, as he does, that we can schematize the category of causation for any but our own forms of intuition because the assimilation of affection to Kantian causation would make it impossible for us to explain how we can be immediately aware of anything without invoking its relation to something that precedes it as a condition of our being affected at all. What Kant calls a thing in itself would really be a phenomenal object that acts on other phenomenal objects. And this would make it impossible to claim that the category of causation can be schematized in different ways according to differences in the forms of sensibility. Both of these textual-cum-philosophical consequences import inconsistencies into two of the central themes of the first *Kritik* that would rob it of philosophical respectability. Cf. chap. 1 for further evidence that affection cannot be causation.

48. A28=B44; A35=B52. Cf. *Prol.*, sec. 9.

49. The prolonged and notorious Trendelenburg-Fischer debate about the interpretation of "transcendental ideality" cannot count as evidence against the claim that the tradition has overlooked the epistemic-ontological distinction. See Vaihinger, *CZ*, 2:133ff. and 294ff., for the chronicle of a debate that does not testify to the humanizing influence of philosophy.

The issue begins (pp. 133ff.) with a description of the Tetralemma: Space and time are either (1) simply subjective activities of our mind, (2) simply characteristics of the objects that we perceive, or (3) both (1) and (2). Kant's proofs in the Aesthetic of the first *Kritik* may show that the forms of our sensibility are subjective. But, so the argument runs, this does not exclude them from also being properties of the objects that we intuit under those forms. Trendelenburg calls this Kant's *Lücke*, adding for good measure that the admission of such a *Lücke* admits alternative (3) of the Tetralemma as a viable possibility.

The problem only superficially resembles the dilemma that the tradition has ignored. Trendelenburg's Tetralemma divides the possibilities of interpretation according to a principle of division that assumes what I have called the ontological view of Kant's arguments. Trendelenburg's alternative (2) is no evidence to the contrary, for it, like the others, assumes that Kant is making an ontological, not an epistemic, claim. The Trendelenburg Tetralemma, so far from anticipating my distinction, is really just another case in which that distinction has been ignored.

Jill Vance Buroker, *Space and Incongruence*, chap. 5, and Henry Allison, "The Non-Spatiality of Things in Themselves," continue this dispute by arguing, each in a different way, that things in themselves are nonspatial. Both ignore, however, a conception of a thing in itself according to which it is an object that remains numerically the same despite alterations in forms of intuition but that may have or lack the characteristics it has in our world when it becomes part of another world. Cf. my "The Crisis of Syntheticity: The Kant-Eberhard Controversy," for an argument, crucial to this view of what a thing in itself is, that Kant's Argument from Incongruent Counterparts must be seen as having two uses not always clearly distinguished by Kant himself. He uses that argument to show the irreducibility of particulars to clusters of properties, relational or non-relational. But he also uses the same argument to reach the quite different though compatible conclusion that space and time are not concepts but rather forms of intuition. The former use of the argument is important because it shows the drastic difference between the traditional and the revised formations of the *TDT*. The *TWT* requires that there be two numerically diverse particulars in any description of perceptual awareness. And this requires us to individuate the particulars we perceive with reference to the forms of intuition under which we perceive them. The Argument from Incongruent Counterparts forbids this because it prevents any characteristics or properties of something to account for what the particular in a perceptual situation is. The traditional interpretation of the *TDT* also runs afoul of the Argument from Incongruent Counterparts. That explanatory alternative of the distinction between things in themselves and appearances merely translates the problem facing us in the actual world in which there are perceptual acts into a description of a possible world in which there are the same kinds of acts requiring an explanation. If such an explanation is to succeed at all, it must succeed in the actual world before we can talk about what goes on in a possible world without duplicating the circumstances of the problem. And none of this implies the conclusion that Kant reaches when he uses Argument from Incongruent Counterparts in the second way. Cf. my "The Sense of a Kantian Intuition," George Schrader's "The Thing in Itself in Kantian Philosophy" and, especially, his "The Transcendental Ideality and Empirical Reality of Kant's Space and Time."

That relation holds between an act of awareness and an object about which we do not know whether it has or lacks the characteristics of our forms of intuition independently of possible experience. The relation of affection does not—indeed, cannot—hold between an object about which we do know that it has the characteristics we perceive independently of possible experience. This fact enables us to say that what we call, *apud* Kant, an appearance is a composite of a thing in itself epistemically interpreted and an act of perceptual awareness. Circularity arises in the appeal to affection as a relation between an object about which we know what characteristics it has in itself as an act of consciousness. Such a claim would prevent the relation of affection from holding, as it must, between a thing in itself and a perceptual act. It would also prevent that relation from explaining how we come to be acquainted with an appearance by forcing us to smuggle the notion of appearance into the explanation of what it is to be acquainted with an appearance.

Chapter 5. Kant's First Antinomy

1. Beginning at A426=B454.
2. Beginning at A428=B456.
3. B454.
4. A504=B532.
5. A33=B49.
6. A26=B42.
7. There is a counterargument according to which the criteriological conception is reducible to the ontological conception of the thing in itself. Thus it might be argued that space and time define what is to count as verifiable. To admit the possibility that things in themselves might be spatial and temporal is to deny that they are things in themselves just because space and time would make them possible objects of human experience. Hence, it might be concluded that the criteriological view is not a separate view of the thing in itself at all. But there is an effective reply to this counterargument. What makes the criteriological conception so different from the ontological conception of things in themselves is that, on the criteriological conception, what defines verifiability is that we must *see* objects in a space-time matrix. Nothing is said about whether they *are* in fact in a space-time matrix apart from possible human experience. And to claim that they are is not ipso facto to claim that they are possible objects of human experience.
8. Cf. the definition of "world" at A334=B391, A605=B633, A418=B446, A419=B447.
9. Cf. A33.
10. Cf. A26=B42.
11. My discussion here will concentrate on (1)—what I call the definition of "transcendental ideality." For if it can be shown that (1) has nothing to do with the conclusion of the First Antinomy, (2) and (3) can be immediately dismissed. (2) follows from (1), although they are not equivalent: If anything is a property of human sensibility, it must be a condition of our being presented with objects. (3) likewise follows from (1): If space and time are nothing but forms of apprehension, then they cannot be substances or accidents of substances. As Kant understands "substance," the self is not a substance. (Cf. B407) And since the self is not a substance, it cannot have accidents. Hence, to show that the conclusion of the antinomy is irrelevant to (1) suffices to disqualify both (2) and (3).
12. Cf. B519 to B521=A491 to A493.
13. A504=B532.
14. A262=B454.
15. There is independent evidence for this in his defintion of "world"; cf. note 7, supra.
16. It is not an argument against my position to say that the last member of the series cannot be exhibited. I concede that such a member cannot be exhibited *as the last member*. But this does not mean that it cannot be exhibited at all.
17. B454.
18. A432n.
19. Smith, *A Commentary to Kant's "Critique of Pure Reason,"* p. 486.
20. Cf. A432=B460; the same point is made in *De mundi sensibilis atque intelligibilis forma et principiis*, para. In.
21. A431=B459.

22. A431=B459.
23. Bertrand Russell, *Our Knowledge of the External World*, p. 161. Henry Allison, *Kant's Transcendental Idealism*, pp. 40–45, records and discusses another Russellian criticism of Kant's argument, according to which we can, contrary to Kant's claim, be acquainted with infinite classes all at once. Classes, infinite or finite, are specified by the defining property which all of their members instantiate. We can be acquainted with this property in one act of awareness; hence, what Kant calls successive synthetic activity is not required in the apprehension of infinitely populated classes. The objection fails because it wrongly assimilates sets or collections to classes. The latter are, to be sure, defined in terms of a common property had by all their members. The former are not. The problem of successive synthetic activity remains.
24. Ibid., p. 194.
25. Ibid., p. 202.
26. Ibid., p. 161.
27. Smith, *Commentary*, p. 486; Jose Benardete, *Infinity*, p. 128; cf. p. 129.
28. Cf. Smith, *Commentary*, p. 485.
29. Benardete, *Infinity*, p. 129.
30. Ibid.
31. Ibid., p. 110.
32. Ibid., pp. 108–9.

Chapter 6. The Duplication Problem

1. Kant gives this argument for time in the *Critique of Pure Reason*, A31=B46. A35=B52 gives the parallel argument for space. (I cite all otherwise unspecified reference to the first *Kritik* only by the pagination of the first or second editions of that work.)
2. A506=B534; cf. esp. A507=B535.
3. A444=B472.
4. Ibid. (Kant's italics).
5. A444=B272 (Kant's italics).
6. A446=B474 (Kant's italics).
7. Ibid.
8. A445=B473.
9. Ibid.
10. Ibid.
11. A447=B475. I ignore Kant's argument at A448=B476, where we are required to acknowledge the fact of freedom because "it is required to make an origin of the world conceivable." I postpone consideration of this until note 13.
12. A451=B479.
13. A447=B475.
14. Whether what Kant calls our forms of intuition are merely properties of the mind (*liegen im Gemüte bereits vor*) or, alternatively, characteristics of things independently of the way in which we intuit them triggered the Trendelenburg-Fischer controversy. Vaihinger, *CZ*, 2:134ff., provides both as complete a description of that controversy as anybody would find philosophically worthwhile as well as a literally exhaustive review (pp. 545–48) of what everybody else had to say about the controversy over a twenty year period. My interest in the Trendelenburg-Fischer controversy is at once narrower and more important for my general thesis about the relation between things in them-

selves and appearances than the general dispute that Vaihinger faithfully records. (See appendix.)

15. Cf. chap. 2 for a fuller discussion of this issue.

16. Cf. chap. 2 for the distinction between a noumenon and a thing in itself that undermines the ontological interpretation of the notion of a thing in itself. The problem here is the relation between a thing in itself qua noumenon and an appearance to which it is supposed to be somehow connected. See this discussion in chap. 1. The issue, however, is what is to count as a case of affection. (See appendix for further discussion.)

17. Peter Krausser, "'Raum' und 'Zeit' als 'Formen der Anschauung' und als 'formale Anschauungen' in Kants kritischer Theorie," offers a speciously plausible way out of all of this. Krausser claims (p. 20) that "Anschauung" in the *Kritik* does not primarily refer to what is intuited but rather to the rules by which one synthesizes or combines what is intuited. He says (p. 25) that space and time are "*qua* primitive Regeln des anschauenden Operierens unseres Geistes nicht selbst Angeschautes, nicht selbst 'Gegenstände der Anschauung' sind und sein können." Krausser's distinction between space and time as objects of intuition and rules combining whatever objects of intuition we have can be conceded for the sake of the argument, but that distinction still does not explicate the very different distinction between things in themselves and appearances. For even if, say, space and time are merely rules for combining things in experience and not themselves items in those experiences, we can still ask about what distinguishes things as they are in themselves from the way in which they appear to us in a world in which there are no space and time. Richard Aquila, "The Relationship between Pure and Empirical Intuition in Kant," clearly sees the relation between space and time as objects of intuition (the Aesthetic view) and space and time as rules of synthesis (the Analytic view) in a way that escapes Krausser's problem and properly focuses the issue on what I discuss here (pp. 275 ff.).

18. The structure of Kant's Third Antinomy is logically strange. He begins by contrasting two incompatible ways in which a time series can be initiated. At A444=B472 he tells us that to say that something takes place is just to say that it follows upon a temporally antecedent event necessarily according to a rule. And at A446=B474 he tells us that a series of events can be initiated whenever something that is not itself an event but is somehow related to an event initiates the first event in the time series. The real problem lies, however, not in how two kinds of temporal series can be initiated, but rather in the relation of any one member of either series to its initiator. The older literature is more sensitive to this strange twist in Kant's argument than what philosophers have—erroneously, I think—regarded as important in the assessment of the Third Antinomy. Ludwig Busse, "Zu Kant's Lehre vom Ding an sich," provides the reportorial basis for this, founded mostly on a German rendition of the extremely important but generally neglected Rikizo Nakashima monograph, *Kant's Doctrine of the "Thing-in-itself."* Busse (p. 91) correctly reports that Kant can resolve the Third Antinomy without having to appeal to a noumenal self of a thing in itself that exists without any temporal characteristics. The unity of the self can be explained without dispensing with temporality. And the acceptance of temporality does not imply universal determinism. The point is as simple as it is incisive. Once you say that the self has temporal characteristics and go on to say, as Busse does, that the temporal characteristics in question are so many abilities the self has of combining the manifold, then the self can be in time without being part of the manifold it synthesizes; hence, even if it is in time, the self is not therefore just one more item subject to the law of causation. That is the thrust of Busse's report.

Having made most of the perceptive distinctions in the Kantian use of "thing in it-self," Nakashima rightly distinguishes between a sense of "cause" in which one event succeeds necessarily upon another according to a rule and a quite different sense of "cause" in which an object acts on our sensibility. If the object in question is a thought object, then we can be caused to act by what we conceive. And this is all that is required for the resolution of the Third Antinomy while conceding that the conception of such an object is a temporal event but refusing to concede that all temporal events are causally determined by antecedent temporal events necessarily according to a rule.

W. T. Jones, *Morality and Freedom in the Philosophy of Immanuel Kant*, argues that noumenal causation makes free action possible without being able to distinguish be-tween a noumenon and a thing in itself. Jones points out that if Kant's theory of free action is to be right, we must be obliged to say that one and the same act is both causally determined and free (p. 9). Jones rightly concludes that any such theory would be a con-tradiction and rejects it in favor of saying, rather, that freedom and necessity must be thought of as somehow united in the same subject, depending upon the way in which you choose to look at the agent (p. 9). Jones seeks to justify this contention by saying (pp. 26–27) that some event (call it *E*) can both be an act of will and a physical change and cause something (call it *E'*) because some event *E* will always be followed by an event *E'* but that the occurrence of *E'* will always be preceded by the occurrence of *E*. Jones gives us a case of constant similarity of effects. He does not, however, give us a case of constant similarity of causes that in turn are constantly similar effects of prior causes. Acts of will are admittedly in the time. And they admittedly cause things to hap-pen. But the question is whether such acts are predictable. Removing acts of will to noumenal selves is just to give us what I have called the duplication problem with a verbal fig leaf.

19. S. F. Barker, "Appearing and Appearances in Kant," argues that Kant's reason for distinguishing between things in themselves and appearances is to reconstruct the dis-tinction between what Barker calls the language of appearing and the language of ap-pearance. Niceties aside, this is Barker's distinction. "*S* perceives *O*" can be interpreted to mean either (a) "*S* perceives, say, an oasis whether it be a mirage or not" or (b) "*S* perceives some other particular that appears to him to be mirage-like." In *a*-cases of perception *every* case of perceptual awareness, veridical or not, involves a particular that exists just as we perceive it to exist. In *b*-cases of perception at least some cases of perception involve a real particular that appears to us to be other than it is. According to Barker (p. 278) the *a*-model (the language of appearances) implies that there is no direct contact with the external and, further (p. 279) that "if one knows anything definite about the nature or existence of things outside the mind, this knowledge must be in-ferential." Kant allegedly vacillates between these two very different conceptions of the relation between things in themselves and appearances. But according to Barker (p. 286) the most plausible reason for distinguishing between things in themselves and appear-ances in Kant's adoption of the language of appearing, pointing out that at Bxxvi through Bxxvii Kant speaks of the "absurd conclusion that there can be appearance without anything that appears."

Yes, there is a distinction between qualitative and existential appearing. But it does not support the Kantian distinction between things in themselves and appearances. For one thing, Bxxx–xxxvi applies equally to phenomenal particulars and their appearing as it does to things in themselves and how they appear to us; hence, an appeal to this and passages like it cannot be used to support the view that what Kant calls the distinction between things in themselves and appearances rests on the existence of the language of appearing. But even waiving this difficulty, bad enough as it is, Barker's distinction between two kinds of perceptual languages does not solve what I have been calling the duplication problem. Existential appearing as well as qualitative appearing can occur in a world containing appearances and things in themselves; hence, Barker's distinction does not ground the distinction between things in themselves and appearances as it has traditionally been understood any more than it provides independent evidence for the existence of such a distinction. Cf. Prichard, *Kant's Theory of Knowledge*, who attacks the notion of affection (chap. 4) in Kant as the structural root of the disastrous distinction between things in themselves and appearances.

20. *The Moral Law: Kant's Groundwork of the Metaphysics of Morals*, p. 106 (Kant's italics). See also p. 109: "But we cannot possibly conceive of a reason as being consciously directed from outside in regard to its judgments; for in that case the subject would attribute the determination of his power of judgment, not to his reason, but to an impulsion." See also pp. 107 and 111. B. Erdmann, *Kant's Kriticismus*, p. 44ff., dimly perceived this whole issue. See also Robert Steffen, *Kant's Lehre vom Ding an Sich*, pp. 42–43. They both hold that Kant applies the notion of causality through freedom to the voluntary action of man only and not to every phenomenon in nature. Both of them fail to distinguish between heteronomous actions that are events according to the Second Analogy and heteronomous actions that proceed from a certain kind of motive, whether predictable or not. See my "Kant's Arguments Against Material Principles," for yet another attempt to make these two senses of heteronomy intellectually accessible.

21. Paton, *Kant's Metaphysic of Experience*, p. 113.

22. Ibid., pp. 113, 116, 117. These passages are significant in that they refer to how the agent conceives of *himself*, not how he conceives of the relation between things in themselves and appearances. The former alone is used as the basis for resolving the antinomy.

23. *Critique of Practical Reason*, p. 55.

24. Ibid., p. 57; see also p. 58: "The concept of an empirically unconditioned causality is indeed theoretically empty since it has no appropriate intuition, even though it is still possible and refers to an indeterminate object."

25. Ibid., p. 55.

26. Ibid., p. 57.

27. See A26=B42, where Kant argues for space that it is the "form of all appearances of outer sense." A31=B46ff. gives the same argument for time. Both arguments apply to characteristics of moments of time and space taken individually. They would hold irrespective of whatever other relations, temporal or otherwise, might hold between any two moments.

28. See A176=B218, where Kant repeatedly begins his proofs by reminding us that "[e]xperience is possible only through the representation of a necessary connection of perceptions." Or, again, he constantly reminds us (e.g., A182=B213) that our "*apprehension* of the manifold appearance is always successive, and is therefore always changing." Cf. A189=B233 and A193=B238.

29. A42=B60.

30. This should be plain from the distinction Kant makes at A70=B95 and later at A80=B106 between the table of what he calls the logical functions of the understanding in judgments on the one hand and the table of categories on the other. And as if that were not enough to alert us to the truth of what I attribute to Kant here, he goes on to

distinguish between the table of categories and the *schemata* of these categories when applied to a description of our world (A137=B176 through A147=B187). See my *Kant, Ontology, and the A Priori*, chap. 4, for a detailed discussion of the importance of these distinctions for Kant's ontology.

Henry Allison, *Kant's Transcendental Idealism*, pp. 181–85, mounts an attack on a theory of schematism that I set forth in my *Kant, Ontology, and the A Priori*, pp. 91–94, 128–29, and offers a view of the doctrine that purportedly escapes the criticisms I give of a theory I reject. The issue turns on the merits of what I have called the third-thing theory of transcendental schematism. According to Allison (p. 181), I hold that transcendental schemata are "referents of the schematized and not the pure concepts," I fail to distinguish two senses of "pure intuition"—namely, form of intuition and formal intuition—and I falsely assume that pure intuition can be understood only as a form of intuition. Thus my objection to the third-thing theory collapses. Allison's alternative: A transcendental schema is a determinate pure intuition, "one that is conceptualized" (p. 184). True, but irrelevant. First, what is embedded in Kant's text as the third-thing theory concerns the characteristics of the referent of the concept of a schematized category itself. Second, the place of importance I assign to the notion of a transcendental time determination is compatible with the view that Allison defends. The two are simply views about different things, not conflicting views about the same thing.

31. This is a logical possibility for Kant's theory, but it is just not ontologically possible for this world given our cognitive apparatus. Gunther Tiele, *Kant's Intellektuelle Anschauung*, (p. 184) argues that our ability to schematize a category in this world in a way different from the way in which we actually do requires our possession of intellectual as over against sensuous intuition. It would, Thiele argues, obliterate the distinctions between concepts and intuitions and real and imaginary objects.

32. St. Thomas Aquinas, *Summa Contra Gentiles*, Book 2, and *Summa Theologiae*, Part 1, Question 46, argues that it cannot be demonstrated whether the world had a beginning in time or not although it can be demonstrated that the world has a first cause.

Chapter 7. Concluding Aporetical Postscript

1. See chap. 2.
2. See chap. 6.
3. There is an ancillary reason for pressing this point. Without it, intellectual intuition as Kant understands it would be logically impossible. If the notion is to be internally coherent, we must be able to define directness of awareness independently of any forms of intuition. See my "Intellectual Intuition: The Continuity Thesis."
4. See chap. 2.
5. W. H. Werkmeister confirms this view in "The Complementarity of Phenomena and Things in Themselves," when he argues that the distinction is not ontological but, as he calls it, perspectival. Werkemeister draws on evidence from the *Opus postumum*; namely, that the distinction between things in themselves and appearances is subjective and not objective (*oppositio sine correlatum realis*), that a thing in itself is an *ens rationis* because it is the concept of a different way of conceiving something from what we are given by our forms of intuition, and that things in themselves are not noumena. Here, as Werkemeister correctly sees, the concept of a thing in itself moves very close to the concept of an object in general. But there remains the distinction between the con-

cept of an empirical object in general and the concept of an object about which we cannot know more than that it is a subject of predicates. The former is the concept of any object under which the manifold can be united. The latter is not.

6. See Prauss, *Kant und das Problem der Dinge an Sich* (chap. 2) for an attempt to understand the distinction between a thing in itself and an appearance in terms of the further and more basic distinction between a transcendental and an empirical sense in which they can be viewed. This confirms the view that affection cannot be assimilated to causation and that causation cannot be used to explicate the kind of relation that holds between a thing in itself and an appearance.

SELECTED BIBLIOGRAPHY

I list here only those works that I discuss in the text. More comprehensive bibliographies are readily available to the reader. The standard bibliography of work about Kant up to the early nineteenth century is to be found in Erich Adickes's "German Kantian Bibliography," which first appeared in *The Philosophical Review* 2 (1893) and 3 (1894). It has been reprinted under the title *German Kantian Bibliography* (Ithaca, N.Y.: Burt Franklin, 1970). M. J. Scott-Taggart covers the recent work in his bibliographical discussion, "Recent Work on the Philosophy of Kant," reprinted in *Kant Studies Today*, edited by Lewis White Beck (LaSalle, Ill.: Open Court Publishing Co., 1969). The most recent work is covered by Karl Ameriks in his "Recent Work on Kant's Theoretical Philosophy," *American Philosophical Quarterly* 19 (1982).

Primary Sources

Any reference to Kant's texts not otherwise specified is to *Kant's gesammelte Schriften*, ed. Königlich Preussische Akademie der Wissenschaften (Berlin, Leipzig: de Gruyter, 1922). In other cases I cite from the following English translations of the relevant works:

Critique of Judgement, translated by James C. Meredith (Oxford: Clarendon Press, 1978).
Critique of Practical Reason, translated by Lewis White Beck (Indianapolis: Bobbs-Merrill Co., 1956).

Critique of Pure Reason, translated by Norman Kemp Smith (London: Macmillan and Co., 1929).

Kant, Selected Pre-Critical Writings, edited and translated by G. B. Kerferd and D. E. Walford (Manchester: Manchester University Press, 1968).

Metaphysical Foundations of Natural Science, translated by James Ellington (Indianapolis and New York: Bobbs-Merrill Co., 1970).

Prolegomena to any Future Metaphysics, translated by Lewis White Beck (Indianapolis and New York: Bobbs-Merrill Co., 1950).

Secondary Sources

Adickes, Erich. *Kant und das Ding an Sich*. Berlin: Pan Verlag Rolf Heise, 1924.

—— *Kants Theorie von der doppelter Affektion unseres Ich als Schlüssel zu seiner Erkenntnistheorie*. Tübingen: J. C. B. Mohr, 1929.

Al-Azm, Sadik J. *The Origins of Kant's Arguments in the Antinomies*. Oxford: Clarendon Press, 1972.

Allaire, Edwin B. "Existence, Independence, and Universals." *The Philosophical Review* 69 (1960): 485–96. Reprinted in *Essays in Ontology*, edited by E. B. Allaire et al. The Hague: Martinus Nijhoff, 1963.

Allison, Henry. "Kant's Concept of the Transcendental Object." *Kant-Studien* 59 (1968): 165–86.

————. *Kant's Transcendental Idealism*. New Haven: Yale University Press, 1983.

————. *The Kant-Eberhard Controversy*. Baltimore: The Johns Hopkins University Press, 1973.

————. "The Non-Spatiality of Things in Themselves for Kant," *Journal of the History of Philosophy* 4 (1976): 313–21.

————. "Things in Themselves, Noumena, and the Transcendental Object." *Dialectica* 32 (1978): 41–76.

Ameriks, Karl. *Kant's Theory of Mind*. Oxford: Clarendon Press, 1982.

Aquila, Richard. "*A priori* Form and *a priori* Knowledge in the Transcendental Aesthetic." In *Akten des 5. Internationalen Kant-Kongresses*, edited by Manfred Kleinschnieder et al. Bonn: Bouvier Verlag Herbart Grundmann, 1981.

————. "Intentional Objects and Kantian Appearances." In *Essays on Kant's Critique of Pure Reason*, edited by J. N. Mohanty and Robert W. Shahan. Norman: University of Oklahoma Press, 1982.

————. "Is Sensation the Matter of Appearance?" In *Interpreting Kant*, edited by Moltke S. Gram. Iowa City: University of Iowa Press, 1982.

————. "The Relationship between Pure and Empirical Intuition in Kant." *Kant-Studien* 68 (1977): 275–89.

————. "Things in Themselves and Appearances: Intentionality and Reality in Kant." *Archiv für Geschichte der Philosophie* 61 (1979): 293–308.

————. "Two Lines of Argument in Kant's Transcendental Aesthetic." *International Studies in Philosophy* 10 (1978): 85–100.

Aquinas, St. Thomas. *Summa Contra Gentiles*.

————. *Summa Theologiae*.

Barker, S. F. "Appearing and Appearances in Kant." In *Kant Studies Today*, edited by Lewis White Beck. LaSalle, Ill.: Open Court Publishing Co., 1969.

Beck, Lewis White. *A Commentary on Kant's Critique of Practical Reason*. Chicago: University of Chicago Press, 1960.

Benardete, Jose. *Infinity*. New York: Oxford University Press, 1964.

Bennett, Jonathan. *Kant's Analytic*. Cambridge: The University Press, 1966.

———. *Kant's Dialectic*. Cambridge: The University Press, 1974.

Berkeley, George. *The Principles of Human Knowledge*. In *The Works of George Berkeley*, vol. 2, edited by A. A. Luce and T. E. Jessup. London: Thomas Nelson and Sons, 1964.

Bröcker, Walter. "Kants Lehre von der aüsseren Affektion." *Forschungen und Fortschritte* 20 (1944): 151–54.

Brysz, Simon. *Das Ding an sich und die empirische Anschauung in Kants Philosophie*. Halle: Erhardt Karras, 1913.

Buroker, Jill Vance. *Space and Incongruence*. Dordrecht: D. Reidel Publishing Co., 1981.

Busse, Ludwig. "Zu Kant's Lehre vom Ding an sich," *Zeitschrift für Philosophie und philosophische Kritik* 101 (1892): 74–113; 102 (1893): 171–232.

Carus, Paul. *The Surd of Metaphysics*. Chicago: Open Court Publishing Co., 1903.

Cassirer, H. W. *Kant's First Critique*. London: George Allen & Unwin Ltd., 1954.

Chipman, Lauchlan. "Things in Themselves." *Philosophy and Phenomenological Research* 33 (1973): 489–502.

Cohen, Hermann. *Kants Theorie der Erfahrung*. Berlin: Fred. Dümmlers Verlagsbuchhandlung, 1871.

Dryer, D. P. *Kant's Solution for Verification in Metaphysics*. Toronto: University of Toronto Press, 1966.

Erdmann, B. *Kant's Kriticismus*. Leipzig: L. Voss, 1878.

Fang, Joong. *Das Antinomienproblem im Entstehungsgang der Transzendentalphilosophie*. N.p., 1957.

Fichte, J. G. *Erste Einleitung in die Wissenschaftslehre*. In *Werke*, edited by I. H. Fichte, vol. 1. Berlin: Walter de Gruyter & Co., 1971.

———. *Grundlage der gesammten Wissenschaftslehre* (1794). In *Werke*, edited by I. H. Fichte, vol. 1. Berlin: Walter de Gruyter & Co., 1971.

———. Review of *Aenesidemus*. In *Werke*, edited by I. H. Fichte, vol. 1. Berlin: Walter de Gruyter & Co., 1971.

———. *Versuch einer neuen Darstellung der Wissenschaftslehre* (1797). In *Werke*, edited by I. H. Fichte, vol. 1. Berlin: Walter de Gruyter & Co., 1971.

———. *The Vocation of Man*. Edited by Roderick H. Chisholm. Indianapolis: Bobbs-Merrill Co., 1956.

Findlay, J. N. *Kant and the Transcendental Object*. Oxford: The Clarendon Press, 1981.

Fischer, Kuno. *A Commentary on Kant's Critick of the Pure Reason*. Translated by Pentland Mahaffy. London: Longmans, Green & Co., 1866.

———. *Geschichte der neueren Philosophie*. 2d ed. Vol. 3. Heidelberg: F. Bassermann, 1869.

Goethe, J. W. *Werke*. 14 vols. Hamburg: Christian Wegner Verlag, 1958.

Gram, Moltke S. "Causation and Direct Realism." *The Philosophy of Science* 39 (1972): 388–96.

———. "Do Transcendental Arguments Have a Future?" *Neue Hefte für Philosophie* 14 (1978): 23–56.

———. "The Crisis of Syntheticity: The Kant-Eberhard Controversy." *Kant-Studien* 71 (1980): 155–88.

———. "Gadamer on Hegel's Dialectic." *The Thomist* 43 (1979): 322–30.

———. "Intellectual Intuition: The Continuity Thesis." *The Journal of the History of Ideas* 42 (1981): 287–34.

———. *Kant, Ontology, and the Apriori*. Evanston: Northwestern University Press, 1968.

———. "Kant's Arguments against Material Principles." *The Personalist* 55 (1974): 30–43.

———. "Must Transcendental Arguments Be Spurious?" *Kant-Studien* 65 (1974): 304–17.

———. "The Sense of a Kantian Intuition." In *Interpreting Kant*, edited by Moltke S. Gram. Iowa City: University of Iowa Press, 1982.

———. "The Skeptical Attack on Substance: Kantian Answers." In *Midwestern Studies in Philosophy VIII*, edited by Peter French et al. Minneapolis: University of Minnesota Press, 1983.

———. "Substance." in *Substances and Things*, edited by M. L. O'Hara. Washington: University of America Press, 1982.

———. "Transcendental Arguments." *Nous* 5 (1971): 20–26.

———. "What Kant Really Did to Idealism." In *Essays on Kant's Critique of Pure Reason*, edited by J. N. Mohanty and Robert W. Shahan. Norman: University of Oklahoma Press, 1982.

Harris, W. T. "Kant's Third Antinomy and His Fallacy Regarding the First Cause." *Mind* 3 (1894): 1–13.

Hegel, G. W. F. *Enzyklopädie der philosophischen Wissenschaften*. In *Sämtliche Werke*, edited by Hermann Glockner, vol. 6. Stuttgart: Fr. Frommans Verlag, 1956.

———. *Die Phänomenologie des Geistes*. In *Sämtliche Werke*, edited by Hermann Glockner, vol. 2. Stuttgart: Fr. Frommans Verlag, 1958.

———. *Die Wissenschaft der Logik*. In *Sämtliche Werke*, edited by Hermann Glockner, vols. 5 and 6. Stuttgart: Fr. Frommans Verlag, 1956.

———. *The Phenomenology of Mind*. Translated by J. B. Baillie. London: George Allen and Unwin, 1964.

Heidegger, Martin. *Kant und das Problem der Metaphysik*. Frankfurt am Main: Vittorio Klostermann, 1951.

Heimsoeth, Heinz. *Studien zur Philosophie Immanuel Kants*. Köln: Kölner Universitäts-Verlag, 1956.

———. *Transzendentale Dialektik*. Berlin: Walter de Gruyter & Co., 1966.

———. "Zum kosmologischen Ursprung der Kantischen Freiheitsantinomie." *Kant-Studien* 57 (1966): 206–29.

Heintel, Peter. "Die Dialektik bei Kant." *Studium Generale* 21 (1968): 450–70.

Herring, Herbert. *Das Problem der Affektion bei Kant. Kant-Studien Ergänzungsheft* 67. Köln: Kölner Universitätsverlag, 1953.

Hicks, G. Dawes. *Die Begriffe Phänomen und Noumenon*. Leipzig: Wilhelm Englesmann, 1877.

Hinske, Norbert. "Kants Begriff der Antinomie und die Etappen seiner Ausarbeitung." *Kant-Studien* 56 (1966): 485–96.

Jackson, Reginald. "Locke's Distinction between Primary and Secondary Qualities." *Mind* 38 (1929): 56–76. Reprinted in C. B. Martin and D. M. Armstrong, eds., *Locke and Berkeley*. Garden City, N.Y.: Anchor Books, 1968.

Jacobi, F. H. *David Hume über den Glauben, oder Idealismus und Realismus, Über den transzendentalen Idealismus*. In *Werke*, edited by Roth F. Köpen, vol. 2. Reprint of 1815 ed. Darmstadt: Wissenschaftliche Buchgesellschaft, 1968.

———. *David Hume über den Glauben, oder Idealismus und Realismus*, edited by Hamilton Beck. Reprint of 1787 ed. New York: Garland Publishing Co., 1983.

Jones, W. T. *Morality and Freedom in the Philosophy of Immanuel Kant.* Oxford: Clarendon Press, 1940.

Kalin, Martin. "Inference and Illusion in Dialectic." *Southern Journal of Philosophy* 15 (1977): 253–66.

Kleist, Heinrich von. *Gesammelte Kurzgeschichten.* In *Sämtliche Werke und Briefe*, vol. 2. München: Carl Hanser Verlag, 1961.

Körner, Stephan. "Kant's Conception of Freedom." *Proceedings of the British Academy* 53 (1967): 193–217.

Krausser, Peter. "Kant's Theory of the Structure of Empirical Scientific Inquiry and Two Implied Postulates Regarding Things in Themselves." In *Kant's Theory of Knowledge*, edited by Lewis White Beck. Dordrecht, Holland: D. Reidel Publishing Co., 1974.

———. " 'Raum' und 'Zeit' als 'Formen der Anschauung' und als 'formale Anschauung' in Kants kritischer Theorie." In *Konkrete Reflexion*, edited by J. M. Broekman and J. Knopf. The Hague: Martin Nijhoff, 1975.

Liebmann, Otto. *Kant und die Epigonen.* Berlin: Reuther und Reichard, 1912.

Locke, John. *Essay Concerning Human Understanding.* 2 vols. Oxford: Clarendon Press, 1894.

Lotze, Hermann. *Metaphysic*, 2d ed. Oxford: Clarendon Press, 1887.

Maimon, Solomon. *Versuch über die Transzendentalphilosophie.* In *Gesammelte Werke*, edited by Valerio Verra. Hildesheim: Georg Olms, 1965.

Martin, Gottfried. *Immanuel Kant.* 4th ed. Berlin: Walter de Gruyter & Co., 1969.

———. *Kant's Metaphysics and Theory of Science.* Translated by P. G. Lucas. Manchester: Manchester University Press, 1955.

Meerbote, R. "The Unknowability of Things in Themselves." In *Proceedings of the Third International Kant Congress*, edited by Lewis White Beck. Dordrecht, Holland: D. Reidel Publishing Co., 1972.

Morgenbesser, Sydney, ed. *Philosophy, Science, and Method.* New York: St. Martin's Press, 1969.

Musil, Robert. *Die Verwirrungen des Zöglings Törless.* In *Prosa, Dramen, Späte Briefe*, edited by Adolf Frise. Hamburg: Rowohlt Verlag, 1957.

———. *Der Mann ohne Eigenschaften.* Hamburg: Rowohlt Verlag, 1960.

Nakashima, Rikizo. *Kant's Doctrine of the "Thing-in-itself."* New Haven, Conn.: Price, Lee & Adkins Co., 1889.

Nietzsche, Friedrich. *Werke in Drei Bänden.* Edited by Karl Schlechta. Munich: Carl Hanser Verlag, 1955.

Paton, H. J. *The Categorical Imperative.* London: Hutchinson & Co., 1965.

———. *Kant's Metaphysic of Experience.* 2 vols. New York: Macmillan Co., 1936.

Pippin, Robert B. *Kant's Theory of Form.* New Haven: Yale University Press, 1982.

Prauss, Gerold. *Erscheinung bei Kant.* Berlin: Walter de Gruyter & Co., 1971.

———. *Kant und das Problem der Dinge an Sich.* 2d ed. Bonn: Bouvier Verlag, 1977.

Prichard, H. A. *Kant's Theory of Knowledge.* Oxford: Clarendon Press, 1909.

Reinhold, K. L. *Beiträge zur Berichtigung bisheriger Missverständnisse der Philosophen.* Jena: J. M. Mauke, 1790–94.

———. *Versuch einer neuen Theorie des menschlichen Vorstellungsvermögens.* Prag and Jena: C. Widmann & I. M. Mauke, 1789.

Rescher, Nicholas. "Noumenal Causality." In *Kant's Theory of Knowledge*, edited by Lewis White Beck. Dordrecht, Holland: D. Reidel, 1974.

Riedel, Otto. *Die Bedeutung des Dinges an sich in der Kantischen Ethik.* Stolp: F. W. Frig's Buchdruckerei, 1888.

——. *Die monadologischen Bestimmungen in Kants Lehre vom Ding an sich.* Hamburg: Verlag von Leopold Voss, 1884.

Riehl, Alois. *Der philosophische Kritizismus.* 2d ed. Leipzig: Wilhelm Englesman, 1908.

Ristititsch, Swetomir. *Die indirekten Beweise des transzendentalen Idealismus. Kant-Studien, Ergänzungsheft 16.* Köln: Kölner Universitätsverlag, 1910.

Russell, Bertrand. *Our Knowledge of the External World.* London: George Allen & Unwin Ltd., 1952.

Schaper, Eva. "The Kantian Thing in Itself as a Philosophical Fiction." *Philosophical Quarterly* 14 (1966): 233–43.

Schelling, F. W. J. *Darstellung des philosophischen Empirismus.* In *Werke,* edited by Otto Weiss, vol. 3. Leipzig: Fritz Eckhardt Verlag, 1907.

——. *System des transzendentalen Idealismus.* In *Werke,* edited by Otto Weiss, vol. 2. Leipzig: Fritz Eckhardt Verlag, 1907.

Schopenhauer, Arthur. *Die Welt als Wille und Vorstellung.* In *Sämtliche Werke,* edited by Wolfgang von Löhensen, vol. 2. Frankfurt am Main: Cotta-Insel Verlag, 1960.

Schulze, Gottlob Ernst. *Aenesidemus.* Berlin: Verlag von Reuther & Reichard, 1911.

Schrader, George. "The Thing in Itself in Kantian Philosophy." In *Kant,* edited by R. P. Wolff. New York: Doubleday Anchor, 1967.

——. "The Transcendental Ideality and Empirical Reality of Kant's Space and Time." *The Review of Metaphysics* 4 (1951): 507–36.

Seidl, Horst. "Bemerkungen zu Ding an sich und transzendentalem Gegenstand in Kants Kritik der reinen Vernunft." *Kant-Studien* 63 (1972): 305–14.

Sellars, Wilfrid. *Science and Metaphysics.* New York: Humanities Press, 1968.

Simon, Josef. "Phenomena and Noumena: On the Use and Meaning of the Categories." In *Kant's Theory of Knowledge,* edited by Lewis White Beck. Dordrecht, Holland: D. Reidel, 1974.

Smith, Norman Kemp. *A Commentary to Kant's "Critique of Pure Reason."* New York: Humanities Press, 1962.

Steffen, Robert. *Kant's Lehre vom Ding an Sich.* Leipzig: A. Edelmann, 1877.

Stenius, Eric. "On Kant's Distinction between Phenomena and Noumena." In *Critical Essays,* edited by Eric Stenius. Amsterdam: North-Holland Publishing Co., 1972.

Strawson, P. F. *The Bounds of Sense.* London: Methuen and Co. Ltd., 1966.

Thompson, Manley. "Singular Terms and Intuitions in Kant's Epistemology." *The Review of Metaphysics* 26 (1972): 314–43.

Thomson, Anton, "Bermerkungen zur Kritik des Kantischen Begriffes des Dinges an sich." *Kant-Studien* 8 (1903): 193–257.

Tiele, Gunther. *Kant's Intellectuelle Anschauung.* Halle: Max Niemeyer, 1876.

Vaihinger, Hans. *Commentar zu Kant's 'Kritik der reinen Vernunft'.* 2 vols. Leipzig: Union Deutsche Verlagsgesellschaft, 1892.

——. *The Philosophy of 'As-If.'* Translated by C. K. Ogden. New York: Barnes and Noble, 1966.

Walker, R. C. S. *Kant.* London: Routledge & Kegan Paul, 1978.

Ward, James. *A Study of Kant.* Cambridge: The University Press, 1922.

Watson, John. *Kant and His English Critics.* New York: Macmillan and Co., 1881.

——. *The Philosophy of Kant Explained.* Glasgow: James Maclehose and Sons, 1908.

Weldon, T. D. *Kant's 'Critique of Pure Reason.'* Oxford: The Clarendon Press, 1958.

Werkmeister, William. "The Complementarity of Phenomena and Things in Themselves." *Synthese* 47 (1981): 301–11.

Westphal, W. "In Defense of the Thing in Itself." *Kant-Studien* 59 (1968): 118–41.

Windelband, W. "Über die verschiedenen Phasen der Kantischen Lehre vom Ding-an-sich." *Vierteljahresschrift für wissenschaftliche Philosophie und Soziologie* 1 (1877): 224–66.

Zweig, Arnulf, ed. *Kant: Philosophical Correspondence.* Chicago: University of Chicago Press, 1967.

INDEX